IRISH CHILD CARE SERVICES

Policy, Practice and Provision

D0898966

IRISH CHILD CARE SERVICES

Policy, Practice and Provision

Robbie Gilligan

Institute of Public Administration

Institute of Public Administration
© Robbie Gilligan 1991

British Library Cataloguing in Publication Data
Gilligan, Robbie
Irish Child Care Services
— Policy, Practice and Provision

  I. Title
  344.1704327

  ISBN 1-872002-90-0 Hbk
  ISBN 1-872002-95-1 Pbk

Published by the
Institute of Public Administration
57-61 Lansdowne Road
Dublin 4
Ireland

Photographs by Derek Speirs
Front cover photograph by Jonathan Hession
Typeset in 10/11 Times
Designed by Butler Claffey Design
Origination by Phototype-Set Limited
Printed by Criterion Press Limited, Dublin

For my wife, Mary Quinn,
our children, Aoife, Sinead and Orla,
and my parents, Oscar and Breda Gilligan

CONTENTS

TABLES

PHOTOGRAPHS

Note: The photographs used in this book do not imply in any way whatsoever any connection between people featured and the services mentioned in the text.

FIGURES

FOREWORD

This book is about the needs of deprived children. However defined, child deprivation remains a serious social problem in contemporary Ireland. Many children experience lives of poverty, educational disadvantage, poor health and family conflict. This book is written to highlight their plight and to demonstrate concrete ways of easing it. It is written primarily for those who have a professional involvement with children, be they nurses, teachers, social workers, doctors, gardaí, psychologists or child-care workers. But it should also interest anyone who believes that one of the nation's primary aims should be to cherish all of our children equally.

The idea of writing this book came to me because I saw no comparable work available to Irish students of child welfare. Certainly, there are useful books published in New York, London and elsewhere, but, quite naturally, they deal with services, structures and issues from the vantage point of their home country. They do not draw on, or relate consciously to, Irish experience and Irish conditions.

In teaching Irish university students about social needs and social problems, I have become increasingly aware of the vital importance of having material written from within the Irish cultural experience, addressing current political and social issues in Ireland. The lack of indigenous material for courses and private study is surely as culturally impoverishing for our students as the absence of Irish-produced newspapers, radio or television would be to the Irish public.

The absence of relevant textbooks undermines the growth and prestige of any discipline. In the case of child welfare in Ireland, I hope this book will help to close the gap. But books such as this must be judged ultimately on whether they improve the care and understanding that children in need receive.

Tackling the problems that face Irish children and families in difficulty requires resources — money and people — and action. But it also requires ideas, which must come from an informed debate about what action and what resources best fit Irish conditions. I hope this book will contribute to such debate. In my view, we no longer need to borrow meekly, in some uncritical and apologetic way, ill-fitting or cast-off practices from other countries. We need to shed our post-colonial diffidence, deference and mimicry. We need to recognise the strengths of 'caring' traditions within our own culture — of mutual aid among family and neighbours; of the rural traditions of co-operation, manifested in the *meitheal* (sharing of labour between neighbours) and the early agricultural co-operative movement; of community development, one of the world pioneers of which was Canon Hayes, founder of Muintir na Tíre; of the credit union movement, which has become so strong in Ireland; of the great missionary heritage of Irish churches (from the Irish scholar monks who brought their learning to continental Europe in early mediaeval times to the work for justice in the Third World today by people like Fr. Niall O'Brien in the Philippines; and of the tradition of voluntary effort in the social services generally.

We should now have the confidence and the competence to analyse our own problems and prescribe our own solutions. This is not an argument for some kind of chauvinistic or isolationist approach to the development of our thinking or practice. But we can best integrate the freshest ideas and the most imaginative and challenging practice from abroad only after we have grasped securely what is most valuable in our own experience.

This book is written deliberately for a wide audience as a reference book, more for dipping into and consulting than for reading straight through. For relative newcomers to child welfare — whether third-level students of any discipline in contact with children, or interested citizens — I hope the book will deepen their interest in the needs of children. For old hands, I hope the book will not only renew their commitment but also refresh and perhaps extend their knowledge.

While drawing selectively from international sources, I have tried to be fairly comprehensive in capturing Irish material and evidence, so that readers may be alerted to their existence and relevance. In my selection of topics, and of my target audience, I have cast my net wide, while still retaining a focus on the core issues of children at risk because of family troubles and/or personal and social problems. This breadth of coverage reflects my conviction that the needs of these children and their families are complex and multi-faceted, and can only be understood and met in ways that reflect this. No single discipline or approach has all the answers. No professional grouping has a monopoly of knowledge or skill in relation to the needs of children. The key to effective work with and for children and their families lies in a common understanding between those involved. I hope this book, if used by different disciplines on their different courses, and subsequently in their practice, will contribute to such a common understanding.

The book is divided into five parts. Part I deals with the relationship between children, parents and society. In the first two chapters, psychological, social and legal aspects of the relationship between parents and children are considered. In the third chapter, evidence of the influence of social conditions on Irish children's chances in life is thoroughly examined. The inescapable conclusion is that lower social class and other adverse factors greatly damage a child's prospects on a variety of fronts. Part I, therefore, provides a context for understanding the later sections of the book, which examine in various ways the services provided to and for children and families at risk.

Part II describes the health care and personal social services system as it affects children (including the work of the voluntary sector), the education system and the juvenile justice system. The role played by different professional groups and specific services is also explored.

Part III focuses on actual ways of helping families with the pressures of living, so that problems do not deteriorate to the point of family break-up and the placement of children in care. Methods of working directly with parents and families, and types of support and prevention services at community level are also explored.

Part IV discusses how to help the child or young person who has to live in care. It considers some of the problems that can arise for these youngsters during and after the period in care and the challenges facing their caretakers.

In Part V, certain principles are formulated which, it is suggested, should guide policy. In addition, some aspects of Irish culture affecting the treatment of children are discussed. Finally, an agenda for urgent reform in public policy for children and families is outlined.

An appendix offers the reader a detailed chronology of developments within the field of child welfare in Ireland over the past 30 years. The bibliography that follows lists the sources and references for the present text.

Having said what the book offers, perhaps it is wise to emphasise what it does not attempt to cover. It does not deal with the housing or income maintenance systems or the tax code. These are obviously important public policy areas of relevance to the welfare of children and families; they are not covered here because they are dealt with in other publications and their inclusion would necessitate leaving out important material that lacks comparable treatment elsewhere. Nor is this book intended as a skills' manual: it does not pretend to teach the detailed application of ideas or techniques discussed. Rather, it has been written more as a 'Michelin Guide' than as a recipe book.

It is also important to say that the book does not, despite its title, address the situation in Northern Ireland. This does not arise from neglect and certainly not from disinterest. The complexity of a separate jurisdiction and administrative system will require another volume and a much more detailed knowledge than I possess of the situation north of the border.

One of the great trials in compiling a book of this nature is that the world keeps changing! The child care field is increasingly subject to developments in law, policy and general climate. The reader must therefore be cautious in assuming that any situation will remain exactly as described. Even where change occurs, however, this book and the sources it cites should help the reader track down the most up-to-date position.

Robbie Gilligan
July 1991

ACKNOWLEDGEMENTS

I owe thanks to a very great number of people who have assisted, often unwittingly, in bringing this book to fruition:

to my wife, Mary Quinn, for her unfailing support and patience in the face of the many demands that the book made on our lives together;

to my children, Aoife, Sinead and Orla who have so often shared, and with such good grace, their father's time with an inanimate and long-awaited embryo;

to my parents, Oscar and Breda Gilligan, for having fostered my interest in learning and my commitment to social justice;

to my fellow staff — academic and secretarial — in the Department of Social Studies, Trinity College Dublin, for their interest, assistance and encouragement, and especially to my supportive head of department, Vivienne Darling, who with colleagues Noreen Kearney, Ruth Torode, Shane Butler and Anthony Coughlan, very kindly facilitated my sabbatical leave for an academic term in the critical early stages of the book's gestation;

to Professor William Duncan, Head of the Law School, Trinity College for his characteristic generosity in reading the legal section;

to the students I have taught, for their interest and inquiries which have so often opened up new insights, issues and ideas for me;

to the library, administrative and security staff of the university for their willing assistance on countless occasions;

to Niav O'Daly, the doyenne of Irish child care social work, who taught me so much of what I know about child care;

to my former colleagues in the South Eastern Health Board, the Eastern Health Board, the Society of St. Vincent de Paul and the Department of Social Science, University College Dublin, for having nurtured many of the interests now reflected in the contents of this book;

to Kay Carmichael, Glasgow, Professor Harvey Gochros, University of Hawaii, and Tom Ward, Belfast, who each at different times tried to convince me that there was a book inside me waiting to get out (it is left to the reader to judge whether they were right);

to John Curry who offered invaluable advice on surviving authorship;

to fellow members on all too many committees in the child care field whose lively debate has taught me so much;

to my friends in social work education and practice, in Ireland and abroad, for their interest and support;

to the many people in many organisations who so willingly and generously assisted me with inquiries in my research for the book;

to Derek Speirs whose excellent photography I am proud to have represented in this book;

and finally to IPA personnel — Jim O'Donnell, Iain MacAulay, Sara O'Hara, Kathleen Harte — whose support and advice at different times was greatly valued. I also acknowledge the assistance of Professor John Jackson, Chairman of the IPA Publications Committee.

I must of course stress the time honoured caveat that the final responsibility for the content rests with the author.

PART I:

CHILDREN, PARENTS AND SOCIETY

Chapter 1

CHILDREN AND PARENTS: NEEDS AND RIGHTS

> When speaking of children's needs and children's rights, we can only distinguish them from the needs and rights of other groups and from human rights generally, because children are special in two respects. Firstly, they are persons *in the process of formation*; secondly, they are *not independent*.
> Task Force on Child Care Services, 1981, p. 34

Children, especially in their first four years, develop at a pace unparalleled at any other stage in life, but this development may be thwarted by factors such as poverty or by the absence of parents. Poverty may lead to poor nutrition or stimulation which damages the child's physical and/or psychological development. Moreover, in these early years the child's sense of time is very different to that of an adult. Relatively brief separations, for example, from parents or familiar surroundings may seem like an eternity to a very young child and may, therefore, have a correspondingly traumatic effect. Children's development is heavily dependent on the availability, resources and capacity of their caretakers.

> . . . a child is more impressionable, more vulnerable, more changeable and more liable to being influenced for better or for worse than an adult: the effects of what happens to him are likely to be more profound and less easily reversible than they will be when he has grown up and matured. To put it more starkly, a child's experience of life, and the way he is cared for and dealt with, determines to a large extent the kind of adult he becomes (ibid).

Children's Needs
The late Mia Kellmer Pringle, a leading international authority on child care,

identified four needs which must be met for the child's satisfactory development (Kellmer Pringle, 1974):

(1) The need for love and security

For this need to be met, the child needs to enjoy a stable, dependable relationship with his or her parents 'who themselves enjoy a rewarding relationship with one another' (ibid. pp 34-5).

> The basic and all pervasive feature of parental love is that the child is valued unconditionally and for his own sake, irrespective of his sex, appearance, abilities or personality; that this love is given without expectation of or demand for gratitude; and that the constraints imposed upon parental freedom of movement, upon time and upon finance are accepted without resentment or reproach. (Occasionally begrudging these constraints is, of course, different from a permanent sense of resentment.) (ibid. p. 35).

The child derives a sense of security from stability and dependability in family relationships, familiarity of surroundings and the predictability of routines. These help the growing child cope with the bombardment of new experiences which he or she must face as an essential part of development.

(2) The need for new experiences

> New experiences are a prerequisite for mental growth, as essential to the mind's development as food is for the body's. From birth onwards, tasks appropriate to each stage of growth are presented to the child, and their mastery provides in turn the stepping stone towards more difficult achievements . . . If denied the opportunity of new experiences, no learning can take place (ibid. pp 41-2).

Play and the development of language are vital in facilitating a child's development. It is essential that the child's family and social environment facilitate the use of play and the growth of language, both of which enable the child to acquire and process new experiences.

(3) The need for praise and recognition

Mol an óige agus tiocfaidh sé ('Praise youth and it will thrive') is an Irish *seanfhocal* (proverb) which demonstrates that traditional culture understood that praise was a vital ingredient in the growth of confidence and competence in the young person.

The insights of twentieth-century social science merely serve to re-affirm this earlier understanding. The praise and attention of those close to him or her is something that the child greatly enjoys and values. These help the child persevere in the face of the pitfalls and setbacks that learning inevitably involves.

> Encouragement and a reasonable level of expectation act as a spur to perseverance. Too little expectation leads the child to adopt too low a standard of effort and achievement; too high a level makes him feel that he cannot live up to what is required of him which produces discouragement and again diminished effort. An optimal level of expectation needs to be geared to each individual's capabilities at a given point in time and stage of growth, at a level where success is possible but not without effort (ibid. p. 53).

This last point highlights the importance of treating each child as a unique individual. Even children from the same family will experience the world and life in that family from their own individual perspectives. While children's needs can be conceptualised in some general and abstract way, the needs of a specific child can only be fully understood by responding sensitively to that particular child's history and experience.

(4) The need for responsibility

> This need is met by allowing the child to gain personal independence, to begin with through learning to look after himself in matters of his everyday care, such as feeding, dressing and washing himself . . . [it] is met, too, through having possessions, however small and inexpensive, over which the child is allowed to exercise absolute ownership . . .
>
> As he grows older, increasing independence means permitting, indeed encouraging, increasing freedom — of physical movement; of taste in food, play and clothes; and, perhaps most important of all, of choice of friends, studies, hobbies, career and eventually marriage partner. Giving such independence does not mean withholding one's view, tastes and choices, or the reasons for them; nor does it mean opting out from participating in and guiding the lives of children; nor, indeed, condoning everything they do (ibid. p. 55).

In childhood and adolescence, the young person is acquiring the skills and rehearsing the roles which will be demanded in adulthood. People can only act with an appropriate degree of autonomy, independence (and inter-dependence) in adulthood if they have been given appropriate opportunities to exercise meaningful discretion, responsibility and choice in earlier life — and to live with the consequences. The concerned adult will not allow adverse consequences of a child's choice to overwhelm the youngster, but nor should the child be unaware of these effects.

Adults must provide children with a secure base and clear limits within which appropriate responsibility can be carried and choices made. These limits should be fair, justifiable and explained to the child. There should be room for negotiation and, on occasion, the adult should risk giving the young person additional degrees of freedom — such as to be allowed play at a further distance than usual from the family home or to be allowed out later than usual to go to a well-supervised disco. Limits, and any related sanctions, should be applied consistently. All of this requires considerable judgement on the part of the adult in order to achieve an often elusive balance between freedom and control, between consistency and flexibility, and between protecting and exposing the child.

Adults must also, as necessary, remind children of the crucial distinction that rejecting some unacceptable piece of behaviour is entirely different from rejecting the child. In addition, the adult must remember that in the end young people are likely to draw their own unforgiving conclusions about discrepancies between what adults say — or demand — and what they actually do.

In this view of childhood, it is seen as a precious time when the future destiny of the adult-to-be is determined. 'Give me the child at seven and I will give you the man' is a well-known maxim. While it may now be considered excessively deterministic (in that there is some encouraging evidence of the resilience of children in the face of adversity and of their capacity to make up lost ground if circumstances change in their favour), the idea that childhood experiences shape the adult is widely held among professionals working with children, even if its

5

profound implications are not yet adequately reflected in society's social and political priorities.

This model of childhood — as the precious and critical source of autonomous adulthood — is one that may be valid within the times and culture in which we live. It is essential to remember however that it expresses a specific ideology about childhood and family life. Many of the principles of fostering self-determination in the child and adult might be quite alien in cultures where, for example, marriages are arranged in the light of a family's wider economic and political interests, as in India today and in parts of Ireland in the past.

The notion of childhood as an extended period of preparation for adulthood is a social construct, formed in response to a specific set of social conditions, rather than a truth universal over time and place. An extended and protected childhood depends, for example, on reasonable expectation of longevity. If life expectancy is not more than 30 years, it would not be surprising to find girls of thirteen marrying and bearing children. It is always worth remembering that the customs, values and beliefs that we find meaningful are not necessarily the only viable or most widely adopted system of such ideas. The dominance of Western ideas in our media, literature and textbooks can lull us into thinking that Western patterns represent the highest or only form of civilisation.

Children's Rights

While children may be regarded differently according to varying economic and cultural conditions, there is an apparently universal acknowledgement that children are in some way special and that their interests, therefore, need some special protection. The evidence for this claim lies in the proliferation of references to the rights of children, and of parents and child-rearing families, in a variety of international documents which seek to exert moral influence over governments and people.

The interests and rights of children may also be advanced by legal instruments — laws, constitutions, charters, whether national or international in character — which seek to offer children and their families legally enforceable rights.

The proclamation of children's rights may seem a rather pointless activity when compared with the plight of so many millions of children around the world today, whose lives are blighted or destroyed by war, famine, preventable illness or poverty. In Ireland, too, there are children — homeless, abused, sick and hungry — whose conditions mock the rhetoric of legal undertakings. Despite the ample grounds for cynicism or pessimism, it is important to remember that, given the reality of the political powerlessness of children, the consideration and securing of their welfare is inevitably dependent on the moral and legal force of such assurances and guarantees.

Rights can be legal or moral in character. Legal rights are enforceable, in theory at least. Moral rights, however, are unenforcable in a strictly legal sense but are intended to exert moral pressure on those in authority to act in a manner which does not infringe such rights. There is certainly evidence that governments are sensitive to scrutiny of their failure to comply with what are promulgated as inter-nationally accepted standards of civilised treatment of children.

There remains the problem of awareness of rights and the real difficulty of effective access to the means of enforcement. The legal mechanisms involved in securing rights are often complex, especially where the protection of the right concerned is sought from a major international institution, such as the European Court of Human Rights, or under a national constitution.

In certain jurisdictions, statute law and case law (which interprets and sets precedents based on statutes) may also contribute to the detailed articulation and promotion of the rights of children. Unfortunately, in Ireland this process has been severely curtailed by the protracted failure of any Irish administration to bring into law new legislation to replace the British-enacted Children Act of 1908. While the Child Care Act 1991, when implemented, will undoubtedly improve matters, the development of case law in this area clearly has been greatly hampered by such a legal vacuum. This means that children have had to rely on the elaboration by the courts of the body of rights, enshrined in the 1937 Constitution and conferred on all citizens by virtue of their citizenship.

Children thus have rights under the Irish Constitution. The country has also adopted certain international instruments that *inter alia* confer rights on children e.g. the International Covenant on Economic, Social and Cultural Rights, the European Social Charter, the European Convention on the Legal Status of the Child Born Out of Wedlock. Nevertheless, in practice children rarely enjoy or can secure rights independently of their parents or caretakers. There are no obvious mechanisms whereby children can independently initiate proceedings to secure their own rights. There is no automatic mechanism for independent representation of the child's interests where disputes arise about the child's welfare or custody, between parents or between parent(s) and a third party or the State. The 1985 decision of the Supreme Court in the case of K.C.v. An Bord Uchtála (1985, Irish Reports 375) stressed the child's right to live in their natural family. This seems to underline an assumption that a child's rights can best be secured on his or her behalf by the child's parents and family. This conforms with the emphasis on family privacy as set out in the 1937 Constitution.

Children's rights are, in practice, qualified in a number of ways. For example, very often parental rights may supersede those of their children. Where children can claim a right, they may be deprived of the means or resources to seek its enforcement. And where a claim of a right is successful within the appropriate legal framework, there remains the problem of having it effected.

In some instances, the inadequacy of social service provision may deprive a child of a right to assistance which both courts and State have acknowledged as due. A celebrated example of this in recent times was the case of a 15 year old girl in the care of the Eastern Health Board. She had committed an offence for which she appeared before District Justice Hubert Wine in Dun Laoghaire Court in late 1989. The District Justice found it necessary to remand the case 10 times until late February 1990 when the authorities were finally able to offer an arrangement for the care of the girl (already, formally, in care) which satisfied him. Because of the girl's various personal problems and the lack of appropriate services, the authorities proved slow in responding to the District Justice's requirement.

7

In practice, therefore, the securing of a child's rights also depends on the feasibility of what is required to give them effect, although presumably where the facts of a case and the capacity to bear legal costs or secure legal aid permit, it may be possible to force such deficiencies to be rectified.

Parents' Needs

Historically, children have been regarded as the chattels or property of their parents, in particular of the father. Children were seen as having few, if any rights independent of their parents. Instead, parents were free to impose demands or punishments on their children as they wished, unfettered by legal or social restraints. In Western societies, the past century has seen a gradual and significant shift in how children are viewed. It has been suggested that this trend was prompted by a considerable improvement in the health and mortality risks facing children: if they were more likely to survive, then it made more sense to be concerned about their destiny (Robins, 1980, p. 312).

While the behaviour of parents is now more strictly regulated, it is still widely accepted across the political spectrum and among all social strata that parents hold the key to their children's welfare. Paradoxically, however, this view has not necessarily been shared so fully by those assuming a professional responsibility for deprived children.

In the history of child care, there has been traditionally a preoccupation with the welfare of children in isolation from their parents. There has been a tendency to take parents for granted. Parents were seen merely as carrying out their biological and socially inherited duties. Where parents seemed unequal to their task, this was taken to reveal some personal pathology since parenting was viewed as no more than a practical expression of civilised humanity in adulthood.

Where difficulties in the family gave rise to concern about a child's welfare, the response was often to write the parents out of the picture. Clearly, it was felt that they had surrendered any right to be consulted or involved, since they had so manifestly failed in their social obligations, the discharge of which was seen as the norm of civilised behaviour. Any departure from these norms meant that parents forfeited the right to be treated as civilised members of society.

In this view, the welfare of children was best served by giving them a fresh start with new caretakers, whether in a family or an institution. By a clean break, children could be spared any further suffering at the hands of their incompetent and unworthy parents.

Gradually, there has grown a realisation that social conditions and experience heavily influence an individual's capacity to parent. It is no longer tenable to believe that normal adults are programmed biologically to perform the role of parent. As Quinton and Rutter (1984, p. 246) observe,

> It makes no sense to view an individual's abilities as a parent as if they constituted an intrinsic character trait. Parenting must be considered in terms of resources as well as skills and social qualities.

There is now a more sophisticated understanding of what constitutes 'good' parenting and of how parenting can be facilitated. There is also a growing awareness of the complexity of the parenting task. This complexity is well illustrated by the following specifications (DHSS, 1974) for a family home, which when functioning well:

*   offers adequate shelter, space, food, income and the basic amenities which enable the adults to perform their marital, child-rearing and citizenship roles without incurring so much stress that anxiety inhibits a confident and positive performance;

*   secures the physical care, safety and healthy development of children, either through its own resources or through the competent use of specialised help and services;

*   acknowledges its task of socialising children, encouraging their personal development and abilities, guiding their behaviour and interests, and informing their attitudes and values;

*   offers the experience of warm, loving, intimate and consistently dependable relationships;

*   assures the mother of support and understanding, particularly during the early child-rearing period, and provides the child with a male/father/husband model which continues to remain important through adolescence;

*   offers children (2-6 years) an experience of group life, so extending their social relationships, their awareness of others and their intellectual development;

*   responds to children's curiosity with affection and reasoned explanations, and respects children through all developmental stages as persons in their own right, so securing affection and respect for others within the family circle and wider social network;

*   co-operates with school, values educational and learning opportunities, and encourages exploration and a widening of experience;

*   supports adolescents, physically and emotionally, while they are achieving relative independence of the family, personal identity, sexual maturity, a work role, relationships within society and the testing out of values and ideologies;

*   provides a fall-back, supportive system for the young marrieds during their child-bearing period.

The performance of this daunting series of tasks falls to parents generally. As the role of parenting is more carefully analysed, its complexity should induce admiration for the great sacrifices made by parents in what is largely an unsung contribution to society.

In this light, instances of parental inadequacy can no longer be seen so clearly as incontrovertible evidence of 'personal pathology'. Rather, they must be considered more a result of deficits in the resources and skills available to parents in their role. As Quinton and Rutter (1984) put it:

> Parenting resources must be considered in terms of such variables as the time available; the person's own emotional state; the presence of other life stresses and problems; the qualities of the spouse and the extent to which child-rearing is shared; the existence of other satisfactions and achievements apart from parenting (as in a job outside the home); the availability of adequate social supports; and housing conditions.

The quality of parenting will be influenced by the parent's own experience of having been parented. In the case of parents encountered by child-care services, it is likely that many may have had parenting that was deficient in some crucial respects. Where parents have had such experiences, it may be necessary for them to be compensated before they will have the emotional capacity to parent their own children adequately. They may need to be 're-parented', to fill emotional gaps remaining from their own childhood, since it may only be possible for parents to reproduce in their own behaviour qualities of which they themselves have had direct experience. They may need to experience the concern, love and attention of another adult before they can bestow these adequately on their own children. Otherwise, they may unconsciously seek to have these needs met by the unsuspecting child. The consequences of this process can be hazardous for the child and may, at worst, produce episodes of abuse as the unsatisfied parent vents his or her poorly understood frustrations on the child.

There is a natural tension between the needs of children and the needs of their parents as individuals in their own right. But in terms of child welfare, this conflict may be more apparent than real, since it is also in the child's interests that the parent's own needs are adequately met. Only in this way can parents renew themselves and their reserves of concern, attention and affection which the child craves.

Children can represent a relentless drain on their parents' emotional energy. Parents are not magically possessed of infinite supplies of this precious stuff: they need recognition, encouragement and affection in their own right (as adults, not just as parents) if they are to be sustained in their role as parent.

Parents will, therefore, need a degree of self-awareness, and a capacity to look after themselves — not at the expense of their children, but in a manner which sustains them as adults in their parenting. They will also need practical information about welfare rights, normal child development, childhood illnesses and so on. They will need knowledge of their own culture and where relevant of other cultures with which they or their children may come in contact.

Parenting demands skills broadly in line with those acquired and needed by adults who are functioning adequately. Pugh and De'Ath (1984, pp 18-19) list the desired qualities:

- the ability to love and undertake relationships, to care, to support and nurture other people, and to be sensitive to their needs;
- flexibility of mind and thinking, the ability to respond and to adapt to changing needs and demands;
- consistency of attitudes and behaviour, a reliable and dependable behaviour that provides a stable and secure environment where responses can be anticipated and rules are clear;
- the ability to communicate, through active listening, giving appropriate non-verbal messages, reflecting on feelings, and negotiating;
- the ability to make decisions and to accept responsibility for them;
- the ability to cope with stress and deal with conflict;
- the ability to apply the knowledge and information — for a theory on how to cope with temper tantrums is no use unless it can be put into action.

Parents' Rights

This discussion on children's needs began with the assertion that parents are the key to their children's welfare. We have glimpsed the complexity of the task of parenting and its crucial social importance. In addition, the notion that parenting is an innate capacity with which all civilised human beings are uniformly endowed has been challenged. The capacity to parent adequately is more correctly seen as a gift, born of positive childhood experiences and adequate support in adulthood, which can only find true expression when circumstances are favourable. Those circumstances are determined by the interaction of the personal qualities of the parent, the resources, physical and emotional, available to them in their social networks and the contingencies thrown up by life's events, such as death, redundancy, illness or disability.

Given the crucial social importance of parents, it is hardly surprising that they are frequently referred to in many documents concerned with the development of humanity and society (UN 1948, 1966; Holy See, 1983; Council of Europe, 1950, 1961).

One of the most significant developments in child-care thinking in recent years has been the re-discovery of 'natural parents'. Growing appreciation of the complexity of parenting, a corresponding sympathy for parents struggling against unequal odds, the influence of the wider consumer rights movement and its manifestations in the social services field — all these have contributed to this emerging awareness.

This trend has an important pragmatic basis, too. It has gradually come to be recognised how very difficult it is to supplant adequately the role of natural parents in the lives of children. Some children in care may end up very damaged by an experience intended to help them and rescue them from harm. This realisation has induced greater humility on the part of at least some professionals and a correspondingly greater willingness to regard parents as real partners in the project of child welfare and child protection, whether the child is at home or in care.

In the Irish context, it may be argued that the Constitution affords very complete (excessive, in the eyes of some) guarantees on the rights of parents. These rights certainly exist — on paper. Many harassed parents do not, however, revel in the benefits of such constitutional assurances. As in the case of many legal instruments, there is a considerable gap between the aspiration and the practical effect. Nevertheless, the existence of these guarantees is of moral, and potentially tangible, significance so long as the courts are given adequate opportunity to explore in concrete terms the practical implications of these provisions. The law in a sense unfolds as the superior courts hand down important decisions of principle about what the law actually is. Unless an actual case presents the courts with such an opportunity, the law on a specific problem or issue may languish unstated or undeveloped for a considerable period. The function of the courts is to interpret what the law is in relation to a given situation by reference to the Constitution, statute law (passed by the Oireachtas) and, where relevant, international sources.

Chapter 2

CHILDREN, PARENTS
AND THE LAW*

In the great majority of cases, parents play their role unencumbered by the State or the courts. In legal terms, those parents are freely exercising their guardianship and custody rights in the rearing of their children. The picture becomes more complicated where children belong to parents who do not have a happy marriage, or who fail to exercise their responsibilities, or who are not married to each other.

Guardianship
A person who is a child's guardian has duties and rights in relation to all matters concerning the child's physical, intellectual, religious, social and moral welfare. In practice, the guardian's rights include decisions about religious upbringing, medical care and authorising the issue of a passport for a child. Parents who are married to each other automatically hold equal rights as guardians until a young person reaches the age of 18. Where the parents are not married, only the mother is automatically guardian but the father may apply to the courts, under the Status of Children Act 1987 (Section 11), for recognition as a guardian.

A young person may contract a lawful marriage at 16 years of age (subject to having parental consent if under 18 years of age). If a girl who has not married has a child when younger than 18, she acquires full guardianship rights in respect of that child despite the fact that her parents retain these same rights in respect of herself.

Almost the only way that a parent may divest herself of guardianship rights currently is in the case of an unmarried mother who signs the consents for the adoption of her child. Her consents pave the way for the making of an adoption order in respect of her child by the Adoption Board. This order has the effect of transferring her guardianship rights to her child's adoptive parents.

*The child protection law described in this chapter is based on the law current at the time of writing (i.e. essentially the Children Act 1908). While the Child Care Act 1991 is referred to, it should be remembered that the sections of this Act will become operational only when signed into effect by the Minister for Health on such day or days as he or she may choose. The full implementation of this legislation will, in some instances, entail complex planning and the government has indicated in the Programme for Economic and Social Progress 1991 that it envisages its implementation being phased in over the seven-year lifetime of the programme. This chapter gives a broad brush impression of the legislative intentions behind the Act. In due course, a separate book will be required which can describe the scope, workings and impact of the total Child Care Act 1991 when enacted and fully operational.

In exceptional cases, married parents may lose guardianship rights where an application is made successfully by adoptive applicants to adopt their child under the Adoption Act 1988. The very stringent requirements of this Act, however, make it unlikely to be a widely employed measure.

Parents may arrange by 'deed or will' to appoint people to succeed them as guardians on the death of either or both parents (Guardianship of Infants Act 1964, S. 7). The courts may also appoint any person(s) on application as guardian to a child who has no guardian (ibid. S. 8).

Custody

Custody refers to the everyday 'care and control' of the child. It essentially means the right to physical care and control. Thus a parent deprived of custody is not prevented from having any further say in the upbringing of his or her child. The right to custody is merely one of the rights that arise under the guardianship relationship (Shatter, 1986, p. 343).

It is not necessary to be the child's guardian to have lawful custody of a child. A child's father, for example, who is not the child's guardian (by virtue of not being married to the child's mother) is permitted to apply for custody under Section 13 of the Status of Children Act 1987. Also, in the case of a child in care, custody resides with those responsible for the day-to-day care, whereas the natural parents retain their role as guardians.

In cases of marital separation, the terms of the legal separation agreement will typically assign custody to one parent and access rights to the other. In the case of disagreement, an application may be made to the court for a direction as to who should be the custodial parent (i.e. the parent with day-to-day care and control of the children). In reaching its decision in such inter-parental (married) custody and access disputes, the court will regard the welfare of the child as the first and paramount consideration. Whatever the outcome regarding custody in the event of marital breakdown, both parents retain guardianship rights in respect of their children.

The Law, Child Protection and Limits on Parents' Rights

Under the 1937 Constitution, parents enjoy substantial rights and guarantees. According to Article 41 of the Constitution the family (based on marriage) shall possess 'inalienable and imprescriptible rights, antecedent and superior to all positive law'. A right is 'inalienable' in that it cannot be voluntarily surrendered. A right is 'imprescriptible' in that it cannot be extinguished because of any failure to exercise it adequately or at all.

However, the rights enjoyed by parents are by no means absolute.

> In exceptional cases, where the parents for physical or moral reasons fail in their duty towards their children, the State, as guardian of the common good, by appropriate means shall endeavour to supply the place of the parents, but always with due regard for the natural and imprescriptible rights of the child (Bunreacht na hÉireann, Article 42.5).

As mentioned above, guardianship rights may be extinguished where certain very specific conditions apply in order that a child may be adopted under the Adoption Act 1988. When the relevant sections of the Child Care Act 1991 are enacted, they will have the effect of restricting the exercise of certain guardianship rights by parents in relation to any of their children who are the subject of care orders. Under these provisions the parents' consent to granting of temporary passport or to medical care for the child may be waived.

Custody rights are subject to greater possible limitation in order to secure the welfare of a child. In exceptional cases, where there has been parental failure or where there are other compelling reasons based on the child's welfare, parents may be deprived of custody by various procedures such as an application for a place of safety order, an application for a fit person order, an application for the committal of a child to a special school or the use of wardship proceedings.

Place of Safety Order

This is an emergency order that permits the removal of a child from immediate risk to a place of safety. The granting of the order does not require absolute proof of danger or harm — but there must be reasonable grounds for suspicion.

> If it appears to a district justice, on information on oath laid by any person who, in the opinion of the justice, is acting in the interests of a child or young person, that there is reasonable cause to suspect that the child or young person (under 17 years of age) has been or is being assaulted, ill-treated or neglected in any place within the jurisdiction of the justice, in a manner likely to cause the child or young person unnecessary suffering, or to be injurious to his health, (Children Act 1908, Section 24)

then the district justice may issue a warrant authorising a garda to search for and remove the child concerned.

The suspicion of certain offences having been committed against the child also constitutes grounds for the making of such an order. In addition, Section 20 of the Children Act 1908 gives a garda emergency powers to remove a child directly from immediate risk where he believes such offences to have been committed.

The use of Section 24 is more favoured because it can be followed by an application for a fit person order (below) in the same case. A place of safety order is intended to give a breathing space to arrange a full hearing of the facts of the case and to protect the child in the meantime. A place of safety can be a home, hospital or the like.

Fit Person Order

Section 58 of the Children Act 1908 provides for any person to bring a child or young person under 15 years of age before a court to apply for a fit person order in respect of that child. The court may make such an order where it is satisfied, basically, that the child has been ill-treated or neglected, or that the parents have failed to exercise 'proper guardianship'. In general, courts wish to hear evidence of physical neglect or ill-treatment; evidence of psychological damage appears to be less compelling for the courts — presumably because of its less objective nature. To make a fit person order, the court must consider the step justified 'on the balance of probabilities', the standard of proof required in civil law cases. (It should be noted that this is quite different from the standard of 'beyond all reasonable doubt' required in criminal law cases).

In practice, fit person orders are applied for by health board social workers (who also tend to undertake applications for place of safety orders). The order, if granted, deprives parents of their child's custody normally but not invariably, until his or her sixteenth birthday (but parents always retain guardianship rights and, therefore, must be consulted on relevant issues). Parents may appeal such an order, by lodging their application to do so within ten days. They may also, at any time, apply to have the order revoked. To do this, they must show that there have been material changes in the circumstances of their case. In some instances, where they consider circumstances justify it, health boards may agree to return children under a fit person order to their parents' custody while they still remain the subjects of an order.

Committal Order

Courts may commit a child to care within a special school or industrial school (or to the care of a fit person) as a response to the child's offending behaviour, non-school attendance or need for protection. The use of the committal order for the latter category has fallen into decline with the increasing use of fit person order applications by health board personnel.

Wardship

Wardship jurisdiction is exercised by the president of the High Court or the Circuit Court. Historically, wardship was most concerned with the protection of the property of minors or those who lacked capacity. Nowadays, no such property interest has to exist for wardship to be instituted.

Wardship proceedings can permit a third party to seek custody of a child against the wishes of a parent or to 'obtain protection for a child against the actions of a parent' (Shatter, 1986, p. 400).

Wardship jurisdiction may be used in a number of circumstances (ibid. pp 401-2):

- where parents seek to prevent a teenage son or daughter from marrying, leaving home, or associating with undesirable persons, they may apply to have them made a ward of court;
- if a child is placed, or is living with, relations, foster parents, potential adopters or any other persons who wish to retain custody of the child, contrary to the wishes of the natural parent or parents, the former may apply for a custody order under the wardship jurisdiction;
- a health board, local authority or other such agency may apply to have a child whose welfare is threatened made a ward of court and seek orders enabling it to have the child assessed or supervised in its place of residence or taken into care;
- to restrict the removal of a minor from the jurisdiction or to have a minor returned to the jurisdiction from where he was brought. Thus the wardship jurisdiction may be invoked by an estranged spouse upon the 'kidnapping' of a child by the other spouse. If it is in the best interests of a ward of the Irish court to leave this jurisdiction, permission will be granted by the court;
- to determine a dispute between spouses as to their child's upbringing or custody. It is normally, however, more appropriate to use the provisions of Section 11 of the Guardianship of Infants Act 1964 for this purpose;
- the most common circumstance in which a minor is made a ward of court is where it is thought desirable to obtain independent protection for a minor's property interest.

Wardship proceedings can be used to plug a legal gap concerning the welfare of young people between the ages of 16 and 18. This arises because the protection of the Children Act 1908 (and therefore the benefits of a place of safety or fit person order) applies to young people aged under 16 because a fit person order can only apply to young people under 16 years of age. Wardship has been used by the Eastern Health Board in cases of sexual abuse involving females aged 16 to 18 (Scully, 1987, p. 138).

Child Care Act 1991

The Child Care Act 1991 is the culmination of a number of attempts since 1985 to update the legislation in the area of child protection and welfare and replace the (British) Children Act of 1908. While the Act has been signed into law by the President, under Section 1 each section will not become effective until signed into operation by the Minister for Health. Thus the implementation of many sections may prove to be considerably delayed. The Government has announced that it proposes 'to implement the Bill, when passed, on a phased basis' (Ireland, 1991, p. 27).

The new legislation will give duties and powers to health boards to promote and protect the welfare of children at risk and to provide child care and family support services. The provisions of the Act are extensive, but *inter alia* they will
- clarify and extend the powers of health boards to intervene compulsorily to protect children on an emergency or longer term basis;
- raise the maximum age for children to remain in care, from their 16th birthday to their 18th birthday and define a 'child' as any person under 18 years who is not married;
- require the establishment of at least one child care advisory committee for each health board;
- require health boards to prepare annual reviews of the adequacy of the child care services in their region;
- introduce a new supervision order, alongside emergency care, interim care and care orders;
- require a court to regard the welfare of the child as paramount and, as far as practicable, to take account of the child's wishes in decisions affecting the child;
- allow a child to be joined in his/her own right as a party to proceedings;
- allow a court to procure a report on a child;
- require a health board to facilitate reasonable access by parents or others with a *bona fide* interest to a child in the board's care, and allow courts to make rulings in relation to access matters;
- provide for the regulation of foster care, residential care and pre-school care by health boards;
- provide for the compulsory review of the cases of children in care, and permit the assistance of such children when they leave care, up until the age of 21 years.

Other legal developments

The Judicial Separation and Family Law Reform Act 1989 strengthens the powers of courts in deciding in the best interests of children whose parents are obtaining a judicial separation. The court may order the procurement of a report on any aspect of the welfare of a child concerned (S. 40). The court is also free to declare a parent as unfit to have custody (S. 41).

The Child Abduction and Enforcement of Custody Orders Act 1991 is intended to prevent the removal of a child from the jurisdiction to another state, where that state is a Contracting State to the Convention on the Civil Aspects of International Child

Abduction 1980 and the European Convention on Recognition and Enforcement of Decisions concerning Custody of Children 1980. The enactment of the legislation means that the Conventions will have effect in Ireland and that attempts to frustrate Irish court orders in respect of children by bringing them to another jurisdiction can be prevented if the other state concerned has ratified the Conventions.

In September 1990, An Taoiseach announced at the World Summit for Children held in New York that Ireland intended to ratify the United Nations Convention on the Rights of the Child, an international human rights treaty on the treatment of children. By ratification, a member government undertakes to adhere to the standards of provision and protection for children and their families on a range of fronts — health, education, vocational training, social security, play and recreational opportunities, the guarantee of the due process of law, family support, special provision for vulnerable children, and, subject to their age and capacity, a commitment to allowing children to have a say in their own lives. Governments of countries which have ratified the Convention will have to submit regular reports and will have their performance reviewed by a Committee on the Rights of the Child, made up of ten independent experts elected by ratifying governments.

Also in September 1990, the Law Reform Commission published its *Report on Child Sexual Abuse*. The report contains a range of proposals for changes in the civil and criminal law, and in the law of evidence. It proposes, *inter alia,*

- a duty on professional workers in specific categories to report suspected cases of child sexual abuse (mandatory reporting);
- immunity from civil and criminal proceedings for any person who, in good faith and with due care, reports a suspicion of child sexual abuse;
- specific duties for health boards and their officials in relation to the management of suspected or confirmed cases of child sexual abuse;
- new powers and procedures for the District Court in cases of child sexual abuse;
- a new offence of *child sexual abuse* which would replace the existing offence of *indecent assault*;
- new measures to facilitate the hearing of children's evidence in a more appropriate manner.

In the months prior to going to press, the government brought in new legislation to regulate inter-country adoption, the Adoption Act 1991, and committed itself to introducing legislation on juvenile justice (An Taoiseach 1991).

Chapter 3

SOCIAL STRESS IN THE LIVES OF CHILDREN

Socio-Economic Factors

Socio-economic factors play a major part in shaping the destinies of Irish children. Social class has an overwhelming, if largely unacknowledged, influence on their chances in life. There is an inexorable association between lower social class and inferior outcome on a whole series of measures, such as infant mortality, general health, educational attainment or employment prospects. Lower social class seems also to increase the risk of exposure to other social problems, to aggravate their effect and to deprive children of the resources which may mitigate the worst effects for their more socially favoured peers. Children from lower social classes are more at risk of becoming involved in drug abuse, delinquency or of being subjected to abuse. They are more likely to live in physical environments that are barren and impoverished.

It is important to stress that not all children from these social backgrounds are destined to experience these problems. But belonging to a lower social class certainly increases the risk.

Children in Low Income Families

Measuring poverty is a difficult task. Are people poor only when they literally have no food in their stomach or no money to put it there? Are people poor when they lack the necessities just to survive? Or are people poor when they cannot expect to enjoy things that are taken for granted by the majority of the population — things such as regular meals with meat, an annual holiday or a colour television?

The 1986 Census of Population reported a total of 976,304 households in the state. According to a major study by the Economic and Social Research Institute (Callan *et al*, 1988), close to one in five (18.9%) of all households in the state may be said to live in poverty. In reaching this figure, the study, of a sample of 3,286 households, counted as 'poor' any household that (i) had no more than 50% of the weekly income of what a sample of households of similar composition in the population had and (ii) could only make ends meet 'with some difficulty'.

The proportion of these poor households that had children was found to have risen dramatically, from 43.3% in 1973 to 67.2% in 1987 (ibid. p. 40). Not only do households with children now make up the major share of all households in poverty, they also carry a disproportionate risk of being poor. Households with children made up 44% of the households in the study population, but they made up between 58 and 61% of poor households (the proportion varying depending on what weighting was given to the cost of maintaining adult and child dependants).

Health
Health care for mothers and infants
A Department of Health survey (1980) of 1,189 mothers in receipt of ante-natal, obstetrical and post-natal care revealed important differences in health histories along class lines.

For the purposes of the survey, women were divided by their eligibility status for health care. The group that qualifies for the means-tested general medical services card (Category 1 eligibility) can reasonably be considered to represent the poorer classes in society. The survey found

> considerable evidence of a higher level of obstetric risk among Category 1 mothers. There were significant differences between the Category 1 mothers and the other mothers in terms of risk factors related to age, parity, marital status and certain events in previous obstetric history, such as a previous stillbirth or neo-natal death, congenital abnormalities in previous live births, and previous obstetric history of caesarean section, toxaemia, anaemia or bleeding (Department of Health, 1982, pp 35-6).

In addition to less favourable obstetric histories, Category 1 mothers tended to make less use of maternal health services than other mothers. They were more likely to have had less than seven ante-natal visits; they were also less likely to go early for ante-natal care, to have had their babies examined soon after discharge, to have had a post-natal check-up soon after discharge, or have had family-planning discussions (ibid. p. 38).

Perinatal mortality rates
Perinatal mortality refers to the number of stillbirths and early neo-natal deaths, and is regarded as a valuable proxy measurement of general health and welfare in a given population. Major differences are found in the rates experienced by groups at different ends of the occupational scale. A perinatal mortality rate of 15.5 per 1,000 for unskilled manual and 22.4 per 1,000 for unemployed groups compared with a rate, in 1986, of 1.7 per 1,000 for higher professionals and 1.6 per 1,000 for salaried employees (Department of Health, 1990).

Such disparities in the experience of perinatal mortality in different social classes provides some of the most powerful evidence of the impact of social class on children's chances in life.

Breast-feeding
Medical opinion now strongly emphasises the advantages for physical and psychological development which accrue from breast-feeding, rather than other forms of infant-feeding.

> In normal circumstances, breast-feeding is considered to be the best way to feed a baby, both physically and, to some extent, emotionally. In its composition and temperature, breast milk is ideal for the newborn infant. Antibodies are transmitted in it, giving some protection against infection in early life, and it may also provide some defence against allergies. It avoids the possibility of over-concentration, which is present with artificial preparations and which may lead to dehydration, as well as the possibility of the laying down of extra fat cells, making weight more difficult to control in later life (McSweeney and Kevany, 1981).

The reasons why a woman may breast-feed or not are complex, but they seem to be related to the conviction and cultural sensitivity with which the pro-breast feeding message is delivered by professionals, the attitudes of key informal sources of information, such as mothers and friends, and the woman's perception of her own sexuality.

There are also practical considerations. Poorer women are less likely to have the energy and unpressured time to devote to breast-feeding which, for all its merits, many women may find a time-consuming, if not exhausting, process (McSweeney, 1986). Stress may affect a woman's lactation and she may become dispirited, at this vulnerable time, by worries about the adequacy of her milk supply, soreness and so on.

Whatever the reasons, it is fairly clear that the health care system has failed to alter substantially infant-feeding practices in favour of breast-feeding, especially among working-class women. The national perinatal reporting system provides data, *inter alia*, on the extent of breast-feeding by occupational group, at the time of discharge from hospital after delivery. In 1986, the rate of breast-feeding among children of the higher professional group (66.8%) was almost five times the rate for the children of unskilled manual workers (13.7%) and almost six times the rate for children of the unemployed (12.01%) and over twice the national rate (31.2%) (Department of Health, 1990, p. 142).

In a survey of women discharged following the birth of their child from maternity hospital during a week in March 1986, McSweeney (1986) found that 37.8% had started to breast-feed and 32.9% were still doing so when leaving the hospital. This figure has increased only slightly since the first such survey in 1981 and the rate of breast-feeding in Ireland remains low compared to other developed countries. Of those who breast-feed, middle-class mothers are among those likely to continue doing so for longer. After 6 weeks, 40% of mothers from non-skilled/ manual, unemployed or unmarried backgrounds who had started breast-feeding had ceased, as against 23% of those from a middle-class background. By 12 weeks, the proportions of those who had ceased had increased to 62.5% and 47.4% respectively (ibid).

21

Irish children generally have less chance of being breast-fed than children in other developed countries, but their chances are diminished even further if they are born into the working class.

Nutrition

A recent study of the diets of 53 families in a working-class area of Dublin with high unemployment found a series of deficiencies (Lee and Gibney, 1989). Fat intake in adults exceeded recommended values, while their fibre intake was below the desirable level, especially in women. Iron intake was very low in adult women and adolescent girls, and many children also had deficiencies in iron. Again, children and women were found to have low intakes of Vitamin C. Overall, women (especially in single parent families) were the group most at risk of nutritional inadequacy.

A 1980 study investigated dietary knowledge and practices among a sample of 394 mothers of young children (McSweeney and Kevany, 1981). It was found that working-class mothers scored less well than their middle-class peers. They tended to have less adequate information about nutrition and they were also more likely to have 'bad habits' (such as eating excessive amounts of fried food, which results in an undesirable intake of fat) in relation to the family diet. The husbands of wives from a non-skilled background were three times more likely to eat a fry at least once a day than their peers from a non-manual background.

Children from a working class background were much more likely to eat sweets. Those over 4 years of age were four times more likely to be given money for sweets each day than their middle-class counterparts. Between the ages of 1 and 4, working-class children were three times more likely to be bought sweets every day (ibid. p. 16).

A study in Dublin primary schools in 1980-81 found that children from working-class backgrounds tended to have less nutritious lunches than those from middle-class or rural homes (McLaughlin, Gormley and Wickham, 1982). In the case of most nutrients recommended, the working-class children's intake was deficient and inferior to that of other children. The study also found that 7.7% of working-class girls had not consumed breakfast on the first study day (i.e. day on which the information was collected), with a figure of 8.6% on the second day. This compared with a mean rate of no breakfast of 4.2% among all the children surveyed.

Dental health

A major study in 1984 looked at dental health among children and young people (O'Mullane et al, 1986). It found that working-class youngsters scored less favourably on a number of measures (ibid. pp 82-90). They were more likely to have dental caries, especially in adolescence (although the children of farmers fared worse again). Working-class children had visited their dentist less recently and less frequently. When asked to choose between a filling or an extraction for a bad back or front tooth, working-class parents of 8-year olds were less likely to opt for the filling than their middle-class counterparts. A similar disparity was maintained between the social groups when the same question was posed to 15-year olds.

Height and weight
A 1971 study of Dublin schoolchildren (N = 412) found that children from less well-off social backgrounds showed a pattern of development in terms of height and weight considerably inferior to that observed among their better-off counterparts (Kent and Sexton, 1973).

Psychiatric illness
Adults: While there is only limited evidence about the extent of psychiatric illness among children, there is considerable information about the position in relation to adults. Where parents suffer mental illness, this clearly may have implications for the quality of parent/child relationships and, in certain circumstances, may produce enduring adverse consequences for the child (see p. 59). Consistently, the evidence points to a disproportionately heavy rate of admission to in-patient psychiatric care for lower socio-economic groups.

Returns for admissions consistently show that the unskilled/manual group have the highest admission rates (O'Connor and Walsh, 1989, pp 9-10). In 1987, the rate for admission to psychiatric hospital for people from the 'unskilled manual' socio-economic group (2,216.50 per 100,000 population) was over six times that for people in the 'employers and managers' group (ibid. p. 20). In the case of a diagnosis of schizophrenia, the disparity was even more marked, with the poorer patients having a rate of such diagnosis more than 21 times that of 'employers and managers' (ibid. p. 26).

Children: A recent study of national schoolchildren in Clare and Limerick (N = 1,361) found that pupils in national schools officially classified as disadvantaged (i.e. situated in and serving disadvantaged areas) had a rate of maladjustment among their pupils twice that of all pupils in the study and over four times that of rural children in the study (O'Connor, Ruddle and O'Gallagher, 1989, pp 55-6).

McCarthy and O'Boyle (1986) assessed the extent of maladjustment of 7-11 year olds (N = 542) in four Dublin schools. They found a rate of conduct disorders (aggression and destructiveness) among working-class children that was double that of their more socially favoured peers.

Drug abuse
Various studies and reports confirm a strong association between concentrations of illicit drug use and social deprivation in the history of the Dublin 'opiate epidemic' of the 1980s. In a study of drug use in Dublin's south-inner city, O'Kelly et al (1988, pp 35-8) observed that

> the sudden rise in heroin use in this ward, as in other central Dublin areas, occurred in a vulnerable community where there are large families with a high level of unemployment and few recreational facilities. Heroin use was most common in local authority flat complexes. Educational achievement was often poor and there was frequently a history of previous contact with the Gardaí and Probation Service.

Another study in Dublin's north-inner city found that of 88 heroin abusers interviewed, only 4 had any kind of educational certificate, 10 could not read or write, and only 4 were employed at the time of interview (Dean, Bradshaw and

Lavelle, 1983, pp 25-6). These Dublin trends are mirrored in reports from Glasgow and Merseyside (Dean *et al*, 1987, p. 141).

Education
Literacy and numeracy problems
Wide differences in reading attainment levels have been found in national school pupils of different social backgrounds in Limerick and Clare (O'Connor, Ruddle and O'Gallagher, 1989, pp 67-8, 81). Almost half of the pupils from a disadvantaged urban area (47%) were found to have a reading age 18 months below their chronological age. This compared with only one in five (20%) for all children in the study (N = 1,361). The rate of severe reading backwardness (i.e. a discrepancy of 30 months between reading and chronological age) was three times higher in the disadvantaged group compared to the whole study population — 16.3% compared to 5%.

In a 1983 study, Dublin inner city teachers reported that one in six (17.09%) of local primary school leavers (generally working class and poor) had not achieved everyday reading skills (O'Flaherty 1984), compared to a rate of 6% in an earlier national study (Fontes and Kellaghan, 1977). Further, albeit indirect, evidence of greater literacy and numeracy problems among working-class children than among their middle-class peers derives from a survey of the estimates of principals of different categories of second-level schools (Hannan, Breen *et al*, 1983, Table 4.3, p. 90). The principals in the survey sample reporting the greater tendency to such problems had higher concentrations of working-class children in their intake. About half of the principals of community schools, but over two-thirds of those in charge of vocational schools, reported that over 15% of school entrants had serious numeracy and literacy problems. By comparison, less than a quarter of secondary school principals reported such a level of problems in their entrants (ibid. pp 90-91).

A similar disparity between pupils in secondary and vocational schools was also established in a 1971-72 study of reading levels (Swan, 1978). Almost one in six (15.9%) of first-year pupils were backward readers, with 8.5% of secondary school and 30.4% of vocational school pupils falling into these categories.

There may well be a form of selection in existence between schools, with the more academically able attracted to the secondary schools. But social class is clearly also a factor to be considered.

Qualification level on leaving the educational system
There is overwhelming evidence from a number of Irish studies that lower social class increases the chances of leaving school early and/or without a qualification.

> Early leaving is quite concentrated in particular kinds of schools: those that cater mainly for working-class children or children from small farms or from the families of unemployed manual workers, vocational schools and schools in which the poorly educible, educationally, are selectively concentrated (Hannan, 1986, p. 30).

While not confined to working-class areas, the problems of early drop-out and school failure are especially concentrated in working-class districts. The rate of early school-leaving is at its highest — almost three times the national average in (working class) central Dublin. But in other large working-class suburbs of Dublin and the other large cities, the rate is also disproportionately high (ibid. p. 24).

One in three young people from working-class Dublin leave school without a qualification (ibid. p. 24). Their fate is considerably worse than that of all young people nationally, of whom 23% of boys and 17% of girls experience such educational failure. The implications of this failure for young people's chances in life are enormous.

> The unemployment rate among those who pass the Leaving Certificate is almost half that of those who fail it or who leave school having passed only the Intermediate or Group Certificate exam, and it is almost three times better than those who failed their junior cycle exams or who left school without taking any exam (ibid. p. 28).

Educational attainment is important not only in determining whether one is likely to get a job. It also influences the quality of employment gained, in terms of conditions and job security (Breen, 1985). Those least qualified (most likely to be from the lower social classes) are least likely to find secure employment.

Participation in third-level education

Major analyses of new entrants to higher education in 1980 and 1986 reveal great inequalities of access to the system (Clancy, 1982 and 1988). In 1986, young people from the socio-economic group 'higher professional' had a share of higher education entrants three times their share of the general population. In contrast, students from the 'manual workers' group were heavily under-represented. Students from 'skilled manual' and 'semi-skilled manual' backgrounds would require a twofold increase in order to gain their proportionate share of entry places to higher education relative to their share in the general population (Clancy, 1988, p. 22).

The trends between 1980 and 1986 point to the stubborn persistence of marked social inequalities in rates of admission to higher education (ibid. p. 25). As things stand, young people from a higher professional background have a chance 19 times greater of entering third-level education than their counterparts from an unskilled manual background.

Employment

The unemployment rate among unskilled workers is estimated to be 15 times that among professional and technical workers (Cullen *et al*, 1987a, p. 213). Furthermore, unskilled workers are likely to have had the largest number of episodes of involuntary unemployment and to have spent the longest period unemployed.

The frequency of unemployment and its cumulative duration increases steadily as one moves down the occupational scale from the professional classes (Whelan, 1980, p. 24). The effects of unemployment are most likely to fall, therefore, on working class children. The evidence available as to these effects is reviewed in Madge (1983).

Juvenile Delinquency

In a 1984 study of 870 young offenders, aged between 16 and 20, who had served custodial sentences in a specific centre, O'Mahony, Cullen and O'Hara (1985) found 'clear-cut evidence of economic disadvantage in the family background of the offenders' (ibid p. 35). The authors discovered that the proportion of offenders in their study whose fathers had a manual occupation (85%) was twice that found in the Census of Population 1981. Close to half of all the offenders (43%) had fathers in unskilled manual positions, a proportion almost six times that in the national population.

Family Violence

Children may be affected by domestic violence in two ways. They may be the direct victims of physical abuse (see pp 60-65) or they may suffer psychological harm from witnessing physical violence against their mother by their father or by some other man with whom their mother is involved.

Wife battering
How do people see the problem of wife battering? In 1986, Women's Aid, Dublin, commissioned the Market Research Bureau of Ireland (MRBI) to undertake a survey of knowledge and perceptions of family violence in the adult population (Women's Aid, 1986). One in four of the adults surveyed, in a representative sample (N = 750), claimed to have personal knowledge of households where violence occurred towards the wife. (One in seven claimed knowledge of a household where a child was the victim of violence.) Despite this level of familiarity with these problems, the respondents regarded them as less widespread than a number of other problems they were asked to consider. The problems of redundancy, emigration, teenage pregnancy and marriage breakdown were regarded by the respondents as at least twice as common as physical violence by husbands against wives.

This problem of violence may not be regarded as seriously in Ireland as it is in many other countries. In a study of European attitudes, only 65% of Irish respondents were willing to regard divorce as justifiable in the case of a violent partner. The comparable figures elsewhere were Northern Ireland, 56%, Britain, 80% and 'all Europe', 77% (Fogarty, Ryan and Lee, 1984, p. 185). However, it is important to recognise that, in this example, the question of attitudes to violence is framed in terms of justifiable grounds for seeking divorce, the possible introduction of which was rejected in a referendum in the Republic in 1986.

How extensive is the problem of wife-battering? Despite its grave implications for the women involved, and their children, there exist no comprehensive data on the scale of the problem in Ireland. For some light on the subject, we must rely on scanty figures of women approaching services for assistance and on limited research evidence, such as the study by Kennedy (1985) which reported that some 215 women sought refuge from violence in two Dublin hostels during 1983.

Another possible source on the extent of wife abuse is the numbers of women seeking, and being granted by the courts, barring orders against their husbands. For a woman to secure such an order, it is necessary for her to satisfy the court of the man's unreasonable behaviour towards her (which, presumably, frequently involves physical violence). Unfortunately national figures are not easily available.

The difficulty in measuring the extent of the problem from the use of legal or social support facilities is that it fails to include the considerable number of women who have not yet been able to bring themselves to the point of publicising their problem through seeking external help. Nevertheless, the evidence suggests that the problem of violence between spouses exists on a significant scale in Ireland. It is worth recalling the figure mentioned in the 1986 survey (above) — one in four members of the public claimed to know of a household where the woman was a victim of physical violence. There is also evidence from an exploratory study by O'Higgins (1974) of 40 deserted women. She found that the problem of violence was referred to by half of the women interviewed. It was the third most frequently mentioned adverse factor in their marriage (21 instances), after 'lack of communication' (25) and 'expectations from marriage not realised' (23).

What effects does this violence have? The deleterious effects of the violence on women, and their children, may be aggravated by an ambivalence on the part of the woman, her relatives or the public. People in Ireland seem unwilling to recognise or address the problem. Even in her exploratory study, O'Higgins (ibid, p. 93) was able to conclude that 'violence had no major significance for our subjects. It was a problem for some but not an insurmountable one. Although not acceptable to the subjects, it was only problematic for a very small number.'

The victim does not seem alone in her low-key or reticent response to the problem of physical violence in her life. By its nature, such violence tends to remain hidden. Its perpetrators are unlikely to publicise it. Its victims may hesitate to seek help through fear, shame or a confusion of feelings towards their partner based on a residue of loyalty or an irrepressible faith that the most recent incident will be the last. Even relatives may be reluctant to become involved because of fear, embarrassment or inhibitions about infringing family privacy. Respondents in the 1986 survey of attitudes to family violence recommended that relatives should not get involved in disputes between husband and wife; help from outside the family circle was favoured (Women's Aid, 1986). It was the view of 61% and 66% respectively that parents and brothers/sisters should not intervene.

The problem of battering in the relationship is very serious for the woman concerned, however privately she may endure her abuse. In a study by Casey (1987) of 127 women who had used refuge facilities for battered women, 48% reported being beaten at least once a week, including the 12% beaten each day. In terms of the violence inflicted, 22% reported bones broken, 56% reported their head had been beaten and 49% had experienced flesh wounds. One in four had been raped by their partner, one in eight had experienced an attempted choking and almost one in ten had been threatened with a knife.

There is evidence of the harmful effect of overt marital discord on the psychological development of children, particularly boys (Rutter and Giller, 1983). There is also the problem that aggressive behaviour on the part of a father figure to whom the child is close may have a powerful effect on the child's behaviour and attitudes. Boys may model their own behaviour, immediately and in the long term, on this aggressive pattern and may internalise the demeaning image of women implicit in the behaviour which the father has legitimised in the child's eyes. Girls,

Table 1: **Forms of violence mentioned by a sample of women users of battered wives refuges, as received in battering during pregnancy* (N = 76)**

Forms of violence	No.	%
Loss of baby	10	13
Threatened loss of baby	17	22
Rape	2	3
Thrown downstairs	2	3
Bones broken	5	7
Flesh wounds	21	28
Abdomen kicked	13	17
Attempted choking	3	4
Head battered	35	46
Threatened with knife	2	3
Dragged by hair	2	3
Black eyes	12	16
Severe bruising	70	92

*These figures do not total to sample size as many women mentioned more than one form of violence.

Source: Casey, M., *Domestic Violence against Women.* Dublin: Federation of Women's Refuges, 1987

on the other hand, may be affected by internalising similarly demeaning images of themselves and, perhaps even more insidiously, an expectation that such experience will be normal 'when the time comes'.

Violence against a mother by her partner puts a child, even in the womb, at risk psychologically and physically. Casey's study (ibid. p. 19) revealed that 60% of the women (N = 76) said that they had been battered when pregnant, resulting in a threatened loss of their baby in 17 cases (22%) and an actual loss of the baby in ten cases (13%).

The battering of a pregnant women may cause death or physical and/or psychological trauma to the child she is carrying. Table 1 gives details of the forms of violence endured by pregnant women in Casey's study. The effects of continuing violence on the child may be severe right through his childhood.

Ninety-six per cent (N = 122) of the unions had children. In 34 cases (28%), the mothers mentioned that the children were severely beaten by their partners. There were 14 confirmed cases of father/child sexual abuse in the sample and a further 5 cases were under investigation (3 of the latter involved older brother/younger sibling abuse). Nine other cases of father/child abuse were reported by mothers, on which action, at the time, had not yet been taken (ibid. p. 20).

It is possible that the experience of violence in one generation increases the chances of its being reproduced in the next. In this study, 62% of the women said there was a history of battering in their partner's family, while 18% reported a similar history in their own family (ibid. p. 22).

The causation of wife battering is complex, but these findings converge with evidence from the international literature that some of its roots lie in the childhood experiences of the protagonists.

Lone Parent Families

Census returns indicate that there are 37,546 family units with children in the age range 0-19 headed by lone parents in the State (Central Statistics Office, 1989); overwhelmingly, these family units, which account for 81,846 children, are headed by women. Besides the global figure for lone parent households, we may know the various possible categories of lone parenthood — widow, widower, prisoner's spouse, deserted, separated or divorced spouse, unmarried or single parent — but we do not know how many lone parents there are in each of these categories nor how many children they have. This is a serious lacuna in official statistics in relation to the family.

There has been a significant increase in the numbers of children in one parent families in receipt of social welfare payments in the 1980s (see Table 2). While these figures are of great importance in social policy terms, they do not tell us the number of children in each category of lone parent family. Firstly, not all one parent families are eligible or willing to claim social welfare payments. Thus social welfare statistics are likely to underestimate the numbers of one parent families in each category.

Secondly, lone parent families represent a sub-group of all one parent families. Some one parent families may live in a household headed by a relative or friend (for example, the family may be living with the child's grandparents, other relatives or friends). Others may live in a household headed by the solo parent, but containing other people in addition to the parent's children (for example, the parent's younger adult sister or a friend).

Lone parent households are of special significance in social policy terms, since the adult in the family must face the challenges of parenthood without the material

Table 2: **Numbers of child dependants on families receiving one-parent weekly social welfare payments by family type 1983–88**

Social Welfare Payments	1983	1988
Widow's (contributory) pension	19,028	15,213
Widow's (non-contributory) pension	6,425	3,661
Deserted wife's benefit	6,526	16,139
Deserted wife's allowance	5,044	8,600
Unmarried mother's allowance	9,851	19,302
Prisoner's wife's allowance	554	653
	47,428	63,558

Sources: Dept. of Social Welfare (1984), *Statistical Information on Social Welfare Services 1983.* Dublin: Stationery Office; Dept. of Social Welfare (1989), *Statistical Information on Social Welfare Services 1988.* Dublin: Stationery Office

and emotional support of another adult. This isolation may put a strain on the family and, many would claim, puts the children at additional risk. Some of this risk may be economic — lone parent households are often low income households. Some of the risk may be social — lone parent households may be vulnerable to social stigma or isolation. Some of it may be emotional, deriving from the causes or consequences of lone parenthood. One UK study found the children of one parent families to have inferior scores to children from two parent families in tests of behaviour, vocabulary and visuo-motor co-ordination at five years of age (Wadsworth *et al*, 1985).

In Irish official statistics on children in the care of health boards, the most frequent reason for admission is 'one parent family, unable to cope', accounting for 825 — one in three of all children in care (Department of Health, 1989). This statistic offers fairly graphic evidence in support of the social stress theory.

There may be ideological reasons for the State's failure to gather sufficient statistical and other evidence on the experience of lone parenthood in our society. Lone parenthood, especially where it occurs by 'choice', constitutes a challenge to the orthodoxy of the two-parent family — an orthodoxy which enjoys constitutional underpinning in Ireland. Article 41.3.1 of Bunreacht na hÉireann states: 'The State pledges itself to guard with special care the institution of Marriage, on which the family is founded, and to protect it against attack.'

Against this background, the hesitancy of public policy in relation to the one parent family and lone parents may be more easily understood. The refusal, for example, until 1983 to allow information to be collected in the Census on separated persons, as well as the long haul to achieve legal reform in relation to illegitimacy, are not irrelevant in this regard.

Defining what constitutes 'the family' is not, therefore, merely a technical, legal or administrative decision. It goes to the very heart of what a society wants to believe about itself. Children in lone parent households may unwittingly find themselves in the frontline of this ideological struggle. While the overall thrust of this discussion is to explain and explore the special disadvantages faced by children of lone parents, it is important to stress that this is not the inevitable or universal experience of all children in all of these families. Many lone parents and their children do very well. The point is, however, that the dice tend to be loaded heavily against them. The fact that some do well is more a tribute to their courage and good fortune than a contradiction of this fundamental thesis — the disadvantaged status of lone parents and their children in our society.

Lone parents may share a common characteristic, but they are by no means an homogeneous group. Age and social class (and certain psychological factors) interact crucially with the status of lone parenthood, to determine the fate of individual children and parents in the different categories.

Single or Unmarried Parents

It is perhaps worth reiterating that not all unmarried parents are lone parents: they may be co-habiting or living with parents, relatives or friends, or they may have placed their child for adoption.

Figure 1: **Births outside marriage as a percentage of total births: 1944-88**

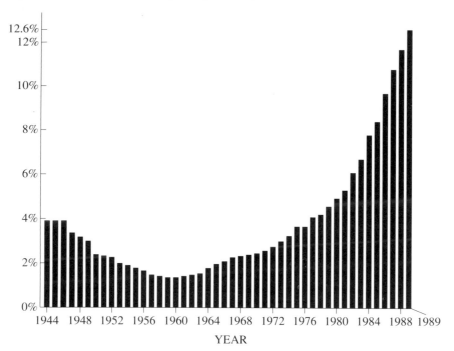

Source: Dept. of Health 1990, *Health Statistics, 1989.* Dublin: Stationery Office; Dept. of Health, *Vital Statistics, 1989.* Dublin: Stationery Office, 1990

There are two interesting recent trends in relation to this group of parents. Firstly, there has been a steady growth since the early 1960s in the number of births outside marriage — in fact, the proportion of all births outside marriage in the period 1960 to 1989 has grown more than sixfold and stood at 12.6% in 1989. (It should be noted that the early '60s represented, for some reason, a low point in the numbers and proportion of births outside marriage since the foundation of the State; see Figure 1.)

The second interesting trend is the dramatic recent decline in the use of adoption by unmarried women as a 'solution' to extra-marital pregnancy (see section on adoption, pp 132-6). Indeed, in a 1983 national study of women giving birth outside marriage, less than one in five (18%) planned to place their child for adoption, while 76% intended to keep the child (O'Hare *et al*, 1987, p. 49). Two studies, in 1986 and 1987, of unmarried women delivered of their babies in the National Maternity Hospital revealed that just over half in each year planned to live with their child at home with their parents — 54.4% in 1986 and 53% in 1987 (Richardson, 1987; Richardson and Winston, 1988). Approximately one in six (15.1% and 17.3% respectively) answered that they planned to live alone with the child on discharge.

It is important to stress that such plans may be subject to change sooner or later. A mother may go on to place her child for adoption, may co-habit with the father or another partner, or may marry.

Social class
The 1983 study (above) also revealed that women from 'semi-skilled' and 'unskilled/manual' backgrounds have a quite disproportionate share of non-marital births when compared to their more socially favoured peers. They accounted for 55% of all such births in 1983, while comprising only 25% of all women in the national population (O'Hare *et al*, 1987, pp 24-5).

Age
If all non-marital births have increased in relative and absolute terms in recent times, the growth has been even more dramatic in the non-marital share of all births to teenage mothers (see Table 4). In 1989, well over three out of every four births (82.2%) to a teenage mother were outside marriage. Non-marital births to teenage mothers accounted for 29.5% of all non-marital births in 1989 (Dept. of Health, 1989). Teenage mothers in receipt of Unmarried Mother's Allowance accounted for 11.6% of all such mothers in 1988 (Dept. of Social Welfare, 1989).

Table 3: **Births to teenage mothers as percentage of all births, 1981, 1983, 1985, 1987, 1989**

Year	Births to teenage mothers	% of all births
1989	2,338	4.5
1987	2,574	4.4
1985	2,621	4.2
1983	2,958	4.4
1981	3,547	4.9

Source: Dept. of Health, *Vital Statistics*, for relevant years

Table 4: **Statistics on non-marital births to teenage mothers**

Year	Non-marital births to teenage mothers	Non-marital births to teenage mothers as % of all births	Non-marital births to teenage mothers as % of all births to teenage mothers	Non-marital births to teenage mothers as % of all non-marital births
1989	1,922	3.7	82.2	29.5
1987	1,925	3.3	74.8	30.2
1985	1,689	2.7	64.4	32.1
1983	1,600	2.4	54.1	35.4
1981	1,507	2.1	42.5	38.5

Source: Dept. of Health, *Vital Statistics*, for relevant years

Research evidence suggests that children born to teenage mothers (4.5% of all births in 1989; see Table 3 for recent trends) tend to be disadvantaged on a number of fronts when compared with children born to older parents (Wadsworth *et al*, 1984). Among the findings reported are greater health problems, lower IQ, inferior physical development and greater behavioural problems.

Presumably these hazards may even be greater for lone teenage parents. Of mothers under 18 delivered of their babies in the National Maternity Hospital in 1986 and 1987, one in six of those keeping their child (6.9% in 1986 and 7.2% in 1987), or a total of 12 young mothers, told the researchers that they planned to live alone on discharge. The intention to place for adoption was not more marked in this age group. The most likely choice of the mothers under 18 keeping their baby was to live with their parents — 81.6% in 1986 and 79.8% in 1987 (Richardson, 1987; Richardson and Winston, 1988). This degree of preference for returning to the family is fairly strong evidence of the easing of the traditional shame and stigma surrounding the birth of a child outside marriage.

On a national level, 541 mothers under 18 gave birth to a baby outside marriage in 1988 — the proportion of these proposing to live alone with their baby is unknown.

Social stress and single parents
The category 'children of unmarried mothers' accounted for one in three (33.6%) of all children in the care of health boards in 1985 (Department of Health, 1990). This proportion is considerably higher than their likely share of the total child population nationally. (It should be noted that these are not necessarily the same children as those belonging to the category of 'one parent families, unable to cope', cited above.)

In her study of unmarried mothers, Darling (1984) found considerable evidence of hardship among her sample of 58 women who were rearing their children. More than four out of five (85%) 'had had problems relating to housing or finance or both', although the author cautions that her findings are not necessarily representative of all women in this category, since her sample was drawn from women in touch with helping agencies.

The children of unmarried lone parents seem more at risk of socio-economic disadvantage and of entering public care. They may also suffer psychologically, perhaps encountering social stigma which dies hard despite legal reforms and social changes, or they may miss out on adequate knowledge of their origins or access to their father.

Children of Deserted, Separated or Divorced Parents
The child of a parent who is deserted, separated or divorced has many adjustments to make in the wake of the tension and conflict (even violence) that inevitably precede, and sometimes continue after, the departure of the other parent. Marital breakdown bequeaths many psychological tasks to the children affected. For example, children must:
- cope with the conflict and events surrounding the break-up;
- come to terms with the collapse of the intimate social world most familiar and important to them and with the loss of 'normal' family life;

- avoid assuming any blame for the rupture of the family (as children are wont to do in the aftermath of calamities in their lives);
- grieve the loss of the absent parent;
- avoid generalising resentment from any unhappy experiences at the hands of an 'errant' parent to all people of the same gender;
- cope with the sense of being 'piggy in the middle' between estranged parents. The skills of diplomacy this may require of the child may be even further tested by embattled parents competing for his or her exclusive loyalty;
- learn to accept the new shape of their family;
- find how to explain the whole experience to their wider social world.

It is clear that the emotional (and often the economic) costs of marital breakdown are considerable for the children involved. Opponents of divorce claim these costs to the child as evidence in support of their case. This is a controversial area in Ireland, but much of the research would seem to indicate that it is marital discord rather than separation or divorce that has the most damaging impact (Rutter & Giller, 1983, pp 190-91). It is suggested that children can cope better with the clear reality of breakdown than with the anger of marital rows (see Klaczynski and Cummings, 1989) or with the veneer and deceit of a pseudo-harmony which barely masks festering and inexorable conflict. Boys seem more likely to be adversely affected by such marital conflict (ibid. pp 309-14).

The actual demands made of the child in the wake of marital breakdown may be influenced by a variety of factors. These include (1) the child's age, gender, family size, birth rank, temperament and social support; (2) the tone and quality of communication, if any, between the parents; and (3) the precise configuration of family relations after the break-up.

The child may continue in the custody of the remaining parent, without contact with the other parent, or with regular access by the other parent, agreed informally between parents or imposed by a court. With the custodial parent, the child may become part of a reconstituted family which, under Irish law, is unlikely to be recognised. In this situation, the child will also have to come to terms with a replacement or step-parent, and perhaps step-siblings, while also possibly remaining in touch with the absent natural parent. The worst scenario for the child is probably for him or her to become embroiled in repeated conflict between warring spouses.

A review of recent international research evidence is relatively pessimistic about the effects of divorce on children (Fine, 1987). Problems in adjusting to step-parents, step-siblings and extended family, greater risk of psychiatric difficulties and problems of trust in adult heterosexual relationships are among those reported in a series of studies, most of which, unfortunately, are based on small numbers, thereby necessitating caution in their interpretation. The message seems to be that it is best if children can avoid being a party to marital breakdown. However, if it occurs in their lives, their interests are best served by facing up to that reality rather than denying it.

Children of Widowed Parents

The loss of a parent in childhood is a serious blow to the child and threatens his or her psychological equilibrium and development. The extent to which the child is scarred or recovers depends on a variety of factors, including age, gender, quality of relationship with the dead and surviving parent, the cause of death (whether insidious or traumatic), the extent of any opportunity for anticipatory grieving where the prognosis is known (Rosenheim and Reicher, 1985), the degree to which open discussion of the expected death is encouraged within the family (ibid.) and, finally, the degree of opportunity to grieve openly and to participate in the rituals surrounding the event of death. (For an excellent treatment of how to help children cope with the death of loved ones and other forms of loss, see Jewett, 1984).

Drugs and Alcohol: Their Effect on Young People

Legal or illegal chemical substances can affect the lives of children and young people in a number of ways. For example, dependent use of these substances by their parents may impair the quality of parenting that the children receive. For the foetus in the womb, alcohol or drug use may produce undesirable side-effects. Children and young people may also use these substances directly themselves and may experience harmful effects associated with such use.

How extensive is alcohol and drug use among young Irish people? Much valuable information was gained from a study of a sample of Dublin second-level students (N = 2,927) and their practices in relation to smoking, alcohol and drug use (Grube and Morgan, 1986). It must be remembered, however, that the findings refer to a Dublin population and therefore do not necessarily represent the national position.

Smoking

The study revealed that one in four (24.4%) of the young people sampled was a 'regular smoker'. The rate for those aged 13 and under was 12.5%; this rose to a peak of 30.9% for 16-year olds. This and earlier studies (Grube, McGree and Morgan, 1984, pp 265-88; O'Rourke, O'Sullivan and Wilson-Davis, 1983, pp 285-9) indicate that the years between 13 and 14 are those when youngsters are most likely to become regular smokers. However, there are differences between the sexes:

> development of smoking among girls appears to parallel, but lags behind, that of boys by several years . . . the percentage of regular smokers has reached its peak by age 15 among boys, while a significant increase in smoking occurs among girls between 15 and 17 (Grube and Morgan, 1986, p. 71).

The rate of smoking among Irish young people appears to have remained relatively stable in recent years, but 'rates reported here are generally higher than those encountered in other countries' (ibid. p. 87).

Drinking

Slightly more than one in three (36.5%) of the study's sample described themselves as 'regular drinkers'. Of the youngsters aged 13 and under, 17.6% reported being regular drinkers. For those aged 17 and older, just over half (53.3%) placed themselves in this category (ibid. p. 92).

The study revealed that

> almost two-thirds of the respondents had consumed an alcoholic drink at some time in their lives, and of those who had tried a drink, the majority had been drunk at least once. In comparison with other countries, it seems that there is a relatively greater number of lifetime abstainers in this sample, while the number who drink regularly is somewhere between the rates reported for high-consumption countries, like France and Australia, and the rate for low-consumption countries, like Israel (ibid. p. 111).

Furthermore,

> lifetime [ever drank] and current drinking rates increased substantially with age and older students reported having been drunk more frequently than younger students. In terms of gender, boys drank more frequently and in greater amounts than girls and also tended to report being drunk more often (ibid. p. 112).

Drug Use

The study revealed that just over one in five (21.9%) youngsters reported ever having used drugs, with marijuana and glue/solvents being the most popular. One in twelve (8.4%) claimed to be a regular user, with peak current use among 16-year olds at 11.1%, compared to 5% among 13-year olds and 9.7% among those aged 17 and over (ibid. pp 114-16).

These figures suggest an increase in the use of drugs among adolescents, since a study in 1970-71 found only 2.3% of the young people sampled claiming ever to have experimented with drugs (Nevin *et al*, 1971, pp 231-7).

Grube and Morgan, the authors of the 1985 study, urge caution in inter-country comparisons, because of possibly significant differences in detailed research designs. But on the basis of their own data, they comment:

> The overall rate of drug use appears to be considerably lower in the Dublin sample than in samples drawn from the United States or France, and somewhat higher than in samples from Scotland, England or Israel. In terms of specific substances, the use of solvents appears to be relatively more frequent among Dublin adolescents than among adolescents from other countries and the use of drugs is less frequent (Grube and Morgan, 1986, p. 134).

While the above data refer to the whole of the Dublin area, there was striking evidence in the early 1980s of serious drug problems concentrated in certain districts within Dublin. One study in North-Central Dublin during 1982-83 found a prevalence rate of drug use of 10.89% among males and 13.04% among females aged between 15 and 19 years (Dean, Bradshaw and Lavelle, 1983, p. 16).

In the period 1979-83, a dramatic increase of 1,745% was recorded in the number of opiate abusers, aged between 12 and 19, attending the National Drug Advisory and Treatment Centre — almost four times the rate of increase for all age groups in the same period (Dean *et al*, 1985, pp 107-10).

It has been suggested that the 'opiate epidemic' of the early 1980s in the Dublin area may now be in decline. The evidence for this is that figures for all attendances at the National Drug Centre registered successive, if relatively modest, decreases in 1984 and 1985, following a relentless and rapid rise in the period 1979-83. Unfortunately, these more recent data have not been broken down by age, so it is not possible to say whether the figures for the younger age groups conform to these global trends (Dean *et al*, 1987, pp 139-42).

The Consequences of Drugs and Alcohol for Young People

Using any one form of drug increases the chances of using other forms (Kandel, 1982, pp 328-47). In some cases, young people may progress through a career of drug use, gradually accumulating experience in the use of a succession of different forms. Such sequential development is by no means inevitable and there is not necessarily any causative relationship between one form of drug use and another (Yamaguchi and Kandel, 1984, pp 668-72).

Volatile substance abuse

The practice of sniffing gas fuels, aerosol sprays, solvents in glue and other solvents, such as correcting-fluid thinners, is hazardous. A total of 385 deaths due to such activities were reported in the UK between 1981 and 1985 (Anderson *et al*, 1986, pp 1472-4). In half of the cases (55%) the direct toxic effects of the substance were held responsible for abuse deaths. Other causes of death were 'intoxicated behaviour (trauma, 15%), the method of inhalation (plastic bag over the head, 16%) or inhalation of stomach contents (16%)'.

In Ireland, Corrigan (1987) estimated that

> there have been at least ten deaths [due to solvent abuse] in Ireland in the last two years. Only one of these deaths has involved glue. It is believed that typewriter correcting-fluid (Tippex) thinners were implicated in three deaths and butane (camping gas or cigarette lighter gas) was implicated in four deaths, while fluid from a disposable cigarette lighter and an aerosol spray were involved in one death each.

Tobacco

O'Connor and Daly (1985) summarise the damning research evidence on the effects of smoking:

> Research has consistently shown smoking to be associated with lung and other cancers, disease of the heart and blood vessels, bronchitis and emphysema. Smoking is known to be associated with a variety of chest illnesses, as well as non-malignant diseases of the digestive system. There is evidence also to suggest that, compared with non-smokers, not only is smokers' life expectancy on average shorter, but their lives are in many respects less healthy . . . Cigarette smoking has become the outstanding single cause of disease in industrial nations.

Children who smoke are much more likely to do so as adults and thereby face increased risks of early mortality, especially in the case of those children who smoke by age 15 (Killen, 1985, pp 7-15).

Alcohol

The purchase of alcohol for their own consumption by young people under 18 is illegal in Ireland. Since it is clear that many young people do, in fact, drink, the legal prohibition on them means that their drinking will be covert and, therefore, less likely to be under adequate supervision. Paradoxically, this prohibition may obstruct the orderly socialisation of young people into sociable drinking. (It is worth noting that in France, for example, young people aged 14 may purchase for their own consumption all alcohol except hard liquor.)

Drinking alcohol in moderation is a pleasant and popular social activity. However, drinking can lead to problems most of which stem from heavy consumption. Excessive drinking can cause health, social, legal and economic problems at a personal and wider level. Many instances of fighting, family violence, road traffic accidents, crime and industrial absenteeism can be traced to problem-drinking.

Adolescence is a period that can involve turbulent changes in physique, identity and perceptions. Excessive consumption of alcohol at this vulnerable stage may aggravate the causes and effects of adolescent turmoil.

Illicit drugs

Illicit drug use may produce physical, psychological, social and legal problems for the young people concerned. Quite apart from the possible toxic effects of the substances physically and the risk of addiction in the case of substances such as heroin, the young person may become enmeshed in the criminal justice system. The possession of such drugs is illegal. In addition, the young person may be apprehended for the pushing of these substances or for other crime committed in order to fund the purchase of the desired drug.

Parental Drug Abuse and its Consequences for Children

Drugs

By its very nature, the extent of illicit drug use is difficult to quantify. One indicator of its prevalence is the number of attenders at services for such drug users. Among opiate abusers aged 20 and over, there was a 381% increase in attenders at the National Drug Advisory and Treatment Centre between 1979 and 1983. Assuming that most drug-addicted parents are in this age group (and knowing of the even more dramatic increase in the 12-19 age group), this suggests an increased risk of children being born into, or living with, parents with such problems (Dean *et al*, 1985, p. 109).

Drug addicts who become pregnant cause particular concern for health services. The ingestion of drugs (and even worse the substances with which street drugs are typically adulterated) poses physical risks to the foetus. Quite apart from the influence of the drugs *per se*, the social circumstances of a 'street' drug addict are likely to be a source of risk to the welfare of the pregnant woman and her child.

Finnegan, an American medical researcher, states (1982) that 40% to 50% of pregnant drug-dependent women present with medical complications. They tend to have neglected their general health care needs and pre-natal care and nutritional needs. As a result they and their foetus suffer. Their babies tend to be born earlier and weigh less than normal babies of the same gestational age.

Mothers-to-be who are addicts are less likely to have, or use, necessary social and health supports. They are considered less likely to attend regularly for ante-natal services, despite having a profile indicating a stronger need for such attendance. When the child is born, there may be greater risk of medical complications. One of the best known of these includes withdrawal which, while it has the potential to cause the new infant considerable distress, is of much less long-term significance than other possible hazards (ibid. p. 69).

Quite apart from medical complications, these children may experience disjointed caretaking due to their parent's lifestyle. There seems to be an increased risk of their being received into care on an intermittent and erratically planned basis, possibly culminating in permanent placement in care.

In a review of a number of follow-up studies on younger children, Finnegan did not find any striking evidence of developmental disadvantage endured by these children. However, she did observe that 'infants fared better if born to heroin-addicted mothers, who were being maintained on methadone [a synthetic equivalent to heroin] and also receiving pre-natal care' (ibid. p. 95).

There is an increased risk of AIDS (Acquired Immune Deficiency Syndrome) among street drug addicts, because of the swapping of needles or prostitution to fund their habit. AIDS is transmitted by the passage of blood, semen or vaginal fluids from an infected person into the bloodstream of another. This obviously places the children of drug-addicted mothers at special risk of being born HIV-positive (i.e. with human immuno-deficiency virus, a necessary precursor of AIDS). The care and management of children carrying the risk of AIDS pose special challenges for the educational, health and child-care systems. There are particular issues to be faced if any of these children require to be admitted to care (Gurdin and Anderson, 1987, pp 291-302; Harrison, 1986, pp 9-10; Russell, 1987).

There have been two Irish reports on the circumstances of drug-addicted mothers and children born to them in Dublin's Coombe Lying-in Hospital. Ryan *et al* (1983) reported on 15 mothers who were delivered of 17 babies (two mothers confined twice) in the period 1973-81. Reflecting the increase in the heroin problem in the early 1980s, 9 of these mothers were delivered in 1981 alone. There was some background data on the mothers and the fathers of their children in 13 out of the 15 cases.

Nine mothers had received treatment for emotional or psychiatric problems in the past. Seven had had hepatitis in the past (one currently) and two had venereal disease. Relying presumably on the information given by the mothers, the authors reported that all but one of the fathers were drug addicts. Half of them were described as 'being in trouble with the law', while a third were classed as 'very violent'. Only two were credited with giving any support to the woman during her pregnancy.

None of the babies was small for gestational age. Six (40%) experienced mild or moderate withdrawal symptoms. They tended to remain hospitalised for longer, to assuage professional fears, but all, with the exception of one placed for adoption, were discharged to their mothers, although it was expected at the time the report was written (1983) that three of the children would be received into care.

Overall, however, the socio-medical profile of the mothers is less unfavourable than might be expected from the international evidence. The authors suggest that this may be due to the comparatively shorter drug-using careers of the mothers seen to date, a pattern which may eventually change to converge with the more adverse findings reported abroad.

A second report from the Coombe Hospital deals with 42 babies born to 29 known narcotic-addicted mothers in the period 1982-85 (Maguire, Thornton and Clune, 1987). The authors reported:

> One woman had 4 confinements during the study period and 6 women had 2. There were 4 sets of twins . . . The maternal age at delivery ranged from 17 years to 32 years. Twenty women were single, 12 were married and 6 were separated at the time of pregnancy. All partners, where an history was available (29 out of 32), were also drug abusers. All the mothers lived in socially deprived areas of Dublin. Some were known to be engaged in prostitution to pay for their drug habit and many had criminal records relating to theft.

The report goes on to state that in the case of 6 confinements, there had been no ante-natal care. Of the 34 singleton babies, 9 were small for gestational age; 32 (85%) showed signs of withdrawal at birth. Of 7 tested for HIV, 3 were found positive and one of these had developed AIDS (as had a sibling of one of the other children in the study). The long-term care prospects for these children did not seem overly encouraging. Of the 42 babies, at the time of the report (1987), 10 were in long-term care of the Eastern Health Board (5 admitted from hospital and the other 5 from home situations which had subsequently broken down). A further 4 children were in the long-term care of relatives.

Fanshel (1975) examined the progress of children of drug-abusing mothers as part of a longitudinal study of a group of children (N = 624) who were in public care in New York. This group represented 7.1% of all the children studied. His findings were less pessimistic than might be expected.

The children of the drug abusers were as well, or better, adjusted at the point of entry to care as the other children. This may have been because parenting breakdown seemed to occur when the child was younger among the drug-abusing mothers. Their children proved comparable to the other children in care, in terms of IQ, the extent of their behavioural problems and the display of symptoms of emotional disturbance. Only in the case of school adjustment did these children score less well than their peers in care.

Once admitted to care, however, children of drug-abusing mothers are the most likely of all categories of children to have an extended stay in care and to be more subject to multiple placement, possibly, Fanshel suggests, due to the chaotic lifestyle of many of the mothers, which impeded orderly planning of the child's care (ibid. pp 604-12).

Alcohol

In an Irish study on smoking and drinking behaviour nationally, O'Connor and Daly (1985) found that 75% of respondents in the sample (N = 2,724) drank, 16.7% had never done so, and 7.3% described themselves as 'former drinkers'. Men were more likely to drink than women — 83% as against 69%.

Of those who drink, 10.8% of males and 1.2% of females are classified as 'heavy drinkers', i.e. drinking more than the safe level (equivalent of 4 pints per day for men and 2.5 pints per day for women). Age and social class affect the prevalence of drinking for men. Men in manual occupations are 40% more likely to drink heavily than those in non-manual positions. In terms of age, the most heavy drinkers are found in the 55-64 age group (12.1%), followed by the 18-24 and 25-34 age groups (10.4% and 10.3% respectively). When compared with drinking patterns in England and Wales, the proportion of heavy drinking among males in Ireland (11%) is almost twice that in England and Wales (6%). On this point, the report noted: 'Overall, Irish drinking patterns tend to be more extreme in that they are characterised by both heavier consumption and greater abstention than those in England and Wales' (ibid. p. 132).

Alcohol consumption by the pregnant woman may produce quite serious adverse effects on the foetus, which are later manifested in the physical and behavioural characteristics of the child (Cooper, 1987, pp 223-7). Women who drink during pregnancy double the risk of spontaneous abortion and increase the risk of stillbirth. Their children may also suffer consequent physical anomalies, such as central nervous system dysfunction (mental retardation), growth retardation (lighter baby) and facial as well as other abnormalities. Behaviourally, children so affected may display hyperactivity, distractibility and short-attention span, which may, in turn, lead to difficulties in school.

Where all of the physical features and a history of alcohol consumption in pregnancy are present, a full diagnosis of Foetal Alcohol Syndrome may be made. In less serious cases, a partial version of the syndrome may be diagnosed. As Cooper reports,

> The incidence of foetal alcohol syndrome depends on the population studied and may vary from 0.4 per 1,000 live births in the general population to as high as 690 per 1,000 among children of alcoholic women. The characteristics of the syndrome do not appear reversible by environmental factors after birth (ibid. p. 226).

Two linked research studies in Sweden have yielded invaluable information about the effects of parental alcoholism on the developing child, as well as on that same individual in adulthood.

The first study, conducted in 1958, compared the circumstances of a study group of 229 children of alcoholic fathers with a carefully matched control group of 163 children (Nylander, 1960). All of the children at that time were aged between 4 and 12 years. The children of alcoholic fathers fared worse than the controls (none of whom had alcoholic fathers). Their fathers were more likely to have psychiatric or criminal problems; their mothers were more likely to have psychiatric problems. There was more likely to have been feeding problems during infancy; the children were more likely to have physical symptoms, such as headaches, stomach aches or tiredness, for which no physical reason could be found. They were also more likely to display child psychiatric symptoms and to have problems in school adjustment.

The second study (Rydelius, 1981) entailed a follow-up of these same children over a 20-year period. (The possibility of undertaking this was greatly facilitated by the standards of record-keeping in Swedish public administration, although inevitably there was some attrition in the two groups due to death and emigration.) The findings of this follow-up study were broadly consistent with those of the 1958 report. The position of the children of the alcoholic fathers was inferior on almost every measure. Boys seemed much more vulnerable to these adverse effects than girls. The boys were more likely to have been registered with the child welfare authorities (42% as against 25% of the controls); they were also more likely to have exhibited alcohol (or drug) problems of their own, to have come under attention for criminal behaviour and to have experienced physical and psychiatric illnesses. Both boys and girls were more likely to have sought social assistance.

Drug and alcohol problems in a set of Dublin parents were the subject of a study by six community care social workers in the south-inner city area of Dublin (Daly, 1986). The social workers wished to examine the influence of drug and alcohol use on the family problems they were confronting. From a total active caseload of 112 families, they found that in 31 families 'drug and alcohol abuse was an identified problem' (ibid. p. 5). Of these families, 'Nineteen . . . had one or more adults abusing opiates and 17 had one or more adults abusing alcohol. This included 5 families where both opiates and alcohol were abused.'

The study reported that a large number of the children in these families had behavioural, emotional and educational problems. Nineteen of the 31 families had children in care. Of these 42 children, all but 11 were in compulsory care (ibid. p. 8).

Smoking

Although it may not be widely appreciated, smoking is a minority activity engaged in by 49.5% of men and 36.4% of women (O'Connor and Daly, 1985). Whether young people smoke seems more influenced by the behaviour of siblings and peers than by that of parents. Nevertheless, in the case of regular smokers, more of their parents smoke than in the case of non-smokers (ibid. p. 93).

Parents may influence their children's behaviour in relation to smoking by their own example and attitudes. In the case of the pregnant mother, her smoking may have even more serious implications since toxic substances in cigarette smoke cross the placenta and affect the foetus directly. There is evidence that

> smoking retards foetal growth . . . Women who smoke cigarettes during pregnancy have more spontaneous abortions and a greater prevalence of bleeding during pregnancy. They also suffer an increased risk of premature delivery . . . Children of mothers who smoked during pregnancy have been found to have a slower growth rate than children of non-smoking mothers (ibid. p. 116).

Overall, the likely effects on children or young people of their own or their parents' drug use cannot be judged in relation to the drug alone. The effects are likely to be heavily influenced by the social circumstances in which the use occurs. Adverse effects are likely to be most severe when use interacts with other unfavourable factors. In general, those most likely to be damaged are those least well equipped socially and economically to absorb the ill-effects.

Physical Environment

Rural Isolation

Children and families in rural areas are likely to encounter greater problems than their urban counterparts in regard to the availability of, and access to, various social services. The relentless trend towards the concentration of schools in urban

centres at the expense of smaller rural schools means that many rural children must spend many hours of each school day waiting for, and travelling on, school transport.

In the case of health care, provision of child-health services (see pp 127-8) has been confined to urban centres with a population of more than 5,000. Access to more specialised health services may entail long, expensive and often arduous journeys for parents with young children. There may be no day nursery or playgroup facilities available or accessible in rural areas. Where children are in care, they may be placed at considerable distance from their family home because many rural counties have no residential care provision of their own. According to 1984 data, seven out of the total of 24 community care areas outside Dublin have no children's home situated within their boundaries (O'Higgins and Boyle, 1988).

O'Mahony (1985), in a study of community care services in the Western Health Board region, found that services tended to be concentrated in urban areas and that the level of service diminished steadily with increasing distance from an urban centre.

The problems of remoter rural areas are aggravated not only by this imbalance in service provision, but also by unfavourable economic and demographic trends which affect the resources available from within a remoter rural community. As O'Mahony, writing before the great resurgence of emigration in the late 1980s, points out,

> In general terms, the more remote rural areas covered in this study are characterised by population dispersal over large geographical areas, demographic imbalances, low incomes, poor employment opportunities and high migration rates . . . The losses in the vital young adult and middle-age groups deprive rural communities of that section of the population by whose efforts the young and the elderly are maintained and supported. The potential sources of voluntary effort in such communities are significantly less than in urban areas (ibid. pp 182-3).

This apparently inexorable trend towards urbanisation and the centralisation of services can lead to problems in the recruitment of staff to work in rural areas, even in the finding of local home-helps. Since voluntary organisations tend to be based in towns, services normally provided by voluntary bodies may simply not exist in rural areas.

The fact that rural areas lack an infrastructure of social services and facilities more commonly found in urban areas is rendered more serious for rural residents by the inadequacy or non-existence of public transport. In this crucial area, access to health services was facilitated in the past by taxi services to out-patient clinics from rural areas. Cuts in public spending have forced health boards to withdraw this service at great cost to the individuals concerned. The failure to restore such a facility, or more reasonably to provide a subsidy to health boards to retain it, must symbolise to rural residents the neglect of their needs at the level of public policy.

The absence of adequate provision is not for the want of successful models. In Glenamaddy, Co. Galway, for example, the local social service council has operated a community bus with some grant aid from the Western Health Board to facilitate, among other things, access by local children to a pre-school playgroup (O'Mahony, 1986, p. 83). In Co. Clare, An Post introduced a post-bus to serve rural areas, similar to well-established schemes in Austria, Germany, Switzerland, Sweden and the UK (ibid. p. 79). In other areas, however, it must be extremely frustrating for rural dwellers to see local school buses lie idle for long periods of the day and the year while local transport needs go unmet (ibid. p. 78).

In rural areas, it may make more sense to bring the service to the users. The play-bus (see pp 165-6) model of provision is an example of a mobile facility which would be suitable to rural needs. Its operation might usefully be combined with the occasional operation of child-health clinics to compensate for the otherwise urban bias in these services.

Thus, while emigration and economic growth have taken a steady toll in Ireland, the neglect or absence of provision in rural areas is not inevitable. Concerted effort at the level of policy and planning could resolve many of the problems.

Inner Cities and Suburban Ghettos

It has been suggested that Ireland's self-image is inextricably bound up with rural or pastoral themes and for this reason urban problems have never been tackled with the necessary degree of conviction. While there may be some truth in this observation, there has been a dawning realisation of the problems of urban deprivation, originating in the mid-1970s. At that time, official recognition was given to the problems of Dublin's inner city, with a new awareness that the capital city possessed urban deprivation akin to that seen in certain cities in the USA and UK. Over the years, it has come to be recognised that Dublin's north inner city (and pockets in the south) have exceptional rates of unemployment, a substantial proportion of decaying housing stock, a concentration of the city's drug problem and a large percentage of the city's and country's total crime.

In the middle of the last century, Engels (1844, p. 40) wrote that 'the poorer districts of Dublin are amongst the ugliest and most revolting in the world'. A more recent review of problems in Dublin (Bannon, Eustace and O'Neill, 1981) emphasised that blackspots of urban deprivation persist in the city and that they are not confined to the inner city, but also a feature of the large working-class estates on the periphery of the city.

The prospects for young people in these areas are particularly bleak. Many leave school unqualified and are thus at greater risk of unemployment. The now widely accepted association between high rates of unemployment and high concentrations of drug use has been confirmed by data from Glasgow, the Wirral on Merseyside and inner city Dublin (Dean et al, 1987, pp 139-42). There is also clear evidence that young people from the inner city are likely to succumb to the clear association now established between low educational attainment, limited work experience and crime (Rottman, 1984, p. 121). The concentration of crime in the inner city is illustrated by the fact that while the area accounts for only 15% of the city's population, its residents account for one-third of all Dublin people apprehended for indictable offences (ibid. p. 193).

The physical environment in these working-class ghettos can be grim. They are

> often characterised by monotonous housing developments, inadequate vegetation and an unattractive visual environment, with consequent social and psychological implications (Bannon, Eustace and O'Neill, 1981, p. 232).

47

These problems may be further exacerbated by insufficient attention to the maintenance of the housing stock and public utilities in these areas or by other factors, such as the local effects of the housing authority's wider allocations or housing management policy.

These issues were highlighted in a survey of such problems on the 1960's Ballymun Estate in Dublin — the only local authority estate in the country with high-rise blocks of flats (SUSS Centre, 1987). During the survey period of January to August 1986, it was found that, on average, one in ten of the 2,814 flats was empty, one in ten of light fittings on the stairs and landings was broken and one-third of the lifts (vital in high-rise buildings) was out of order. Rubbish disposal systems are also important in flat complexes, yet the report found the proportion of disposal chutes broken had increased from 22% to 24% in the survey period.

The data also confirmed a high degree of transience in the population, with one-third of residents declaring an intention to leave Ballymun. In addition, there was evidence that the housing authority's policy had resulted in Ballymun getting a disproportionate share of all lettings to single parents and single men in the city as a whole. Many of the parents were young unmarried mothers and many of the men had been recently discharged from long-stay care in psychiatric hospitals. The report complained that no additional social amenities or facilities had been provided to cater for the needs of these new residents, who were likely to have above-average social needs. These problems were not made easier by the weakness of the local economy, with an unemployment rate almost three times the national average (Ballymun Job Centre Project, 1986, p. 15).

Urban disadvantage is also a stark feature of many more conventional local authority housing estates. Dublin County Council commissioned a study in 1986 of social need in 24 neighbourhoods chosen by county council officials who judged them to be among the most socially disadvantaged in the council's area (SUS Research, 1987). This judgement was vindicated by the research findings (which referred only to households occupying local authority accommodation in these districts). On a number of indicators, the average score for these areas and the range of individual scores confirmed a high concentration of social disadvantage in these peripheral estates.

The level of unemployment in these areas may be gleaned from the fact that, on average (all 1987 figures), only 37.9% of principal earners in households were employed; the figures ranged from a low of 25.6% to a high of 47.1%. It was calculated that over half (55.1%) the households had a gross income of less than £100 a week; one in ten (10.8%) had a gross income of less than £60 a week. At the other end of the scale, just under one in five (19.6%) had a weekly gross income in excess of £150.

One in eight households (12.5%) were headed by a single parent, dependent on either unmarried mother's or deserted wife's allowance. This proportion varied at the level of local estates, from a low of 4.7% to a high of 26.8%.

Households were, on average, 4.4 weeks in arrears in the payment of rent. At the local level, this ranged from 1.7 weeks to a maximum average for one neighbourhood of 9.4 weeks.

Road Traffic Accidents
An average of 75 children die and 1,000 are injured each year in Ireland in road traffic accidents. In the period 1977-82, child deaths in such accidents accounted for 12.9% of all road deaths in the country (McCarthy, 1985, pp 1, 14, 42). This proportion represented the second highest in a survey of 16 member-countries of the Organisation of Economic Co-Operation and Development (OECD). The age group most vulnerable are those between 5 and 9 years. The most typical accident scenario is that of a child dashing out from behind a parked vehicle.

Traffic accidents account for more than half (54%) of child deaths in Ireland due to accidents by external cause — traffic, fire, drowning, scalding. Mortality rates for traffic accidents have been rising steadily since 1950, while the reverse is true for other causes of accidental death (Kirke, 1984).

Homelessness

'Homelessness' is a broad concept which ranges from sleeping rough to living in highly insecure or unsatisfactory conditions. The greatest burden borne by homeless young people is the lack of any sense of belonging to roots, of having a place called 'home' — where the young person is accepted and will not be turned away — of having adults who are constant and reliable figures in his or her life and who can defer attention to their own needs when the youngster's needs require it. These youngsters may have poor relations with their parents and have episodically run away from home. Homeless young people may be sleeping rough, living in a squat or under the immediate threat of eviction, or they may be leaving care without any prospect of permanent accommodation.

Homelessness is not just a physical state; it is also a psychological fate that produces serious physical, moral and psychological dangers. Commonly, it represents a path along which young people travel en route to serious involvement in problems such as drug abuse, prostitution or crime. Not all of the victims of such problems have been homeless nor do all homeless youngsters inevitably proceed to these difficulties, but the association between homelessness and other social problems remains very strong. This is why the issue of youth homelessness requires such attention.

There have been a number of major studies of the extent of youth homelessness in Ireland. A national study (excluding Eastern Health Board) was sponsored by a campaign group, Streetwise National Coalition (1988), and entailed a national census of youth homelessness in one week during November 1987. A total of 306 young people aged 18 and under were identified. Of these, 225 (73.5%) were actually homeless and 81 (26.5%) were at risk of homelessness during the census week. Young people were classified as homeless if they were sleeping rough, squatting or 'dossing' with friends or relatives, or if they were living in a flat without parent or guardian and unable to cope. To be classified as 'at risk of becoming homeless', young people would either have been waiting to be admitted to a care facility, facing imminent discharge from care without secure accommodation arrangements or have been intermittently out of home (i.e. been out of home at least twice in the past six months).

Of the total of 306 young people who were homeless or at risk of being homeless, two in every three were male. One in seven (14.4%) were under 15 years of age. Almost one in five of the total (18.9%) were sleeping rough during the census week; of these 58 youngsters, 46 were male, 12 were female, 15 were under 16 and most tended to be concentrated in the larger cities. Of the actually homeless group, more than one in three (34.8%) had been homeless for over six months. Those professionals (health board social workers, juvenile liaison officers, day-centre workers, etc) who helped the researchers identify the 306 youngsters cited three major reasons for the young people's plight — family problems (62.1%), alcohol or substance abuse (14.4%) and education (10.1%).

A Dublin study (unpublished but summarised in Streetwise National Coalition) was undertaken by social workers of the Eastern Health Board between January and June of 1987. They identified a total of 406 cases involving homeless young people under 18.

Among the most significant findings when the two studies are compared is that 35 young people (8.6%) in Dublin and 43 (17.7%) outside Dublin were found to be sleeping rough (nature of accommodation not known in 100 Dublin cases). Almost a third of the homeless young people in both studies were found to be under 15 (age not known in 24 of the Dublin cases), with 38 in Dublin and 10 outside Dublin under 13 years. Other trends noted were a younger profile among the Dublin group and in both studies a predominance of males in the younger age groups.

In another more recent study of the young homeless in Dublin, Focus Point and the Eastern Health Board conducted research into all young people (18 and under) who came into contact with either agency because of homelessness in a 54 day period between October and December 1988 (Focus Point and the Eastern Health Board, 1989). Of the 77 young people in the study, 54.5% were male, 45.5% female, and 36.3% had not been in contact with either agency before. Almost two thirds (61%) came from the greater Dublin area and two thirds were aged between 15 and 17 years. By the end of the 8 week research period, 71.4% were still out of home. A high rate of mobility was found among the study group. An association between homelessness and anti-social and self-destructive behaviour was also noted. Of the 71 youngsters, significant proportions were 'known or suspected to be involved in' prostitution (25%); drug abuse (18%); solvent abuse (21%); shoplifting and petty crime (39%) and alcohol abuse (31%) (ibid, p. 42-3).

A study in Limerick in May 1989 identified 25 homeless young people aged 14 and over; 18 were male and 7 female (Keane and Crowley, 1990). The association between other social problems and homelessness found in the 1988 Dublin study is also evident in the Limerick findings; 10 of the 25 had been convicted of an offence, 22 of the 25 were out of school and in 49% of cases family problems (marital/parental) were seen as the root cause of the youngster's difficulty. Over the whole year in 1989, an action research project on youth homelessness in Limerick had 57 referrals and undertook intensive work with 33 homeless youngsters in 16-18 age range. While numbers sleeping rough may be small, the project found 'a large number of young people with no regular base, drifting from one insecure situation to another' (ibid).

Children in Homeless Families

While some (usually older) children may become homeless in their own right, others (usually younger) may become homeless as part of their family unit. Family units may be homeless through any combination of poverty, family violence, eviction or migration.

A recent census of (homeless) hostel dwellers in Dublin identified 51 women and 35 children staying in emergency hostel accommodation for women and their children (Murphy *et al*, 1988). Many of these women were victims of family violence. These 86 people represented an occupancy rate of 162% in the emergency hostels (i.e. there was gross overcrowding). A further 90 women and 23 children were resident in the only hostel providing emergency long- and short-term accommodation for women alone and for women with children.

The report by Murphy *et al* (ibid. p. 29) criticises the lack of any facilities in the Dublin area to accommodate homeless families together (i.e. husband, wife and children). The absence of family hostels means that many families who are out-of-home have to be separated at great social, personal and emotional cost, and this at a time in their lives when families are already under stress.

Disability

Children may experience stress arising from disability or handicap in their own lives or in the lives of their siblings or their parents. In turn, the other members of the family system will be affected by disability in one of the children in the system.

Disability may vary in several ways, such as its severity; its implications, e.g. loss of mobility, sight or full sexual function; its form, viz. physical disability, mental handicap, long-term mental illness; and its source, e.g. trauma, disease or inheritance. The effects on the individual child will depend on these factors, as well as on social reaction to the disability in the child's social networks and more widely. In addition, the effects will be influenced by the child's age and temperament, and the range and relevance of social supports available to the child and the family system.

The World Health Organization (WHO) has proposed a useful classification of terms in this area (cited in Department of Health, 1984):

Impairment: any loss or abnormality of psychological, physiological, or anatomical structure or function.

Disability: any restriction or lack (resulting from an impairment) of ability to perform an activity in the manner or within the range considered normal for a human being.

Handicap: a disadvantage for a given individual resulting from an impairment or a disability that limits or prevents the fulfilment of a role that is normal (depending on age, sex and social and cultural factors) for that individual.

Physical Disability

Unfortunately, no comprehensive data exist on the extent of physical disability in the child population of Ireland. Some lifetime conditions arise in the neo-natal period.

Approximately 2 per cent of all infants are born with a major abnormality. Many of these die after birth, while others have conditions which are amenable to treatment by conventional medical or surgical intervention. In most cases, the problem of physical disability in the neo-natal period mainly relates to the conditions of spina bifida and/or hydrocephalus, and cerebral palsy (Department of Health, 1984, p. 26).

Spina bifida: This condition involves a defect in the formation of the spinal column. It occurs in about the fourth week after conception and in most, but not all, cases nerve fibres in the spinal cord are affected (Bamford, 1986). Where they are affected, children are unlikely to survive unless treated surgically in infancy. They will be likely to have any or all of the following problems: inability to walk independently, impaired intelligence, spinal deformity and incontinence of both urine and faeces.

In Ireland, the incidence of spina bifida is estimated to be 2.7 per 1,000 live births, with only 45 per cent of these children surviving into adulthood (Department of Health, 1984, p. 26).

Cerebral palsy: This is an evolving disorder of motor function that occurs secondary to non-progressive brain damage in infancy and adulthood (Rosenbloom, 1986). The form of motor disorder can vary widely and may change over time in the one child with age, and as a result of treatment. The most common symptoms seen alone or in combination are weakness or floppiness, stiffness (spasticity), involuntary movements (athetosis) and a lack of co-ordination (ataxia). Children with cerebral palsy are quite likely to be subject to other disorders of physical or mental capacity.

It is estimated that there are 2.5 cases per 1,000 of the population in Ireland (Department of Health, 1984, p. 26). Improvements in medical and maternity services have meant that the condition is now seen less frequently and in less severe forms.

Communication Handicaps
According to estimates, there are 4-4.5 deaf children and 4.5-5 severely hard of hearing children per 10,000 of the school population in Ireland (ibid, p. 46). In addition, 900 children and young people under 19 years of age suffer partial or total blindness (ibid. p. 27).

Mental Handicap
Mental handicap varies in its severity and in the extent to which it may be accompanied by additional sensory or non-sensory handicaps, such as epilepsy. The current WHO classification of degrees of handicap has been recommended for use in Ireland (Trant, 1980). This system uses four grades of handicap: mild (IQ range 50-70), moderate (IQ range 35-49), severe (IQ range 20-34) and profound (IQ range below 20).

Traditionally, assessments of mental handicap have relied on measurements of deficiency in intelligence, although this is now regarded as unsatisfactory. The American Association on Mental Deficiency has recommended that mental retardation be considered present only if a person is deficient in both measured intelligence and adaptive behaviour (cited in Trant 1980, p.6). The degree of primary handicap and the extent of additional handicaps will determine the consequences for the individual. Mental handicap may mean that everyday routines taken for granted by the general population become quite daunting projects or tasks which either require careful preparation, rehearsal and practice or are beyond the reach of a person with such a handicap. A predictable environment that offers unobtrusive support but reliable routine and the minimum of stress is likely to prove most helpful. People with milder handicaps can function in many respects quite normally and their handicap may pass unnoticed. For those with more serious handicaps, considerable improvements in functioning can be achieved through training and the use of imaginative and sophisticated techniques. Sometimes, the effects of over-protective family or institutional life are confused with those of the condition itself. Where the handicap is more severe, it may seriously limit a person's capacity for independent functioning.

> Most mildly handicapped children are able to acquire the basic scholastic skills of reading, writing and arithmetic, although their levels of attainment tend to be below those for children of normal intelligence. Youngsters with moderate handicap may acquire some meagre skills in the 3Rs, but their understanding is usually severely limited. On the other hand, most can achieve reasonable proficiency in mechanical tasks. Severely handicapped children are likely to gain limited social skills, while most of the profoundly handicapped remain completely dependent on other people even for toileting, washing and dressing (Rutter and Gould, 1985, p. 314).

A census of mentally handicapped people in 1981, together with an earlier one in 1974, have provided important information about the extent of the condition in Ireland (Mulcahy and Reynolds, 1984). The results for 1981 indicate a total of 22,979 persons with some degree of handicap, which represented a prevalence rate of 6.7 per 1,000 population in 1981. Children under 15 years made up three in ten of all cases returned in the census. They constituted one in three (35.7 per cent) of borderline/mild cases and one in four (26.8 per cent) of the more severely handicapped. Fewer severely handicapped children were reported in 1981 than in 1974 (ibid. p. 20).

Down's syndrome is one of the most important mental handicap conditions. The incidence of the condition in Ireland has been shown to be 1.7 per 1,000 live births (Connolly, 1977) — a rate that conforms to international trends (McCarthy, Fitzgerald and Smith, 1984).

Mental Illness

Most of the more serious psychiatric illnesses tend to appear in adulthood or late adolescence, and in general the conditions seen in children are less severe than those observed in adults.

> Childhood emotional difficulties become evident in many ways. While there are some children with definable mental illness, in the great majority of cases the symptoms reflect an interaction of factors specific to the individual child. A diagnostic list would include childhood anxiety and phobias; depression and compulsive disorders; conduct disorders including truancy, stealing and running away from home;

developmental delays and disorders; habit disorders; hyperactive children; children with psychosomatic disorders; and some with specific educational disorders associated with emotional problems. A small number of children also suffer from psychotic disorders, including autism and childhood schizophrenia (Trant 1985).

The rates of psychiatric disorder reported in international studies range from 5 to 29 per cent (Vikan, 1985). In addition to his own study, Vikan also reports the findings of eleven other studies of varying methodological adequacy. The most satisfactory are Vikan's own study and the comparative studies by Rutter *et al* (1975) of 10-year-old urban and rural populations. The results of these studies tend to corroborate other findings of considerably lower rates of disorder in rural rather than urban populations. Vikan found a prevalence rate of 5 per cent in a rural Norwegian study, compared with a finding by Rutter *et al* of 6.8 per cent in a rural British setting (the Isle of Wight) and 25.4 per cent in a London population.

McCarthy and O'Boyle (1986) undertook a study of Dublin schoolchildren aged between 7 and 11 (N = 542). They found a rate of marked conduct disorder of 17.3 per cent and of marked disorders of emotion (i.e. continuous anxiety or emotion) of 11.9 per cent. Teachers were asked to rate the children's behaviour on a long-established and widely validated set of research instruments. The children were drawn from four schools of different social composition. Rates of maladjustment were lower among girls and among children from more affluent backgrounds. Overall, the prevalence found in this study falls within the international range.

A study of a sample of primary schoolchildren in Limerick and Clare (O'Connor, Ruddle and O'Gallagher, 1988), where N = 1,361, yielded an estimated rate of psychological maladjustment of 14 per cent. There was considerable variation by area, with a rate of only 7 per cent being found among pupils in rural schools compared with 28 per cent in urban schools which had been classified as disadvantaged. Again, these findings seem to conform with international trends.

Autism
This is a severely incapacitating condition which requires specialist intervention and support of the family. First described by Leo Kanner in 1943, there has been much controversy about the causation of the condition, which it is now recognised continues into adulthood. Autism is characterised by marked deficits in language and social development, the avoidance of eye contact, idiosyncratic patterns of body movement and communication problems generally. The condition can be difficult to diagnose, since children with other conditions may display some comparable symptoms.

Autism is primarily of organic origin and is associated with language disorder (Trant, 1985).

While it does seriously affect the learning capacity of children, it is distinct from global mental handicap. Some autistic children are also mentally handicapped, but most mentally handicapped children do not have autism. While between a quarter and one-third of autistic children have been shown to have an IQ within the normal range, they frequently do poorly on verbal tasks and on those requiring abstract thought and logic. Some of these children display special abilities in computation and at rote memory, as well as puzzle-type tests; others can have special artistic or musical abilities (ibid. 99).

One study in Ireland has found a rate of 4.3 autistic children per 10,000 children in the age groups of 8-10 years in the eastern part of the country — findings that are broadly similar to those of other European studies (McCarthy, Fitzgerald and Smith, 1984).

The Wider Consequences of Disability

Consequences for the disabled child

The fact of disability may carry wide implications for a child's personal development. Disability may impose practical limits on mobility and thereby on opportunities for social outlets and contact with peers. The child may experience stigma from the reaction of others to a visible impairment. Children who display similar external characteristics may be stereotyped and subjected to 'batch treatment' by professionals and others. An example of such trite images might be the idea that all Down's syndrome children are necessarily of a sunny disposition. The danger is that failure to differentiate ignores dissimilarities between people with similar conditions. Such differences may be of much greater importance in determining the significance of the disability for the individual.

Disability seems to give rise to less emotional disturbance in children affected than might be expected. Except in the case of conditions with brain disorder, these children seem not to differ markedly in terms of adjustment from their non-disabled peers. The cumulative effect, however, of immobility, stigma and possible parental over protection may be a high degree of social isolation. Educational opportunities may be limited and achievement may be below par for ability. In some cases, children may be subjected to unreasonable expectations from parents who may see educational achievement as a means of compensating for, or denying, the full impact of the disability. Philp and Duckworth (1982) give a comprehensive review of the literature on these issues and an amplification of the points made here.

In general, it seems that the child's adaptation is influenced not only by constraints imposed by the disabling condition *per se*, but also by his or her personality and age, and the reactions of parents, family and wider social systems, such as school and peer group. Where reactions are supportive, the inhibiting effects of the condition may be minimised and the child may succeed in functioning at a much higher level on a variety of fronts than another child with a similar condition but who lacks such a favourable environment.

Consequences for parents

Disability in a child may impose many physical and financial costs on parents, quite apart from the worry and stress that can spill out into other relationships within the family. Parents may be confronted with problems about the adequacy of housing, the need for special adaptations or equipment and a variety of problems concerning special diet and transport to hospital and school, with their attendant costs. Most of all perhaps, there is the physical strain of coping with problems such as incontinence and of being bound to the home when a child's disability is severe; respite care may not be readily feasible, even where it may occasionally be available.

At an emotional level, parents may experience guilt in the face of their child's disability, frustration at the limitations it imposes on his or her future, worries about the effect preoccupation with the disabled child may have on siblings and/or on the marital relationship. In addition, parents are often deeply concerned about the care arrangements available for their child when they grow too old or when they die. On a day-to-day basis, they may respond by being over-protective or over-indulgent, both of which may give rise to behavioural problems in the child and associated tensions in the family system.

All of these burdens produce great pressure on parents, especially where additional 'normal' stresses (financial or others) are also present. Most parents cope, some at a high price which can include considerable social isolation. Some may adapt very well to the demands. Others may fail to come to terms with the child's disability and, in extreme circumstances, may reject the child and refuse to undertake day-to-day care.

Increasingly, the support and resources available to parents are seen as critical. In understanding family difficulties, Philp and Duckworth (1982) note that the focus should be on the practical assistance a family requires rather than on seeing its problems in coping as a sign of pathology. Only a few exceptional families can manage without outside help.

It is important also to recognise that for some parents the adaptation to the needs of the disabled family member may prove an enriching experience.

Consequences for siblings
At first sight, it might seem likely that other children in the family may have to pay quite a high price for disability in a sibling. Research findings have tended to corroborate this view, with the following tendencies being among those observed.

Siblings may receive, or perceive themselves as getting, less parental attention since so much time and energy is devoted to the extra needs of the disabled child (Philp and Duckworth, 1982, pp 62-9; Van Dongen-Melman and Sanders-Woudstra, 1986, pp 160-61). He or she may be 'let away' with behaviour that is not tolerated from the other children. Reactions of resentment and anger, which may occasionally well up, may be quickly followed by pangs of guilt. Siblings may carry a greater burden of domestic responsiblities than peers in other families without a disabled child. They may also experience the shadow of stigma directed towards the disabled child by the outside world. Finally, they may lack clear information and understanding about the full nature of the disability.

Despite these possible difficulties, two research studies tend to dispel the notion that chronic disability or illness in one child necessarily produces disturbance or undue stress in the siblings (Ferrari, 1984; Gath and Gumley, 1987). Indeed, Ferrari's study found that siblings of chronically ill children were rated by their teachers as most socially competent and concerned among their peers in school. Many parents also reported that the presence of a chronically ill child had engendered greater compassion and understanding in the remaining children.

In determining the risk faced by siblings, it seems necessary to differentiate between the effects of various disabling conditions and the other problems and resources of a family which may be aggravated or drained by the presence of a disabled child. It is also necessary to regard each sibling individually, since the effects of a disabled child's presence in a family are unlikely to be spread uniformly throughout the sibling group.

Consequences of Parental Disability for Children
Parental mental illness

Children of mentally ill parents bear various risks. They may inherit a genetically transmitted predisposition to a particular mental condition. They may be at greater physical risk. They may also be vulnerable to psychiatric disorder arising from discord and disruption within the family due to mental disturbance in one or both parents.

A child with one parent who is schizophrenic carries a 10 per cent chance of developing the condition ultimately. (The chances increase to 50 per cent where both parents are schizophrenic.) However, it now appears that children of schizophrenic parents may actually be at less risk of psychiatric disturbance than children of parents with other mental disorders, such as personality disorder, chronic or recurrent depression or emotional disturbance (Rutter and Cox, 1985). In a review of research on maternal depression, Puckering (1989) notes that depression and educational and behavioural problems are among those reported in the children of depressed mothers.

The present understanding of psychiatric risk to children arising from parental mental disorder has been summarised by Rutter and Cox (1985, p. 71):

> It is evident that parental mental disorder constitutes an important psychiatric risk factor for children. However, the risk is far from inevitable. It seems to be greatest when both parents are ill, when there is substantial family discord and disruption, when parenting is overtly impaired and when parental symptoms directly impinge on or involve the children. It appears least when these factors are absent and when the child maintains a good harmonious relationship with at least one parent.

Parental mental handicap

The proportion of adults with mental handicap (excluding the mild range) who have children is likely to be small. The proportion who rear those children is likely to be even smaller, once again excluding those parents in the mild range.

In assessing the effect of having a mentally handicapped parent, it is necessary to distinguish between genetic and environmental effects. The quality of parenting is a major factor in the non-genetic or environmental influences on a child's developmental prospects. Where mental handicap is mild, the parent's handicap *per se* may not be a direct source of difficulty especially if there are no special financial or social problems. Nevertheless, lower intelligence represents a serious deficit in the range of resources that a parent requires in order to perform his or her complex role adequately. Mild mental handicap tends to be associated with lower socio-economic class (Rutter and Gould, 1985, p. 313) and it is the interaction of mental handicap with other sources of adversity that may impair parental performance. In those circumstances, parental skills of coping, problem-solving and general alertness and sensitivity to their children's needs may be deficient. Such problems may be mitigated where a second parent is capable of supplementing adequately the efforts of the first. Gath (1988) has reviewed parenting by mentally handicapped people.

Chronic physical disability or illness in a parent
As in the case of mental handicap, the effect on children of having a chronically ill or disabled parent can only be considered in the context of deficits in other resources which may accompany disablity in a parent. Where there is another parent who copes, where finances are not a problem and where there is a clear and relatively benign prognosis (e.g. not a progressive or terminal condition), it seems likely that any adverse effects can be minimised. But the corollary applies presumably with at least equal force. Information about the parent's condition, disclosed in a sensitive manner, may help children cope better with any anxiety. Rosenheim and Reicher (1985) found that there was lower anxiety among children informed clearly of their parent's terminal illness than among those not so informed.

Violence and Children

Child Abuse
Conventional views
Child abuse has become a dominant concern of child welfare services in most industrialised countries. Services are provided on the assumption that a well-organised and regulated system of child protection ensures that children do not suffer death, harm or neglect at the hands of their parents or caretakers. Child-care legislation first emerged in most countries towards the end of the last century or early this century. It represented a major breach in the dogma of the privacy of the family and responded to concerns about rescuing children from dangerous or unsavoury circumstances. In general, this phase of child-care legislation seemed geared to protect children from neglect due to parental ignorance or inadequacy rather than from any wilful act of harm.

In the early 1960s, an American paediatrician, Henry Kempe, wrote an influential paper with some colleagues in which he drew attention to the risk to children of deliberate injury by parents or caretakers (Kempe *et al*, 1962). He introduced the concept of the 'battered baby syndrome'. Initial professional hesitation and public shock gave way to a resolve on the part of legislators and professionals, in most countries, to address this newly perceived phenomenon. Gradually, the terms 'non-accidental injury' and later 'child abuse' gained currency. In addition, the definition had broadened beyond Kempe's original focus on serious physical abuse resulting in 'permanent injury or death'. There was increasing concern with the emotional as well as the physical consequences of failings in parental or caretakers' behaviour, as well as with the risk of sexual abuse.

The Department of Health's most recent description (1987) of child abuse exemplifies this broader view:

> Parents, carers (i.e. persons who, while not parents, have actual responsibility for a child) or others can harm children either by direct acts or by a failure to provide proper care, or both. Such acts include physical injuries, severe neglect and sexual or emotional abuse.

A panoply of legislation, regulations, procedures and services has emerged in many countries. These reflect a commitment to protect children and a belief that such measures can indeed constitute a comprehensive basis for the prevention of abuse. An important debate has emerged, however, about whether the phenomenon of the physical abuse or neglect of children is actually susceptible to such a response. Critics argue that the stresses which give rise to such forms of abuse are largely ignored in a model of intervention that focuses almost exclusively on the behaviour or pathology of the offending adults. This focus conveniently diverts attention from the social/structural sources of such stresses onto the personalities and relationships of the unfortunate parents in whom the symptoms of stress manifest themselves. Critics contend that responses to child abuse must go well beyond psychological treatment of the individual abuser. Since social and economic stress have frequently triggered the problem behaviour, the sources and symptoms of this stress must also be tackled, if child abuse is to be prevented.

Critics also question the degree of concern expressed about the welfare of children in the context of child abuse when compared with the hazards children must endure in relation to, for example, road traffic and industrial pollution, both of which on first appearance would seem more amenable to resolution by public policy and intervention. Class differences in exposure to a whole host of health risks, from higher infant mortality to smaller size, are well documented for children, yet this deeply ingrained pattern of inequality affecting children in society remains ignored despite its involving infinitely greater numbers than might ever experience child abuse in all its forms.

This double standard needs to be explained and the critics of the highlighting of child abuse argue that its real function is to serve as a focus for a moral panic among conservatives about what they perceive as the decay of family values in society, especially among the poor. In this analysis, the machinery of the child-protection system may be viewed as serving a political function, far broader than the protection of vulnerable children. Anxieties about child abuse provide a mandate for the policing by state services of what are seen by neighbours or other state agencies as 'troublesome' and 'anti-social' families who threaten the fabric of society. Clearly, critics are not implying that children who are abused should be left prey to their circumstances, but they are arguing that intervention, realistically, must recognise the social context in which the manifestations and definitions of, and the responses to, child abuse arise.

The relationship between the physical abuse of children and poverty may be disguised in another way also — by the idea that child abuse occurs fairly randomly throughout all social strata in society. This idea has been decried as 'the myth of classlessness'.

> Both evidence and reason lead to the unmistakable conclusion that, contrary to the myth of classlessness, the physical abuse and neglect of children are strongly related to poverty, in terms of prevalance and of severity of consequences. This is not to say that abuse and neglect do not occur among other socio-economic classes or that, when they do occur, they never have severe consequences. However, widespread reports suggesting that abuse and neglect are classless phenomena are unfounded and misleading.

The myth of classlessness persists not on the basis of evidence or logic, but because it serves certain professional and political interests. These interests do not further the task of dealing with the real problems underlying physical abuse and neglect; adherence to the myth obscures the nature of the problem and diverts resources from its solution (Pelton, 1985).

Recognising the different forms of Child Abuse and Neglect
Commentators may differ about how it is caused or defined, but the effects of child abuse, in its different forms, can be very real for its victims.

Physical abuse and neglect
Children who experience serious physical abuse may suffer fractures, burns and scalds (from cigarette butts or 'dunking' in scalding water, for example), as well as poisoning. In its 'milder' forms the main immediate effect of abuse may be bruising. Children of any age, even infants, may be victims.

In the case of neglect, there may be evidence of inadequate nutrition, inattention to urgent medical needs, developmental delays, the child being left unattended and alone or with inadequate arrangements for care. Neglect usually involves a variety of factors, although in extreme cases only one factor may be present.

Emotional abuse
This is the most difficult to define and identify. An emotionally abused child may suffer from a surfeit — or serious deficit — of attention from parents or primary caretakers. Such attention that is given may be manipulative, exploitative or demeaning in character. The child may be made a scapegoat, exposed to regular and possibly public ridicule or measured by quite unreasonable and possibly shifting expectations. In some cases, an older child may be forced to assume constant responsibility for the care of younger siblings without any regard for the individual needs, rights or preferences of the child concerned.

Emotional abuse can be categorised as emotional neglect, in that the emotional and psychological needs of a developing child are seriously frustrated or ignored. The often subtle, elusive and apparently infinite character of the symptoms makes for great difficulty, as well as danger, in the assessment and identification of emotional abuse. Cultural attitudes and differences can heavily influence perceptions of professionals and others. Consequently, the interpretation of symptoms and evidence may often diverge significantly. In addition, the frequently intangible quality of emotional abuse does not readily suit it to the standards of proof required by courts.

Sexual abuse
This form of abuse has been defined as

the involvement of dependent, developmentally immature children and adolescents in sexual activities which they do not truly comprehend, to which they are unable to give informed consent or that violate the social taboos of family roles (Kempe and Kempe, 1978, p. 60).

It can encompass forms of sexual activity other than intercourse, including fondling, mutual masturbation, digital penetration, oral-genital contact and involvement of children in photography or filming for pornographic purposes.

Sexual abuse may be perpetrated by a member of the victim's family or household. It may also occur outside the family network, where it can be occasioned by a young person or an adult in a position of trust, such as a neighbour, youth worker or a child-care worker or, very rarely, a stranger.

There is a discussion of work with cases of child sexual abuse in pp 178-82.

The Effects of Abuse
Physical abuse and neglect
The research evidence tends to be increasingly uncertain about the precise implications of physical abuse or neglect for a child's development. Augustinos (1987) found that previous assumptions — that abuse necessarily precipitated developmental deficits — had to be qualified by recent findings. More sophisticated research methods have pointed to the possible importance of other factors in the child's make-up or environment in terms of mitigating, potentiating or aggravating the effects of abuse *per se*. She cites two studies which suggest that a higher IQ in the child, or the presence of play materials in the home or maternal involvement may somehow act as or be associated with protective factors for the abused child. Augustinos also drew attention to the need for greater clarity in distinguishing between the effects of abuse and neglect.

In the past, researchers have assumed that negative developmental outcomes were due to physical abuse. But there is increasing evidence to suggest that many of the observed deficits in abused children may be more properly attributed to undetected neglect. Furthermore, some researchers are now suggesting that neglect may be potentially more damaging to development than abuse (i.e. if abuse is not associated with death or neurological impairment), particularly in the areas of language development, psychosocial development and empathic responsiveness (ibid).

Sexual abuse
Factors which bear on the severity and durability of the effects of sexual abuse seem to include its frequency, intensity and duration, as well as the relationship of the victim to the perpetrator. The nature of the abusive act may also be important: it should not be assumed that the most damage is caused by the grosser forms of abuse. Some children may be deeply damaged by relatively 'light' forms of abuse.

The effects of sexual abuse are only beginning to be unravelled. An immediate risk is the removal of the child from the home where abuse is within the family. In such instances, the victim suffers twice over, first having their trust betrayed by the abuser and then losing their place in the family. Some children may have their self-esteem further undermined by the response to the disclosure of abuse. Denial of the fact of abuse or over-reaction to it may aggravate the original damage caused. Clumsy and repetitious investigations may be as traumatising for the child as the original incidents.

In the long term, sexual abuse seems to leave victims at risk of a legacy of serious harm, although conclusive proof of the causal link between abuse and specific damage is awaited. One study of adult women who had childhood experiences of abuse, and who were receiving therapy in adulthood, found that they had experienced a wide range of problems (Jehu, 1988). These included disturbances of mood (low self-esteem, feelings of guilt, depressive episodes), self-damaging behaviour (attempted suicide, self-mutilation, substance abuse, eating disorders), interpersonal problems (isolation, insecurity, discord, inadequacy), stress disorders giving rise to various psychological problems (e.g. panic or anxiety states or psychosomatic disorders) and sexual difficulties (problems of sexual dysfunction or orientation, subsequent experience of rape, involvement in prostitution or compulsive sexual behaviour).

The difficulty is knowing, first, whether these problems are all attributable to the abuse or to surrounding circumstances, and, second, whether these women are representative of all women who experience abuse as children. It is also important to note that not all victims are female (see below).

Child Abuse in Ireland

The only available data relating to the extent of child abuse nationally are those of cases reported to the Department of Health following referral to, and investigation on behalf of, local directors of community care. It should be noted, however, that all reported cases are unlikely to correspond with all actual cases. Given the present state of knowledge, it is difficult to estimate what proportion of actual cases the reported cases represent. The powerlessness of the victims, the typical secretiveness of the abusers and the reticence of third parties who may come to suspect abuse will all tend to inhibit the reporting of actual cases.

The available data, however, reveal that in the period 1983-87, the number of new confirmed cases annually had grown from 156 to 763 — an almost fivefold increase (see Figure 2). The numbers of these confirmed cases involving sexual abuse had grown in the same period from 37 in 1983 to 456 in 1987 — an increase by a factor of 13. The share of confirmed cases by those involving sexual abuse had also grown. In 1983, they constituted less than one in four (23.7%) of all confirmed cases, whereas in 1987 they made up more than half (59.8%).

These increases may, however, reflect the influence of other factors as much as a true increase in child abuse. They may be due to, for example, greater professional alertness and/or greater civic spirit, or a fuller appreciation of the adverse consequences of child abuse on the part of members of the public who initiate referrals and/or fuller awareness by the professionals of the procedures laid down in Department of Health guidelines on child abuse, which have been in effect, with regular revision, since 1976.

The increase in referral figures may also be accounted for by an expansion of the category of child abuse. As now defined, it may take a physical and/or emotional and/or sexual form. This wider definition could also contribute to the steady upward trend, especially in the absence of standardised categories for the identification of cases.

A study of child sexual abuse cases in the Eastern Health Board region in 1988 gives valuable information about the nature and extent of the problem. Examining all cases known to community care social workers where child sexual abuse was a

Figure 2: **Numbers of new cases of alleged and confirmed child abuse reported to the health boards in Ireland, 1984-87**

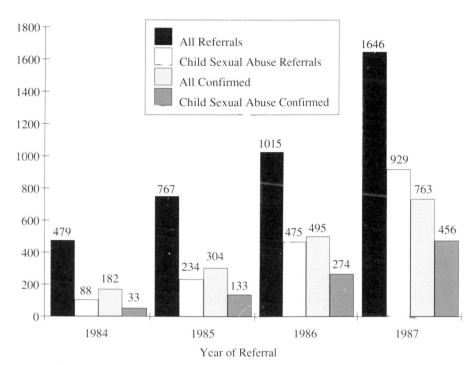

Year of Referral

Source: McKeown, K. and Gilligan, R. (1990), from *Statistics on Child Abuse, 1984; 1985; 1986; 1987*, Department of Health

concern, the researchers identified 990 such cases of which 512 (52.0%) had by the end of the year been confirmed by agreed official procedures as actual cases. This total of confirmed cases yields a rate of sexual abuse among children of 1.2 per 1,000 children. (It should be noted, of course, that many cases may remain unknown and others of the known group wait to be confirmed so the actual extent of the problem is likely to be greater than these figures suggest.) Of the confirmed cases, one in four involved boys and one in three children aged six and under. In 90% of cases, the abuser was male, in 2% of cases the abuser was female and in a further 7% the child was the victim of both male and female abusers. In 60% of cases the abuser was a relative, and in 51% of cases the abuser lived in the same household (McKeown and Gilligan, 1990).

Children and AIDS

Children may be affected by AIDS in two ways; they may have the condition themselves or their parents or caretakers may have it. A person with AIDS —

Acquired Immune Deficiency Syndrome — lacks normal immunity against certain illnesses. AIDS is caused by the Human Immuno-Deficiency Virus — HIV — which attacks the body's immune system and renders it vulnerable to various infections. These infections will ultimately prove fatal to a person with AIDS. This is because of the steady weakening of the normal defences of the body which is characteristic of AIDS.

While there is a lot of public anxiety about how easily HIV may be passed from one person to another, there are only four proven routes for possible infection. Two of these routes are determined by the behaviour of the individual, viz. engaging in intimate sexual contact, whether heterosexual or homosexual, where there occurs an exchange of body fluids with an infected person. The remaining two are beyond the control of the individual, viz. being born to a mother who is herself HIV+; or having injections or transfusions which use blood or blood products from an infected person (a risk run particularly by 'street' drug users).

It now seems that a person who is tested as HIV+ will eventually get AIDS, but they may enjoy many years of good health in the meantime, especially if they take good care of themselves.

Children may become HIV+ by being infected by their mother in the womb or by having intimate sexual contact (where body fluids are exchanged) with an infected person. Clearly a child or young person risks this infection if they are sexually active in their own right; but there is also a risk, in theory at least, that sexually abused youngsters who are not otherwise sexually active may be infected by their abuser.

In Ireland, by the end of December 1990, seven children had been diagnosed as having AIDS. They had been born to mothers who were intravenous drug users. Of these seven, five had died (Dept. of Health 1991). As of the end of July 1990, another 68 children had been found to be HIV+ (Dept. of Health 1990). Unfortunately there is no information available on the precise age or general social background of these children, although it seems reasonable to speculate that most of these children are from the same type of deprived working class backgrounds as most chronic illicit drug users. Children who are HIV+ face daunting problems quite apart from their prognosis. Their conditions impose great demands on their families. If there are other serious problems pressing on the parents or family, they may not be in a position to look after the child. In such circumstances, a child may have to go into the care of the local health board, which must then find a foster family or children's home willing to provide care for the child. Given public anxiety and confusion about the risks surrounding AIDS and HIV+, it may not prove easy to find a suitable placement for such a child.

Social Prejudice and Children of Minorities: The Case of the Travellers

Ireland is a relatively homogeneous society. It lacks the racial and other cultural differentiation which in many societies gives rise to prejudice, bigotry and conflict. The impact of such differences is not remote from the Irish experience, however, in that the inter-communal tensions in Northern Ireland impinge regularly on our consciousness.

The apparent absence of serious problems of social prejudice may reflect reduced opportunity rather than any national virtue of tolerance. In the United States, the immigrant Irish have a reputation for racism. Even at home, the research available points to a not insignificant degree of intolerance lurking beneath the surface of our society.

The children most likely to experience social prejudice are those who belong to the travelling people. In a study of social attitudes in the general population Davis, Grube and Morgan (1984) found that over 70% of the random sample (N = 2,359) 'would be reluctant to buy a house next door to an itinerant.' The report also found that this negative attitude towards the travellers was 'a widespread tendency in the population as a whole, rather than only in certain subgroups' (ibid. p. 99).

These findings support the results of earlier work by McGréil (1977) on prejudice in Dublin. He found that

> itinerants rank very low on the respondents' order of preference. Their standing is particularly low in regard to kinship, i.e. over 70% of the respondents would not welcome itinerants into their family and 6.6% would deny them Irish citizenship. Two reasons were given for this negative attitude towards itinerants — 'not socially acceptable' by 62.1% and their 'way of life' by 32.4%. Because of the high refusal to admit them into the family and the reasons put forward as justification of this, it would seem that itinerants are perceived as a lower social caste in modern Dublin society.

In many respects, travellers in Ireland seem to occupy a position comparable to the 'out group' status of indigenous or immigrant social minorities in other societies, such as the aborigines of Australia, the maoris of New Zealand, the native Indians of North America, the Romany gypsies of continental Europe (Liegois, 1987), the Lapp people of northern Scandinavia and the immigrant workers today in countries such as Germany, Switzerland and France.

Living within a dominant host society that rejects and even despises their culture, such minority groups internalise the low esteem in which they are held. In order to cope, they may often resort to patterns of behaviour, such as heavy drinking, that are ultimately destructive of the remaining fabric of a once viable culture.

According to the 1986 census of travelling people in Ireland, there are 15,888 travelling people, belonging to 2,861 households. Four in ten (41.2%) of these households are accommodated in local authority houses, while more than a third are living in caravans on unserviced sites (13%) or on the roadside (25.7%). More than half (51.9%) of all travellers are under 15 years of age compared to 28.9% of the general population (Barry and Daly, 1988).

Living at the economic and social margins of society produces many problems which are linked with, but go far beyond, the original problem of prejudice. Typically, the travelling community must endure harsh living conditions which, in turn, lead to health, educational and other difficulties.

The infant mortality rate among the travelling community (18.1 per 1,000 live births), is more than twice the rate in the settled community (7.4 per 1,000 live births), according to *The Travellers' Health Status Study* (Barry, Herity and Solan, 1989). Mortality rates are higher for travellers than for the settled population. A male traveller faces twice the risk of dying in a given year, compared to his settled counterpart; a female traveller three times her's (ibid). Life expectancy is considerably lower for travellers than for settled people, 9.9 years less for male travellers and 11.9 years less for female travellers (ibid). It has been suggested that there are unusually high rates of illness and hospitalisation among the children of travelling people (Ennis, 1984, citing Dr. J. Kiely). In addition, there is evidence that the rate of physical growth among traveller children falls behind norms for the population of children generally (Creedon, Corboy and Kevany, 1975). Furthermore, the growth rate of individual traveller children has been found to fall below their personal projected developmental trajectories. Their growth rate fails to measure up to the potential scope for growth based on measurements in early childhood (Carroll *et al*, 1974). It is also believed that life expectancy among adult travellers is considerably lower than that of the population as a whole. Thus, traveller children face a higher risk of experiencing the death of a parent.

The health problems of the travellers are related to their living conditions (Rottman, Tussing and Wiley, 1986). Almost half (48.1%) have no piped water supply and more than half have no use of a hot water tap (61.6%), no fixed bath or shower (62.5%), no toilet facility (50.3%) and no connection to the public electricity supply (54.4%). The picture varies by health board region, with the worst conditions obtaining in the region covered by the Eastern Health Board (i.e. in Dublin city and county, and counties Wicklow and Kildare).

These startling data not only provide graphic evidence of the basic deprivations endured by travellers relative to the settled community. They also indicate the impossibility of securing the primary health care of travellers under such conditions. Safe water and basic sanitation are two of the eight essential elements of primary health care as set down by the World Health Organisation (Levine, 1984).

The authors of the most recent major study on the conditions of Irish travellers do not mince their words (Rottman, Tussing and Wiley, 1986):

> The central conclusion of this study is an inescapable one: the circumstances of the Irish travelling people are intolerable. No humane and decent society, once made aware of such circumstances, could permit them to persist. The clear implication is that the system and structure of responsibility existing at the time of the 1981 Census of Traveller Families failed to provide an acceptable solution to the problems experienced by the most underprivileged population group within Irish society.

The disadvantages facing travellers are not confined to standards of health or accommodation. It seems that approximately 50% of traveller children of school-going age are not attending school (Travelling People Review Body, 1983, p. 64). Only 10% remain in school beyond the age of 12 (ibid. p. 68). This state of affairs seems to be due to a number of possible factors, including the transient lifestyle of many travelling people, parental doubts of the relevance of formal education for traveller culture and the limitations in the relevance of the school curriculum for traveller children. (See pp 74-5 for a discussion of educational provision for traveller children.)

PART II:

SOCIAL SERVICES FOR CHILDREN, YOUNG PEOPLE AND THEIR FAMILIES

Chapter 4

THE EDUCATION SYSTEM

Under Irish law, incorporated in the School Attendance Acts 1926-67 and an extending order of 1972, children must attend school between the ages of 6 and 15. In practice, a substantial number of children begin school at an earlier age than 6: more than half of 4 year olds (55.7%) attend school and in the 5 year old group essentially all do so (see Table 5). These trends are due presumably to the absence of alternative pre-school, kindergarten or nursery school facilities, which in other developed countries frequently serve as a formal introduction to the educational system. In France and Belgium, for example, 95% of 3-5 year olds attend publicly funded pre-schools, while in Italy and and Denmark, the equivalent proportions are 88% and 87% respectively (McKenna, 1988, p. 83).

Table 5: **Estimated percentage of persons in selected age groups receiving full-time education by age, percentage**

Age on 1 Jan. 1989	*Percentage Participation*
3 and under	1.1
4	55.7
5-14	99.7
15	95.8
16	87.5
17	73.2
18	44.5

Source: Dept. of Education, *Statistical Report* 1988/89, p. 3.

Table 6: **Number of pupils (ordinary classes) in national schools by class size, as percentage of all pupils**

	0-19	%	20-29	%	30-39	%	40 and over	%	Total
1988-9	15,053	(2.7)	135,968	(24.8)	371,420	(67.7)	26,182	(4.8)	548,623
1985-6	18,165	(3.3)	157,295	(28.3)	347,481	(62.5)	32,898	(5.9)	555,839

Source: Dept. of Education (1988), *Statistical Report 1985-86*. Dublin: Stationery Office; Dept. of Education (1990), *Statistical Report 1988-89*, Dublin: Stationery Office

Parents are free to select the school of their choice (subject to the availability of a place) and are accorded a constitutional guarantee of freedom from state interference in this regard. Article 42.3.1. of Bunreacht na hÉireann states:

> The State shall not oblige parents in violation of their conscience and lawful preference to send their children to schools established by the State, or to any particular type of school designated by the State.

There is no charge for attendance at national schools and in all but a minority of secondary schools. However, the shortfall that may arise between grant-aid and actual running costs may mean that in many schools there is a strong emphasis on fund-raising and possibly even on 'voluntary contributions' by parents. The levels of funding available to the national schools system also means that many children must attend large classes. Two out of three children (72.5%) in national schools are in classes of 30 and over (see Table 6). This unsatisfactory pupil teacher ratio has long been a feature of Irish education.

Sponsorship and Management of Schools
Within the primary sector in Ireland, the national school system dominates almost completely, with only 2% of schools being run privately (i.e. fees are charged and the school receives no state funds). There are 3,261 state-funded primary national schools and they are almost all under denominational control, with 93.2% under the patronage of the local Roman Catholic bishop (Dáil Debates, 1988).

Two major exceptions to this denominational pattern are the ten model national schools run directly by the State and the small, but growing, multi-denominational sector, whose schools are under the direct control of parents and supporters. The first of these multi-denominational schools was established in 1978 in Dalkey, a suburb of south Co. Dublin, and as of 1990-91 eight others had opened in Bray, north Dublin (Glasnevin and Kilbarrack), south Dublin (Ranelagh), Cork, Kilkenny, Limerick and Sligo. Hyland (1989) gives an account of the evolution of this small sector in the national school system.

Another development in recent years has been the strong interest among parents in Irish-medium primary schools. By September 1989, 62 Gaelscoileanna had been established, with the recognition of the Department of Education, outside Gaeltacht areas (Bord na Gaeilge, 1989), frequently in the face of formidable obstacles. Of particular interest is the fact that demand has often been strongest in urban working-class areas, not traditionally the stronghold of active supporters of the Irish language.

There are 843 schools at secondary level. The denominational pattern at this level is less complete in what is a more complex organisational picture. Over half (56.2%) of second-level schools are under Catholic religious management; a further 2.6% are under the management of other religious denominations. Just under one-third (30.9%) of second-level schools are under the control of local vocational education committees (VECs). These VEC schools were intended to provide technical education as a way of preparation for careers in the trades. In addition, there are 47 community schools and 16 comprehensive schools, which combine elements of the vocational and non-vocational sectors. Community schools have often evolved from the merger of existing schools, while comprehensive schools have been established in rural areas where previously there had been no second-level provision. The secondary school system is completed by 22 schools under private lay management (National Economic and Social Council, 1990, p. 308; Dáil Debates, 1988).

Denominational trends and the pattern of Church/State relations that had begun to emerge under British rule mean that historically the State has gradually accepted responsibility for the funding of schools, while leaving their day-to-day management, in the majority of cases, to the local bishops, their representatives or to religious orders.

In the non-Catholic school sector, these patterns are mirrored. The exceptions to denominational management include the vocational sector, which is theoretically non-denominational. (Remarkably, the Vocational Education Act 1930, under which this sector was established, remains the only legislation bearing on the operation of the school system in the State.) The other exceptions to denominational control are the State-run model primary schools, the secondary schools under private lay management, the embryonic multi-denominational sector at primary level and some special national schools sponsored by voluntary bodies.

In the national school system up to 1975, the local parish priest (or his equivalent in other denominations) acted on behalf of the patron (the local bishop) as school manager. Boards of management were then introduced at the behest of the Department of Education, to give a voice to the interests of elected parents, teachers and nominees of the patron. The initial structure of these boards was such as to ensure a majority for the appointees of the patron but this was revised in 1981. In schools of 6 teachers or less, a board consists of three nominees of the patrons, two representatives elected by parents and the principal. In larger schools, the patron nominates four members, parents elect two and teachers one, and the principal also has a place.

Children with Special Needs
Handicapped or disabled children
Some 8,480 children with physical or mental disabilities that impinge on their learning capacity are catered for in 120 special schools in Ireland. These schools enjoy favourable pupil/teacher ratios, with some 937 teachers being employed in this area (Dáil Debates, 1988).

Children of the travelling community
The policy of making pre-school provision for children of the travelling community is gradually being implemented. The number of pre-schools has grown

from 18 in early 1984 to a total of 41, catering for over 500 children in the school year 1987-88 (Committee to Monitor the Implementation of Government Policy on Travelling People, 1989). There are 3,953 traveller children enrolled in national schools. They are provided for in three different ways:

  i) in special classes (29.8%);
 ii) integrated in ordinary classes (34.5%);
iii) partly integrated but with extra separate tuition (35.7%) (ibid.).

School attendance by children of travelling people is significantly below the norm. It is estimated that only slightly more than one in ten post-primary age traveller children attend school. The picture is considerably better at primary level, but problems remain (ibid.).

Pastoral and Welfare Needs of Pupils
Remedial teachers
The Department of Education makes available a certain number of remedial teacher posts to supplement the resources of schools where there are concentrations of children with needs for remedial tuition. The remedial teacher may have a number of functions within a school: assisting in the identification and diagnosis of learning problems among pupils, devising and reviewing special programmes of help which may be operated by the remedial teacher alone or in conjunction with a class teacher, assisting with pupils who present behavioural or low self-esteem problems, acting as an adviser on resource material, and liaising with parents and outside agencies as necessary in relation to individual children (Department of Education, 1987). Remedial teachers may conduct a full-time class or may work by giving sessional attention to children who otherwise attend the normal class for their age group.

The number of remedial teachers' posts approved varies from year to year. During 1990 there were approximately 890 remedial teachers serving in the region of 1,100 national schools (Primary Education Review Body, 1990, p. 62). Some second-level schools may also have access to remedial teaching posts by means of a special ex-quota provision.

Guidance teachers
In second-level schools, teachers may be assigned to guidance counselling duties. The function of guidance teachers is to provide a pastoral care service to individual pupils and to offer information and advice about career planning.

In the school year 1987-88, there were a total of 293 ex quota guidance teachers' posts approved by the Department of Education (secondary schools, 193; community and comprehensive schools, 49; vocational schools, 51). Ex quota posts for guidance teachers are permitted in schools of more than 500 pupils. This means that the school gets a guidance teacher post in addition to the quota of teachers it is due on the basis of its pupil numbers. In schools that do not qualify on this basis, school authorities must decide whether to redeploy teaching resources in order to provide a full- or part-time guidance teacher post.

Schools' Psychological Service
The Psychological Service of the Department of Education employs 25 psychologists, serving 819 schools in the post-primary sector. Their duties and functions are:

• to monitor, advise on and support the provision of guidance and remedial education in post-primary schools;
• to assess pupils with psychological or educational difficulties as requested and to advise parents, schools and teachers accordingly;
• to advise schools and teachers on the provision for exceptional children, e.g. the disabled or disadvantaged;
• to provide teacher in-service training, e.g. basic training in remedial education as well as short-term in-service training for teachers (Dáil Debates 1987).

In addition to these duties, the psychologists contribute to the development of various programmes, such as vocational and training courses, as well as social and personal programmes for pupils (e.g. education on drugs and substance abuse) and programmes to promote equality of opportunity for boys and girls. They also engage in research and development of educational materials (ibid.).

From this outline, it will be clear that the schools' psychological service does not serve the primary school sector. Not surprisingly, there have been calls for this anomaly to be remedied and for the expansion of the currently threadbare provision for secondary schools. Among the organisations calling for such reform are the Psychological Society of Ireland (1974), the Irish National Teachers' Organisation (1979), the Committee on Discipline in Schools (de Ris, 1985) and the National Parents' Council/Primary (1987). In 1989, the Minster for Education announced her intention of establishing two local three-year pilot projects for a schools' psychological service over three years each (Dáil Debates, 1989). These are sited in West Dublin and South Tipperary and got under way during 1990.

Social Problems and the School
Truancy
The School Attendance Acts provide for school attendance committees which may oversee their operation. There are four such committees in 1990, in the cities of Dublin, Cork and Waterford, and in the borough of Dun Laoghaire. While these committees employ school attendance officer(s), in the remainder of the country, it falls to the gardaí to enforce the Acts, a situation which has been the subject of much criticism (Costello, 1985). Substantial reform of provision to monitor and secure school attendance has been proposed by, *inter alia*, Costello (ibid), the Task Force on Child Care Services (1981) and the Primary Education Review Body (1990).

The courts may commit a child to care as a sanction in a case of persistent truancy, although the use of this sanction is in decline and seems to be used only where other welfare considerations also indicate the measure.

Discipline problems
The use of corporal punishment in schools has been forbidden since 1982. In the case of a continuously disruptive pupil or of a serious breach of discipline, the

pupil may initially be excluded for a maximum period of three days. In special circumstances, this may be extended for a period of ten days by a special decision of the school's Board of Management. In exceptional circumstances, a further period may be permitted. Also, importantly, no pupil may be struck off the rolls in one school without an alternative place in another school having been found for him or her in the locality (Department of Education, 1988).

Social education for young people
In the past, schools have been subject to criticism of their failure to equip young people with the necessary knowledge to cope with the pressures of modern living. In response, many schools have made serious and imaginative efforts to promote programmes of social education and development for their students.

Some of the social skills or life skills programmes which have emerged have been attacked for what is seen as an amoral ethos. Critics wish for students to be instructed in unambiguous and definitive moral precepts. In defence of these programmes, it has been argued that moral development requires a process of personal struggle and discovery, during which an adolescent begins to formulate and internalise a set of values which derive from the ethos of his or her family, school and community. The task of life skills' work is to assist in that process. From this perspective, didactic approaches to moral formation are seen as crude, blunt and ineffectual.

The Department of Education has intervened in this debate to stress that the primary responsibility in this area lies with parents, who may look to schools for assistance (Department of Education, 1987). In their approach, schools must develop a corporate approach which reflects the consulted views of parents and a clear moral dimension, to be informed by religious principles. In the Department's view, the provision of 'sex/relationships education' cannot be considered as 'a purely secular activity'. Its policy is addressed to second-level schools and stresses the need to avoid having 'pupils discuss and consider issues which would be beyond their understanding at a particular age or stage of development'. This would seem to suggest that the Department is unwilling to contemplate the implications of these issues for the primary sector, even in the upper age classes.

Special Initiatives to Tackle Educational Disadvantage
Youth Encounter projects
Some of these projects began to be established in 1977 by the Department of Education, on the recommendation of the Task Force on Child Care Services (1975). Their brief was to explore whether certain young people at risk could be catered for effectively in day facilities rather than in residential care.

There are now four such projects — in Finglas and the north-inner city of Dublin, and in Cork and Limerick. They 'cater for boys and girls in the age group 10-14 who were persistent truants or had been involved with the law or were likely to become involved with the law' (ibid. pp 151-2). Classified as 'special schools' administratively, they are relatively generously staffed with teachers, a social worker (seconded from the Probation and Welfare Service), a community worker and a housekeeper.

The further development of this approach to educational disadvantage has been widely commended by Costello (ibid. pp 154-5), Burke *et al* (1981) and the National Planning Board (1984). The projects were the subject of an evaluation completed in 1984, which was broadly favourable in its assessment of their contribution to the treatment and prevention of delinquency and of their cost effectiveness (Seanad Debates, 1985).

Rutland Street Project
In 1969, an experimental pre-school action research project got underway in Dublin's inner city. It was to prove a major venture in terms of educational and social policy development in Ireland. It attracted interest from abroad and produced knock-on effects not only on participating families but also in the wider educational system.

The findings showed an impressive impact on parental perceptions of education. The children gained in terms of IQ levels during their period of pre-school education relative to controls who did not benefit from such intervention. Unfortunately, follow-up studies, undertaken when the children were 8 years of age, showed that some of these gains had been lost and that overall scholastic performance was less influenced than might have been hoped. Seamus Holland, a Department of Education official close to the project, saw the findings not as grounds for pessimism but rather as further evidence of the need for a multifaceted approach to educational disadvantage which would transcend formal educational intervention.

> The Rutland Street Project confirmed what educationalists have long believed: that a solution to the problem of educational disadvantage will require concerted action, involving a number of statutory agencies and local communities. There are, however, grounds for optimism about the project and its possible outcomes. There are many signs that so-called disadvantaged parents have the capacity to play a more active role in their children's education, and the children themselves display a range of positive personal qualities in sharp contrast to their indifferent scholastic records (Holland, 1979 p.107).

The spin-off effects of the Rutland Street Project included related experiments in seven other schools in disadvantaged areas of Dublin, as well as in Kilkenny and Limerick. In total, all of these initiatives have led to greater sophistication in approaching educational disadvantage through the school system in Ireland (ibid; Archer, 1984).

Schemes of Special Provision for national schools in disadvantaged areas
Two schemes operate to bring extra resources to national schools in disadvantaged areas. The first offers financial assistance (worth £1.5 million in 1991) for (i) grants for books/equipment, (ii) promoting home-school liaison and (iii) special in-service training of teachers; the second offers additional teaching posts and benefits 181 schools (Primary Education Review Body, 1990, p. 65) out of a total of more than 3,200 national schools. This present compensatory provision has been criticised as anomalous and inadequate (Irish National Teachers' Organisation, 1989), and its expansion was recommended by the Primary Education Review Body (1990).

Chapter 5

THE JUVENILE JUSTICE SYSTEM

In 1989, 3,660 youngsters aged 7 and under 17 were convicted or found guilty of offences, giving a rate of offending of 5.3 youngsters in trouble per 1,000 youngsters in this age group (compared to 6.0 per 1,000 persons aged 17 and over). Children and young people aged 7 and under 17 make up one in five of both the general population (19.6%) and of all persons 'convicted or against whom charge was held proved and order made without conviction' (20.5%) (derived from CSO, 1987; Garda Commissioner, 1990).

Young people in trouble with the law may be dealt with in a number of ways. Obviously, the first stage of contact involves the gardai, who have some discretion about how they should proceed especially in relation to a minor offence. The other elements that go to make up the juvenile justice system include the courts and the probation and welfare service of the Department of Justice, together with various residential centres and community projects which are devoted partly or exclusively to the needs of young people in trouble with the law.

Garda Síochána

The gardaí do not operate juvenile bureaux as is the practice in many police forces abroad. The gardaí have no special unit that deals exclusively with young people following their apprehension. However, under the Criminal Justice Act 1984, when interviewing a young person under 17 the gardaí are generally obliged to do so only in the company of a parent, guardian, relative or other responsible adult who is not a member of the force (Treatment of Persons in Custody in Garda Síochána Stations, Regulations 1987, Section 13).

The absence of a special unit to deal exclusively with all juvenile cases may present certain difficulties. While undoubtedly most cases are handled perfectly adequately, the Garda Complaints Board expressed some concerns in this area in its first annual report (1988):

> About one in six of the cases with which the Board dealt during the year [1987-88] involved children or juveniles, and it would appear that the standards which should apply in dealing with such cases are not universally appreciated within the Force. The Board will be keeping a close eye on such cases in the future and will expect that the letter and spirit of the regulations regarding young people will be fully observed in all cases.

Garda Juvenile Liaison Scheme

This scheme was initiated in 1963 to deal with first-time or minor offending by youngsters. Its aim is to identify youngsters at risk and, by advice and counselling, to divert them from further delinquency or contact with the courts and the wider juvenile justice system. It provides for the cautioning, instead of prosecution, of juvenile offenders involved in minor offences (mainly larceny, burglary and malicious damage) subject to the following conditions:

- the offender is under 17 years of age;
- the offender admits the crime/offence;
- the offender either has no criminal record or has a criminal record that is not serious;
- the offender gives a commitment to co-operate with the Juvenile Liaison Officer;
- the parents or guardians of the offender agree to co-operate with the gardaí by accepting any help or advice about the juvenile's future;
- the injured party agrees (Whitaker Committee, 1985).

Under this scheme, a Superintendent or Inspector administers a formal 'caution' to the youngster in the presence of a parent or guardian. When admitted to the scheme, a youngster remains under supervision for a period of two years. During 1989, a total of 2,716 young people (2,315 boys and 401 girls) were admitted to the scheme. Since its inception in 1963, a total of 38,473 young people have been referred. One measure of the scheme's effectiveness is the low rate of re-offending recorded among young people admitted to it (Garda Commissioner, 1989). Over the full period of the scheme, the rate of such re-offending has been 10.8%, with an annual figure for 1988 of 12.3%.

The scheme employs a total of 79 officers on a full-time basis (Dáil Debates, 1985). Each receives four weeks additional training for their role and carry out their duties generally in plain clothes.

The Courts

When dealing with youngsters under 17 years, a court is required, under the Children Act 1908 as amended by the Children Act 1941, to sit in a different place or at a different time from the ordinary sittings of the court. Dublin has the only full-time Children's Court, which deals with children aged up to 15 years and young persons aged 15 and under 17.

Under the provisions of the Summary Jurisdiction over Children Act 1884, these courts have jurisdiction to deal summarily with a child or young person charged with any indictable offence other than homicide. The district justices who hear these cases are lawyers who have been appointed to the bench and they hold full-time salaried positions. It is possible for any child of 7 years or over to be brought before a court for an offence. The position is explained by Shatter (1986):

> A child may be held criminally responsible for his acts from the age of seven. Under common law, there is an irrebuttable presumption that a child below that age cannot commit a criminal offence, in that a child could not distinguish between right and wrong. From the age of 7 to 14 years, there is a rebuttable presumption of innocence, i.e. a presumption that a child lacks criminal capacity or is 'doli incapax'. To override this presumption, it must be established that at the time of committing the act charged, the child knew it was wrong.

An age of criminal responsibility of 7 years is low by comparison with other jurisdictions. For example, in Northern Ireland it is 10 years, as it is in England and Wales; in Germany, it is 14 years.

The Children Act 1908, enacted under British rule in Ireland, remains the law in relation to young offenders, despite its age and its frequent updating in the UK jurisdiction. The Child Care Act 1991 does not deal with young offenders although new juvenile justice legislation has been promised (An Taoiseach 1991). The 1908 Act gives the court the following dispositional alternatives in dealing with young offenders. Section 107 of the Act allows the case to be dealt with by either:

- dismissing the charge; or
- discharging the offender on his entering into a recognisance; or
- so discharging the offender and placing him under the supervision of a probation officer; or
- committing the offender to the care of a relative or other fit person; or
- sending the offender to an industrial school; or
- sending the offender to a reformatory school; or
- ordering the offender to be whipped [a disposition which has fallen into disuse]; or
- ordering the offender to pay a fine, damages or costs; or
- ordering the parent or guardian of the offender to pay a fine, damages or costs; or
- ordering the parent or guardian of the offender to give security for his good behaviour; or
- committing the offender to custody in a place of detention provided under this part of the Act; or
- where the offender is a young person, by sentencing him to imprisonment; or
- dealing with the case in any other manner in which it may be legally dealt with.

The Criminal Justice (Community Service) Act 1983 provides courts with the additional non-custodial disposition of community service, by which an offender of 16 years and over may be sentenced to a certain number of hours of community service (e.g. painting/decorating community facilities).

There is little known about the relative importance of different dispositions. An analysis of 1982 data from the Dublin Metropolitan Court found that 'there had been 498 decisions involving custodial or residential care out of a total of 15,663 cases heard, reflecting an incarceration rate of 3.2% overall' (Caul, 1985). The study also noted that this rate of incarceration was lower than that obtaining in Northern Ireland.

Using 1985 data, Farrelly (1989) found a slightly higher incarceration rate, of 5.2% in 12,628 cases. In addition, analysing new cases appearing in March 1987, Farrelly found that one in four offenders were aged 17 and over, i.e. they had been charged with somebody under 17 thus allowing them be brought before a children's court; this fact should presumably be borne in mind in interpreting these incarceration rates, since older offenders may be more liable to be sent away.

The Probation and Welfare Service

The current Probation and Welfare Service of the Department of Justice began with a single post in 1961. It now has an establishment of 169 posts. A substantial part of the service work is devoted to offenders under the age of 16. In relation to this age group, the service performs a number of functions:

*   preparing social enquiry and other reports for the courts;
*   supervising offenders in the community (on probation, on adjourned supervision and under Community Service Orders);
*   assisting with and helping to set up community-based facilities (hostels, etc) for those in the care of the service and providing a welfare input to special schools, Youth Encounter Projects, etc;
*   assisting in the resolution of family difficulties in civil cases (e.g. marital problems), which obviously impinge on children where their parents are involved.

Offenders may come under the supervision of probation and welfare officers in three ways (Whitaker Committee, 1985). First, there are offenders who are the subject of a 'probation order' under Section 2 of the Probation of Offenders' Act 1907. This order is the main basis of the work of the service in the courts.

> It generally contains a condition that the offender be under the supervision of a named probation officer and such other conditions as the court considers necessary 'for preventing a repetition of the same offence or the commission of other offences' (Section 2(2), as amended, of 1907 Act). The supervising officer endeavours to challenge the attitudes and behaviour of the offender through counselling and support, with a view to developing his self-awareness and self-responsibility. Younger, more immature offenders may not respond readily to such an approach and for them the development of sustaining relationships through indirect means, such as the use of educational or recreational programmes, is encouraged (Whitaker, 1985, p. 335).

Second, offenders may be placed on 'adjourned supervision'. In such cases, the court chooses to defer sentence on condition that the offender complies with supervision from a probation officer. A date is fixed for a review and the penalty is then decided by the court in the light of the progress report from the officer concerned. This disposition is purely informal and has no statutory basis.

In 1988, young people under 16 accounted for 22.4% of all persons placed on probation or on supervision during deferment of penalty (adjourned supervision) (Department of Justice, 1990).

The third way in which offenders may come under the supervision of a probation and welfare officer is as a result of a 'community service order', a disposition that is available to the courts for offenders aged 16 and over. The offender's progress is managed by a probation officer and any breach of the sentence may be reported to the court, which can then impose a custodial sentence.

Probation hostels and workshops
For many of the clients of the probation and welfare service, material problems to do with work and accommodation can bear heavily on whether the person stays out of trouble. Practical services can be an essential adjunct to the personal attention of a probation officer. For this reason, the Probation and Welfare Service has been steadily increasing its support of a still relatively modest range of residential and day centres which cater for young offenders (Department of Justice, 1990). In 1988 a total of 7 hostels offer approximately 60 places to youngsters under 17 years who are under the care of the Probation and Welfare Service; five cater for boys and two for girls. The only hostels outside of Dublin are in Cork and Waterford; both cater for boys.

The Probation and Welfare Service uses places in other hostels from time to time for which it pays a capitation fee. It also promotes or supports a number of ventures geared to providing training, education and personal development activities through day programmes to young people at serious risk.

Special Schools
Only five centres now perform the functions of what were formerly known as reformatories and industrial schools for young offenders. Two of these provide remand and assessment facilities — St Michael's Assessment Unit, Children's Centre, in Finglas (for boys) and Oberstown Assessment Unit in Lusk (for girls). Two provide longer term care for boys — St Laurence's Children's Centre in Finglas (for a maximum period of two years) and St Joseph's in Clonmel (for periods up to a youngster's sixteenth birthday). Trinity House in Lusk, opened in 1983, is a secure unit offering 30 places for 12 to 16 year olds.

Prisons and Places of Detention
Generally, prisoners must be 17 years old before being sentenced to prison or a place of detention. A young offender aged 15 and under 17, however, may be sent to adult prison where he or she is certified under the Children Act 1908 as 'of so unruly a character that he cannot be detained in a place of detention provided under this Act, and that he is of so depraved a character that he is not a fit person to be so detained.'

In 1987, 103 boys and 16 girls were committed to prison on this basis. Twenty-nine of these were sentenced to a period between one and under two years, and eleven for a period of two years and over (Department of Justice, 1988, p. 123). In 1988, 10 boys and 22 girls were committed, 17 of the 32 for periods of more than one year (Department of Justice 1990).

St Patrick's Institution in Dublin is a 'place of detention' or young adult prison, which serves 17-21 year olds. However, 16-year olds may be sent there in the absence of a suitable legal alternative. In 1988, 166 males in this age group were committed to St Patrick's, representing one in five (18.9%) of all committals (ibid. p. 137).

Chapter 6

YOUTH SERVICES

Youth in Society
Ireland's population is a youthful one: young people between the ages of 10 and 18 make up 17.5% of the population, while close to half (46.4%) of the total population is under 25 years of age (CSO, 1987).

Adolescence is a challenging period for many young people, as they gradually assume the roles of adulthood. Young people must learn to play many parts — student, employee/trainee, sexual being, consumer, perhaps parent, and possibly victim of long-term unemployment, emigration or alienation.

Unemployment
Young people face an increased risk of unemployment. One in four young people under 25 (25.5%) in the labour force are unemployed, compared with just over one in six (17.4%) of the whole labour force (Sexton, Whelan and Williams, 1988). This risk of unemployment is not evenly spread among young people; the highest risk is borne by those who leave school without qualifications: 28.4% compared to 9.7% in those with a Leaving Certificate according to 1982 figures (ibid. p. 26).

Research in Ireland confirms international evidence about the adverse effects of unemployment on young people. One study included comparisons between a sample (N = 135) of employed and unemployed young people, aged 16-23 (Cullen *et al*, 1987b). The unemployed smoked more than their employed peers; they were also more likely to worry about the future and to feel more resentful, burdened and unsupported than those in employment. One in four of the unemployed males exhibited symptoms of minor psychological disorder, compared with none of their counterparts with jobs. Unemployed females were less physically fit than females at work.

Another study of unemployed young people found that two in every three (67%) were experiencing acute psychological distress, compared with one in three of a sample of young people in blue-collar jobs or one in five of a sample in white-collar employment (McCarthy and Ronayne, 1984). Financial hardship and dissatisfaction with the use of time seemed to be the two factors which rendered young people most vulnerable to the adverse effects of unemployment. Unemployed females seemed to be more vulnerable than males to the psychological ill-effects of unemployment (ibid. p. 30).

Emigration
The stemming of emigration and indeed the return of many emigrant families to an expanding economy in the 1970s gave way during the 1980s to a revival of the emigration pattern which has been a feature of Irish society for close on 200 years (Fitzpatrick, 1984). The latest wave is thought to have peaked in 1988-89: 46,000 people emigrated in the year ended mid-April 1989 (Central Statistics Office, 1990).

Follow-up studies of cohorts of school-leavers indicate that a certain proportion (about 4%) of these young people are emigrating, a figure which may be an under-estimate according to Jackson (1986). There is no precise information on the age or family status of those emigrating, although it seems possible to identify two distinct groups in the current wave of young emigrants. The first group is composed of young graduates, attracted abroad by favourable employment conditions and opportunities. In 1988, one in five of new graduates chose to emigrate (Higher Education Authority, 1989). The second group of emigrants is considerably less well equipped — it is composed of those with no marketable training or skills.

A study of 248 young Irish people in touch with welfare agencies in London revealed a variety of problems (Connor, 1985). One in four (28.2%) had had accommodation problems (17.5% had spent their first night sleeping rough, with 27% spending 'some time' sleeping rough since their arrival in London). Just under one in four (23.4%) had experienced unemployment in London and one in five (20.1%) had had problems with money or obtaining social benefit. Just under one in four in the sample had no educational qualification, although a third had their leaving certificate. Work was not always the reason cited for leaving Ireland. More than three in every ten gave psychological or social reasons — 'depressed with Ireland' (20.6%), 'family and personal problems' (10.5%) and 'trouble in the community' (4.4%).

Alienation
Many young people living in urban ghettos feel little allegiance to an adult society which seems indifferent to their lot. These youngsters leave school unqualified and join the long-term dole queues, with perhaps some brief diversions through short-term training courses. In their eyes, the institutions of society, ranging from school to the gardaí to the media, seem largely unable to comprehend their experience of the world. Indeed, the only time they seem to receive attention is when evening newspaper headline writers scream shock-horror at some crime attributed to young people. Delinquency, joy-riding, drug-taking and the like seem merely to be part of a search by these youngsters for excitement and meaning in lives otherwise devoid

of these experiences. They want to count for something and yet they know they do not really count in a society in which, as they see it, they are allowed to have no stake.

Daily living needs of young people making their own way
One in four young people (24.9%) are living away from the family home two years after leaving school. The likelihood of living independently varies between different categories of young people — 56% of students do so, compared with 20% of those with jobs and only 7% of those who are unemployed (Corcoran *et al*, 1986). Most of these young people must seek accommodation in what has been a steadily shrinking private rented sector, which now provides for only 6.3% of households (NESC, 1988). The Irish housing system has an extraordinarily high proportion of owner occupation — 82.3% in 1984, compared with 9.7% in the local authority rented sector (ibid).

These trends in the housing system militate against young people setting up their own household, since their traditional sector (private rented) is shrinking and owner occupation is beyond their reach. Only young people who themselves are parents are likely to be even considered for a local authority tenancy in their own right. The Housing Act 1988 is the first legislation to refer to the housing needs of young people, albeit in a very restricted way. In assessing housing need, Section 9 of the Act requires local authorities to have regard to the needs of, *inter alia*, 'young people leaving institutional care or without family accommodation'. The Act also gives wide powers (but not duties) to local authorities to provide housing for these young people and other groups.

Not only may young people encounter difficulty in securing housing in their own right, they are also likely to find problems in securing an income in their own right if they are not in a job. For all practical purposes, young people under 18 are not entitled to any social welfare payments. (The one rare exception would be where a young person has accumulated sufficient social welfare insurance credits, or 'stamps', to be entitled to unemployment benefit should they be out of a job.)

For most young people under 18, therefore, the only practical possibility of financial support from the State is under the Supplementary Welfare Allowance Scheme. Payments under this scheme, however, are entirely at the discretion of individual community welfare officers. If refused payment, the young person, as with any claimant aware of the right, may institute an appeal, but there is no guarantee that it will be successful.

Youth Work and Services
In most countries, there is a long tradition of youth work. This grew mainly from volunteer roots and in some countries has been transformed into a full-time professional service, working with young people outside the school system in various settings. A strong strand of provision in some cities around the world is 'street work' or 'unattached work', where the youth worker leaves behind the structure of a specific premises and seeks to contact alienated young people who would not otherwise be in touch with a friendly adult. The hope is that this 'outreach' contact may attract young people to avail themselves of other services and facilities offered by the youth service.

One British review of professional youth work envisages four functions for the youth worker (HM Inspectorate, 1987, pp 20-21):

- to identify and proffer to young people a range of appropriate experiences;
- to create the situations in which young people can learn from those experiences;
- to muster the resources for both the experience and the learning;
- to support young people while they undergo the experience and learn from it.

In Ireland, the strongest tradition of youth work lies in the voluntary sector and is built on the work of voluntary youth leaders, of whom there may be up to 17,000 according to the O'Sullivan Committee (1980). There is no definite figure for the number of full-time youth workers, but one informed source estimates a figure of 400 (National Youth Council, 1988a). Many of these would be employed in administrative and training positions at regional and national level in the major voluntary youth organisations, such as the National Youth Federation, Foróige and the Catholic Youth Council, Dublin. Unattached youth work has been relatively rare in Ireland.

While there has been a gradual improvement in the level of statutory funding for youth services in Ireland, practice has been dogged by the erratic and fitful evolution of policies. Many policy reports are produced, but the reality is that professional youth workers, working with the most disadvantaged youth, are still few and far between. Those there are must generally cope with insecure employment conditions, inadequate resources and a constant search for funding from a bewildering array of sources.

Existing Irish youth services may be classified in different ways. I propose here to arrange them in four main categories: activity centred services; information, advisory and counselling services; employment and training related services; and youth projects and programmes aimed at 'at-risk' youngsters.

Activity Centred Services

These services encompass the classical forms of youth provision — youth clubs and uniformed youth organisations (scouts, guides, etc). But they also include cultural and sporting groups geared to young people.

A 1984 MRBI survey of young people aged 15-24 indicated that one in three (32%) participated in some form of youth group, as defined above (National Youth Policy Committee, 1984). Overall, the local youth club, followed by a sports club, were the most likely groups to attract membership (see Table 7). Youth club members tend to be under 17, still at school and living with their parents. Sports club members tend to be male and over 18. Members of uniformed groups tend to be under 17 and living in urban areas.

Almost invariably, voluntary youth leaders run the programmes of youth clubs and the uniformed organisations. These groups are generally affiliated to a regional and/or national structure, which offers training and other support services provided by full-time staff. The following are brief profiles of two particularly active youth clubs run by volunteers.

Ghostbusters Youth Club, Portlaoise
Founded in 1986, this club operates in a district previously unserved by youth clubs. It caters for 12-18 year olds and, as in other clubs affiliated to Foróige, much

Table 7: 'Youth Group' participation; percentage distribution of youth participants in different youth organisations; percentage of age group active in each organisation

	All youth aged 15-24 % active in each organisation	All youth participants % active by organisation
Local youth club	13	41
Sports club	9	30
Uniformed groups		
(Scouts, Guides, etc.)	4	12
Cultural/Music/Drama	not given	8
Political	not given	2

Source: MRBI survey cited and summarised in National Youth Policy Committee, 1984, pp 61-63

emphasis is placed on members organising things for themselves with the help of voluntary youth leaders.

The Ghostbusters Club meets for two hours one night a week and among its activities to date have been a tree-planting week, a jumble sale, a sponsored walk to fund a visit to Lourdes by a disabled person, a darts competition and an inter-club soccer competition (National Youth Council, 1988b).

St Mark's Youth Club, Tallaght
This club is unusual in that its focal point is a farm which is run for its 1,000 members. Besides contact with farm animals, the members also have access to the more usual youth club facilities. In addition, photography, drama, hiking and canoeing are popular with older age groups. Occasional activities have included staging a play, excavating a well and researching the history of the farm. The club is run by ten volunteers and its premises are made available for other community purposes, which further strengthens its local identity (Bennett, 1987).

Information, Advice and Counselling Services
Youth Information Centres
Dublin Corporation opened the country's first Youth Information Centre, as part of its library service, in 1982. By 1989, approximately 25 youth information/advice projects were under way or being developed throughout the country. Of these, 9 are well established full-time centres. Sponsors are usually local voluntary youth services affiliated to a national or regional structure. Funding comes from a variety of sources including the National Lottery and employment training schemes (National Youth Council of Ireland, 1989).

Youth counselling and support services
Counselling and support services specifically for young people are only available on a geographically limited basis. Where there is no such service, young people must rely on the adult psychiatric service. In Dublin psychiatric services for adolescents are being developed (see below).

The Mater Dei Counselling Centre, sponsored by the Catholic Archdiocese of Dublin and partly funded by the Eastern Health Board, is the only centre in the country of its type. What is unique about the centre is that counselling services are offered outside the psychiatric services, thus reducing the risk that young people confuse what are normally temporary problems of adolescence with more serious disorders. The psychologists and social workers who staff the centre accept referrals from all over Dublin from parents, professionals and young people themselves. They hold a special brief to help young people who may be experiencing problems arising from drug use and in the prevention of substance abuse.

Young people are seen individually and there is also strong emphasis on involving parents and on family therapy techniques. The centre can also offer advice and support to professionals concerned with problems within the brief of the centre. The Mater Dei Centre has opened an additional part-time outreach service in the Clondalkin area on the west of Dublin city since early 1990.

Ballymun Youth Action Project was founded in 1981 in response to drug problems among young people in the Ballymun community. Through preventive education and through counselling and support to young people at risk and their families, the project aims to enable those affected to come to terms with, and ultimately resolve, problems stemming from drug use. The project has a constant struggle to raise its running costs (mainly spent on staff) from a variety of voluntary and statutory agencies.

Psychiatric services
Only in Dublin are there any services specifically dedicated to the needs of adolescents. On the south side of the city, the psychiatric services are under the auspices of the Cluain Mhuire Child and Family Service, and on the north side, under the aegis of St Vincent's Psychiatric Service in Fairview. Elsewhere, young people must seek assistance from child or adult psychiatric services.

During 1987, 803 young people aged 19 and under were admitted to psychiatric in-patient care, all but 99 to an adult psychiatric unit (O'Connor and Walsh, 1989). The rate of admission for young people aged 15-19 was less than one-third that of the rate of admission for all ages.

Employment and Training Services
Community Training Workshops
In 1986, there were 78 community training workshops, with 50 offering 1,638 places to early school-leavers and 28 offering 604 places to young travelling people. These workshops offer training in basic skills and aim to enhance the job prospects of youngsters. There is also strong emphasis on the personal development of the young person, with attention to life and social skills. Workshop instructors are expected to work closely with the young people and not just be concerned with the technical content of the training. Where necessary, the workshops also offer remedial, literacy and numeracy teaching. Workshops are generally sponsored by a voluntary body and have a local management committee.

Galway Community Training Workshop is an example of such community training schemes. It is sponsored by Galway Youth Council and funded by FÁS.

Its main activities include woodwork, car maintenance, home economics, horticulture, social skills and work experience. Six full-time staff, and a part-time literacy tutor, work with the 40 trainees (Youth Employment Agency, 1987).

An evaluation of the community training workshops concluded that they were being successful on two counts at least (McGennis, Drury and Murray, 1986). Firstly, youth participants in the 29 workshops surveyed seemed pleased with the workshops: 86% of girls and 73% of boys declared themselves 'happy' or 'very happy' with the workshops. Other opinions expressed included 'learning useful things' (98%), 'feel I matter as a person' (88%), 'treated as an adult' (83%) or 'just like school' (28%). Secondly, the workshop places seemed to be going to those for whom they were intended. Trainees were unemployed (75%) for a month prior to the programme, aged 18 or under (83%) and often from a home with an unemployed father (56%).

Youthreach
An estimated 10% of students leave school without any certification each year. Youthreach is a joint Department of Education/Department of Labour programme launched in 1989 to respond to the needs of these 6,000 early school-leavers each year. Initially, 1,000 places have been created in 11 Vocational Education Committee areas. Places are open to young people who have dropped out of school at least six months previously.

The curriculum of Youthreach includes general studies, vocational studies and work experience (Dáil Debates, 1989).

Youth Projects and Programmes for the Disadvantaged
Neighbourhood Youth Projects
These projects were recommended by the Task Force on Child Care Services (1981) as a means of reaching out to youngsters at risk in their own community. Three of the original five projects survive in 1990 — two in Dublin's inner city and one in Mayfield, a suburb of north Cork city. They are funded by the local health boards.

In order to pre-empt the need for admission to care or to reduce the risk of court appearances, three to four people work intensively with a group of roughly 24 youngsters aged 12-16. The work also incorporates a family dimension and attention to the needs of the peer groups of the core members of the project. A variety of activities (e.g. outings, holidays and adventure sports) are typically used as a basis for attracting and retaining the interest of the target youngsters. Also recommended by the Task Force on Child Care Services (1981) were Youth Encounter Projects (special schools for disadvantaged young people. There are currently four in operation (see pp 77-8, section on education system)).

Community Youth Projects
This title embraces a range of community-based projects with a baffling variety of funding arrangements. They are usually located in disadvantaged areas and were got underway due to some local initiative. Typically, they limp along financially, struggling from year to year to piece together a shoestring budget from a variety of

statutory and voluntary sources. This insecurity has serious implications for the morale of the staff and management. Fundamentally, it betrays a lack of a committed public policy to fund properly a professional youth service in disadvantaged areas. As things stand, the most significant proportion of these projects' budgets often derives from grants for the support of a community training workshop — see above. The following are profiles of three different community youth projects.

Togher Youth Development Centre, Cork
This centre caters for 60 regular users and has approximately 200 youngsters on its books in the age range of 15-25 (National Youth Council, 1988b). The local catchment area has high unemployment and previous attempts to engage the interests of local youngsters have not always been successful. The centre's programme includes a drop-in facility open six days a week, outdoor activities, advice and counselling, a part-time craft workshop, a coffee bar, a 'grinds' service, youth exchanges with youth groups in Northern Ireland and Wales, and an 'outreach' service aimed at improving communication between the centre and adult and youth members of the community.

The centre operates under the auspices of Ógra Chorcaí (Cork Youth Association) and has two full-time staff and a small number of part-time and voluntary workers.

Rivermount Youth Link Project, South Finglas, Dublin
This project is one of six community youth projects funded by Comhairle le Leas Óige — the Dublin Youth Service Board, a sub-committee of the City of Dublin Vocational Education Committee. It has three full-time workers who are involved in a range of activities. One example is the generation of local support and outside funding for a 'horse/city farm' project — in an area where there has been concern about young people's ability to care properly for horses, which have long been almost a cult interest for many local youngsters. Other activities have included a community newsletter, an adventure sports course for local young people and a drop-in centre, open two afternoons a week.

Candle Community Trust, Ballyfermot, Dublin
Founded in 1977, the Candle project has a particular concern with young men in trouble with the law and who, in addition, may have other social difficulties in their lives (Ronayne et al, 1986). In its purpose-built premises, the centre operates a drop-in day centre, open twelve hours a week, a part-time skills training workshop and a community training workshop. It also offers other services, including information, counselling and literacy/numeracy work. Approximately 50 young people participate at any one time; of these, 60% are between 16 and 20 years of age.

The primary source of funding for the Candle project is the Department of Justice's Probation and Welfare Services, with support for the community training workshop coming from FÁS. Various other statutory and voluntary agencies also lend their support.

Chapter 7

THE HEALTH AND PERSONAL SOCIAL SERVICES SYSTEM

The health services in Ireland were re-organised under the Health Act 1970 with the establishment of eight regional health boards. These operate under a variety of legislation and carry out a diverse set of functions, ranging from the provision of general practitioner services on a means-tested basis, to public health nursing, residential care for dependent groups, the prevention of infectious disease, child health services, health education, the implementation of food hygiene regulations, the support of voluntary organisations and the provision of various personal social services.

Each health board is run by a mixture of elected public representatives, nominated by local authorities within the board's region, elected representatives of approved professional groups and some ministerial appointees. The boards are responsible for policy decisions and for monitoring their implementation by the board's staff. The Chief Executive Officer is responsible to the board for the day-to-day running of services under its aegis. In some specific areas, such as personnel matters, he or she exercises sole or reserved powers. The administration of services is conducted through three programmes each with its own manager: community care, general (acute) hospitals and special (long stay) hospitals.

Community Care Programme
The community care programme is sub-divided into three sub-programmes (O'Connor, 1987, p. 28):

> (1) The Community Protection Sub-Programme covers prevention of infectious disease, child health examinations, immunisation, drug controls, health education and other preventive services.

(2)   The Community Health Services Sub-Programme covers general practitioner services, including drug supply and refund schemes, home nursing services, dental, ophthalmic and aural services.

(3)   The Community Welfare Sub-Programme covers cash payments, grants to voluntary welfare agencies and personal social services. Cash payments include those to disabled persons and to persons with certain infectious diseases. The term 'personal social services' refers to all those social services (other than health, education, income maintenance and housing) that are directed towards meeting people's social support needs, usually on a community basis. Included under this heading are services provided by social workers, home helps, meals on wheel organisers and the staff of day care services.

The country is divided into 32 community care areas, which represent the focal administrative units for the provision of community care services. These services are delivered by different categories of staff (with administrative support), viz. public health nurses, medical officers, social workers, community welfare officers, home helps, health inspectors, rehabilitation personnel and dentists. In some instances, staff also include community workers and/or homemakers and/or child care workers. In charge of each community care area is a Director, who under present policy must be medically qualified. The heads of most of the foregoing disciplines report to the Director of Community Care who, in turn, reports to the programme manager (see Figure 3). The directors are also charged with liaising with general practitioners and voluntary organisations in their area.

The term 'community care' in this context serves a catch-all administrative purpose. In many instances, community care services may be community-based only in the sense that they are non-institutional. The home help service is obviously delivered in people's own homes and some other health services are also substantially domiciliary in character (public health nursing, social work). Other services, however, are largely centre- or clinic-based, and this may require people to travel long distances, especially in rural areas, to avail themselves of needed services.

There are some institutional services that fall within the ambit of community care, viz. children's homes. There are also many community-based health services relevant to children which may, for bureaucratic reasons, come under the management of the hospital programmes, viz. child guidance clinics and community-based mental handicap services. It is also necessary to stress that not all care in the community is provided exclusively under the auspices of the health boards' community care services. While community care services sponsored by health boards are of special relevance to children and families in need, there are other possible sources of care and support that are of considerable importance.

Sources of Community-based Social Care
Statutory sources: In addition to community care services, children and families may be in receipt of other health services, such as hospital out-patient services or child guidance. They may also be in contact with welfare services provided by many local authority housing departments or the Department of Justice Probation and Welfare service. It is also possible that they are benefiting from activities such as adult education sponsored by vocational education committees.

Figure 3

HEALTH BOARD AREAS AND POPULATION DENSITIES

THE GENERAL STRUCTURE OF IRELAND'S HEALTH CARE SYSTEM

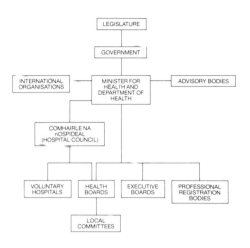

COMMUNITY CARE STRUCTURE

HEALTH BOARD PROGRAMME STRUCTURE

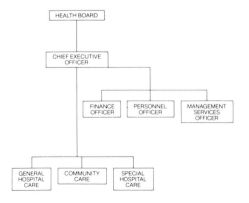

Source: Health, the Wider Dimensions, Dublin: Dept. of Health, 1987

Voluntary sources: These can take three forms:

- *Non-statutory organisations* offer the services of full-time professional staff whose salaries are funded usually by some combination of grant-aid from health boards under Section 65 of the Health Act 1953 and/or from other statutory bodies and/or direct fund-raising from the public.
- *Voluntary groups* provide services largely or exclusively through volunteers. Again, they depend for income on a combination of fund raising and support from health boards.
- *Foster parents* are an important group in personal social services for children. They are essentially volunteers although they receive modest payments from the health boards. But increasingly they and the boards recognise that the payment in no way reflects the market value of the service provided. In effect, the payment is a form of refund of expenses, and the motivation of foster parents in most cases resembles that of specialist volunteers.

Commercial sources: Since many of the families most dependent on personal social services are poor, there is little incentive for intervention by the private or commercial sector to meet their needs (unless, as in the case of general practitioners, someone else, in this instance the State, undertakes to pay for the services provided). It is difficult to calculate the importance of the commercial sector in this area, although it is in day care that its presence is likely to be strongest. However, child-minding by a local woman in her home as an attempt to supplement her own household's slender income is a far cry from a private sector hospital which, in social policy analysts' terms at least, may be more representative of profit-motivated health and social services. The extent of more fully commercial provision of day care is impossible to gauge at the moment because of the absence of any system of public regulation or inspection although this should change with the implementation of the Child Care Act 1991.

Informal Sources: Families, friends or neighbours may be the most significant source of support and assistance for children and families in need. A child who runs away from conflict in his or her own family may find the appropriate degree of shelter and sympathy from an aunt or granny. A depressed mother may find encouragement and support in the cups of tea and chats she has in her neighbour's kitchen. Some very isolated and troubled families, however, may lack such supports. They may have a threadbare social network or may have alienated potential sources of help because of the apparently intractable nature of their difficulties.

Health Boards' Community Care Services

If 'care' can take different forms, so also can the concept of 'community'. In this context, it can refer to a neighbourhood or parish, or to the population living in an administrative district. It can often, in practice, refer to unpaid care by women of their relatives or neighbours — on an informal or formal voluntary basis. O'Connor (1987, p. 31) suggests that community care policies are often predicated on two assumptions: firstly, that 'the family has primary responsibility for the care of its dependants' and, secondly, that 'the community is actually caring through informal networks and that these are spontaneous'. The first assumption ignores the effects on women's lives of this expectation. It also ignores demographic trends towards smaller families and expanding participation of women in the labour force over their lifetime, both of which carry clear implications for their availability. The second assumption may not be grounded in fact. In so far as it is true, it may only apply to those people (often elderly) whose problems and personality attract and retain the interest and sympathy of informal helpers. Such support may not be so forthcoming or sustained for a family with serious problems, whose reputation or behaviour may attract rejection rather than sympathy.

In many senses, it is true to say that the hopes invested in the original concept of community care services have not been fully realised. Some of these difficulties stem from inadequacies in levels of funding; in particular, they stem from the failure to secure any meaningful shift of spending within the health services from institutions to the community. There have also been obstacles stemming from the organisational structures and system adopted.

Despite these considerable impediments, community care services have greatly extended the range of professional services and support available to families in need. Most parts of the country now have access, in principle at least, to professional services, which were unknown prior to the inception of community care teams. This is a very considerable achievement, notwithstanding the frequent and usually inexplicable variations in the depth of coverage by various services between, and even within, different community care areas. Though patchy in some parts, a foundation has, nevertheless, been laid for the comprehensive provision of a variety of personal health and social services by a range of professionals.

Criticisms of Community Care Services
The community care services may have managed to assemble an array of professional services, but many commentators have been sceptical of whether these resources have been organised or mobilised to best effect. Criticisms have been levelled at the community care services as they currently operate. They have been faulted for:

• The unevenness of service provision and availability (NESC, 1987, p. 7). This may lead to a mismatch between needs and resources: the areas with highest social disadvantage may be receiving a lower level of service, a problem which may be most acute in remote rural areas (O'Mahony, 1985). Cuts in public spending may further aggravate any tendencies to inequity in the distribution of services. Consumers of personal social services may lack the political or legal clout to prevent cuts in what are discretionary (rather than statutorily required) services to them (O'Connor, 1987, p. 123).
• The residual status of personal social services. This is attributed to the persisting medical bias in the orientation of services, despite the overwhelmingly social character of the problems (e.g. child sexual abuse, family violence, addiction) which increasingly present to community care services and which demand a social rather than a traditional clinical medical intervention (Garland, 1983, p. 15).
• The inadequacy of planning for policy and service development (ibid. p. 35).

Related to this has been a failure to tailor specific packages of services for groups in need which have already been targeted (NESC, 1987, pp 10-12).

- The pre-occupation with crisis management and the consequent priority for services which substitute rather than support the efforts of families under pressure (ibid. p. 6). Whatever service development there is tends to be on an *ad hoc* and piecemeal basis, with little attention to prevention or overall community needs (O'Connor, 1987, p. 80).

- The ineffectiveness of organisational structures and management systems (McInerney, 1982). The inadequacy of information systems, which has been noted, is both a cause and an effect of management deficiencies (O'Connor, 1987, pp 121-2).

- The failure to forge a strong and cohesive team identity among the disparate disciplines that operate community care services (O'Connor, ibid, p. 123, Commission on Health Funding 1989, p. 40). At an informal level, working relations may, in some instances, be reasonably good among various personnel, but not necessarily any better than those with workers in other agencies with whom regular collaboration or liaison is required. (In other words, shared team membership is not a necessary pre-requisite of effective working relations among front-line workers.) It is clear that these teams have not become an effective mechanism for the management of local services (McInerney, 1982). Predictable strains in working relations between staff of different status and orientation have been exacerbated by practical problems, such as separate accommodation. It has been observed that shared accommodation, not surprisingly, improves working relations (ibid, pp 10).

- The failure to conduct relations with voluntary organisations, which play an often crucial part in service provision, in a uniform and agreed manner (National Social Service Board, 1982, pp 16-23; O'Connor, 1987, p. 124).

- The inadequacy or absence of criteria to determine eligibility for community care services, other than general practitioner services (NESC, 1987, p. 7).

- The non-integration of general practitioners into the work of community care services, despite their pivotal role in the delivery of primary care (Department of Health, 1984, pp 70-6; McInerney, 1982, p. 12).

- The arbitrary separation from community care administration of important health board community-based services. Many non-institutional services do not actually come under the umbrella of community care, despite being based in the community and/or having a major domiciliary dimension to their work. Mental handicap and child guidance are examples of relevance to children's services (Gilligan 1984, p. 70).

There is evidence that change is afoot in the organisation and planning of community care services as part of a general re-vamping of the health services (Department of Health, 1987, Commission on Health Funding, 1989). This is likely to lead to an upgrading of personal social services, a streamlining of relations between the health services and voluntary agencies, and greater attempts to integrate general practitioners into the community care system. There has also been agreement to remove the embargo on non-medically qualified personnel holding the post of director of community care.

PROFESSIONAL DISCIPLINES IN THE COMMUNITY CARE SERVICES

Public Health Nurses

Public health nurses are important figures in the practice of child welfare. Their role brings them into routine contact with all young children and their mothers. They are also available to families to offer support and advice as required. In addition, they may be involved in the operation of child welfare clinics and school health examinations, both of which perform valuable screening functions in the prevention of illness and disability in childhood.

The Public Health Nursing service has a brief that extends beyond children. Public Health Nurses also serve the sick and disabled and the elderly. These nurses function as the primary contact point between the public and health board services in the community. Entrants to the one-year diploma course in public health nursing are required to have general nursing and midwifery training.

The origins of the current service are to be found in a variety of provisions for maternity care and the care of young children which were enacted gradually since the middle of the last century. A number of religious and philanthropic organisations played an important part in the development of district nursing services, which were eventually subsumed into the State services. Figure 4 outlines the stages in the development towards a comprehensive service which began to take shape in 1956 and was finally consolidated by the Ministerial Circular of 1966. This sought to ensure that a public health nursing service was available to every family in the country.

The number of nurses engaged in the public health nursing service has grown steadily over the years, from 509 in 1964 (Department of Health, 1975, p. 3) to 755 in 1972 (ibid. p. 67), and to 1,379 in 1985 (Department of Health, 1986, p. 80). This represented an increase of 171 per cent over the 21-year period covered and had permitted the creation of a career structure within the service and the deployment of certain nurses to specialist posts, such as health education, drugs counselling and mental handicap counselling. The cutbacks announced for the health services in the spring and summer of 1987 have meant that the number of posts has been reduced and that nurses have been withdrawn from some of these specialist posts to resume mainstream duties. By mid 1988, there were 1,282 Public Health Nurses nationally, a cut of almost 100 on the 1985 figure. The availability of these nurses varies between the different health board regions. The North Western and Western health boards have the highest availability and the Eastern and Southern the lowest (see Table 8).

Important information about the work of public health nurses generally was provided by the results of a national survey published in 1975 (Department of Health, 1975). Work in relation to children consumed 34.5% of their time (excluding travel time), with home-visiting occupying 10.6%, maternity care, 1.0% and work at clinics, dispensaries and schools, 22.9% (ibid. p. 95).

O'Mahony's local study (1985) examined the operation of the community care services in the Mayo area. In an analysis of referrals to three disciplines of the Health Board's field staff, she found that referrals for 'neo-natal' services

Figure 4: **Landmarks in the evolution of the modern public health nursing service**

1851	Poor Relief (Ireland) Act enables local authorities to appoint midwives to act as auxiliaries to district medical officers.
1907	Notification of Births Act heralds beginnings of child welfare service.
1915	Notification of Births (Extension) Act 1915 gives national effect to 1907 Act and makes grants available for the employment of nurses to visit mother and children (under five years of age).
1919	Public Health Medical Treatment of Children (Ireland) Act lays the basis for school health service.
1924	School health examinations, as provided for under the 1919 Act, are instituted.
1947	Section 102 of the Health Act provides that a health authority may, with the consent of the Minister, make arrangements for the provision of a nurse or nurses to give to any person requiring the same, advice and assistance on matters relating to health and to assist sick persons.
1956	Minister of Health urges health authorities to make nursing services (including home nursing and midwifery) available in each area.
1966	Ministerial circular (27/66) sets down policy for the development of the service. It envisages, among other things, a service available to families in each area of the country and a ratio of one nurse to 4,000 population. Among the services to be provided are the public health care of children from infancy to the end of the school-going period.
1966	Six-month training courses under the auspices of An Bord Altranais is instituted. Later extended to twelve months.
1970	Section 60 of the Health Act imposes a duty on health boards to provide without charge a nursing service to give to those persons (with full eligibility, or in other categories as specified by the Minister) advice and assistance on matters relating to their health and to assist them if they are sick.
1975	A major report on the workload of public health nurses is published (Department of Health, 1975). This remains one of the most important source documents on the operation of the service.
1980	Institute of Community Health Nursing is founded.
1986	'Public Health Nursing Services in Ireland: Discussion Document' is issued by the General Medical Service Division of the Department of Health.
1987	National University of Ireland Diploma in Public Health Nursing commences at University College Dublin (replacing Bord Altranais course).

accounted for 20.1% of all referrals to the nurses. The neo-natal category was the only one of those used by O'Mahony directly attributable to children, although undoubtedly they also accounted for a certain proportion of referrals assigned to other categories.

The major policy document in relation to the public health nursing service dates back to the Ministerial circular 27/66. This set down various functions for public health nurses. In the case of children, these included

> follow up of 'at risk children' in association with the general practitioner; . . . 'duties relating to the care of mentally handicapped children at home'; . . . 'health education and propaganda among families in her district with a view to encouraging them to avail of immunisation, maternity and child welfare services, school health

Table 8: **Public health nurse posts in regional health boards, and population nurse ratios, various years, superintendent and senior public health nurses excluded**

	1978		1983		1985		
Health Board	Posts approved	Posts approved nurse/ population ratio	Posts approved	Population/ posts approved ratio	Posts approved	Population/ nurses ratio	Range of population ratios recommended in 1975
Eastern	294	3,957	354	3,375	356	3,459	3,014 - 2,458
Midland	74	2,673	77(1)	2,625	79	2,631	2,509 - 2,419
Mid-Western	101	2,977	107(2)	2,880	103	3,058	2,823 - 2,453
North Eastern	101	2,700	108(3)	2,676	107	2,819	2,743 - 2,412
North Western	96	2,125	96	2,169	99	2,146	2,402 - 2,315
South Eastern	136	2,695	133	2,816	133	2,577	2,619 - 2,479
Southern	142	3,364	136	3,862	128	4,191	2,922 - 2,460
Western	144	2,331	143	2,387	148	2,349	2,456 - 2,335
Total	1,091	3,084	1,154	2,933	1,153	3,067	2,616

(1) Includes 2 public health nurses who work as counselling nurses with the families of handicapped people.
(2) Includes 5 members of a religious order who provide a nursing service.
(3) Includes 3 public health nurses who work as counsellors for the handicapped.

Notes: The *higher* the ratio the lower is the provision of public health nurses relative to population. The 1985 population/nurses ratio is based on the 1986 census results.

Source: O'Connor, S., *Community Care Services. An Overview* (Part 2), Dublin: NESC, 1987

> examination services etc; ... duties in connection with Child Welfare Clinic and School Health Examination Services, including where possible, attendance at clinics and examinations in respect of children resident in their district.

Nurses endeavour to make domiciliary visits to children born in their district as soon as possible after return from maternity hospital and then at three, seven, nine, twelve and eighteen months of age and later at two and three years of age. Priority is given to children who may be considered at risk in some way and where necessary close liaison is maintained with social workers and general practitioners.

An important asset for the public health nurse in the different facets of her work is the acceptability of her role in the community. As part of a study of social need in the burgeoning Dublin suburb of Tallaght, Lavan (1981) sought the views of mothers on aspects of service provision. In a sample of 251 mothers, 210 could recall contact with a public health nurse. Of these, two-thirds rated visits from the nurse as 'very helpful' (51.9%) or 'helpful' (15.2%).

Two recent initiatives by the Eastern Health Board point to interesting possibilities for the future role of public health nursing in the delivery of services, information and support to groups who traditionally may have proved 'hard to reach' in terms of the conventional model of public health nursing care. One of these is the assignment of some public health nurses to a mobile health care team to serve the travellers' community exclusively. The second is a scheme headed by a Family Development Nurse (specially assigned public health nurse) to train mothers in selected working-class districts as local health educators, to impart and reinforce health education promotion messages to young and new parents about the problems of coping with the care and management of infants (Eastern Health Board Community Mothers Programme, 1989). The assumption is that the messages will have greater impact because of the local accessibility and credibility of the women relaying them.

Social Workers

Professional social work is a product of Western society in the twentieth century, although it has its roots firmly in the Christian tradition of service to others. It grew out of the efforts of philanthropists, active in various charitable bodies, concerned with poverty and poor housing.

In Ireland, the first social workers were appointed to posts in the Welfare Department of Jacob's Biscuit Factory in Dublin in 1917 and to the Adelaide Hospital, also in Dublin, in 1921. Until the 1960s, the employment of social workers tended to be confined to hospital settings (Darling, 1972). As late as 1972, the then Minister for Health was lamenting the fact that only 43 social workers were in the employment of health boards in community services (*Irish Times* 11 June 1973).

Since the early 1970s, there has been a remarkable growth in the numbers of social workers employed, although the rate of increase has been halted by the impacts of recent cuts in public spending. The greatest increase has been in posts within the health boards and within the probation service. There has also been growth within services contracted out to voluntary agencies, such as mental handicap. Only in the area of social service councils has the early growth been reversed, with most health boards choosing to employ generic social workers directly rather than grant-aid their employment by these agencies. It is important to note that there is wide regional variation in the availability of health board community care social workers (See Table 9).

The social work task

In its development, social work has been influenced by ideas from a diverse range of sources, including psychoanalysis, psychology and, more recently, sociology, community development and adult education. A complete and precise definition of social work is elusive. This may in some way reflect its relative youth as a discipline. It also reflects the fact that the practice and philosophy of social work cannot be divorced from values and ideas about individual people and their relationship with wider society, and about the sources of the problems which social work is asked to address.

If one believes that people's potential is thwarted and that their problems are created or aggravated by social inequality and social structures, then one's definition of social work is likely to emphasise the importance of social change. Thus, such change will be seen as an intrinsic element and aspiration of the

Table 9: **Number of social workers employed in community services by regional health board, in 1981 and 1987**

Health Board	Number of social workers 1981	Number of social workers 1987	Population/ social workers ratio 1981	Population/ social workers ratio 1987
Eastern	114	128	10,480	9,619
Midland	21	23	9,402	9,037
Mid Western	29	15	10,628	21,000
North Eastern	14	14	20,641	21,541
North Western	28	30	7,436	7,080
South Eastern	26	31	14,135	11,058
Southern	30	31	17,508	17,307
Western	35	37	9,752	9,398
Total	298	309	11,555	11,447

Notes: The higher the ratio, the lower is the provision of social workers relative to population. The figures include a very small number of community workers and senior social workers; the censuses of 1981 and 1986 were used for the 1981 and 1987 ratios respectively.

Source: O'Connor, S., *Community Care Services: An Overview* (Part 2). Dublin: NESC, 1987

enterprise of social work, with emphasis on helping people to influence the 'system' for themselves rather than having them depend on the brokerage of the social worker.

Others may have a more muted vision of the project of social work. They may believe that social work's task is to help people adapt to the *status quo* since that is in their own best interests and in the interest of the wider society which, while needing occasional adjustments and reform, is seen as fundamentally sound.

There is, of course, a core of practice and principles that hold true irrespective of the philosophical orientation of the social work practitioner. Yet social work is not some set of value-free or neutral techniques, the practice of which can be easily divorced from the personality and philosophy of their exponent. One of the great resources of social work is the personal commitment and individual style of each practitioner. The consequent variety of approach may actually be social work's greatest strength rather than a fatal weakness. It may be that only a discipline with the broad sweep, flexibility and diversity of social work can hope to respond in any satisfactory way to the bewildering range of tasks and social problems which it is called upon to address. These assets may also mean that social work is better placed to adapt to the impact of social change in our society.

Despite the difficulties of achieving a comprehensive and widely endorsed definition of social work, Pincus and Minahan (1973) offer the following view, which is likely to be broadly acceptable to different shades of opinion.

> Social work is concerned with the interactions between people and their social environment which affect the ability of people to accomplish their life tasks, alleviate distress and realise their aspirations and values. The purpose of social work therefore

is to (1) enhance the problem-solving and coping capacities of people, (2) link people with systems that provide them with resources, services and opportunities, (3) promote the effective and humane operation of these systems, and (4) contribute to the improvement and development of social policy.

Heus and Pincus (1986) suggest that the essence of social work is:

- connecting people and resources;
- creating new resources;
- making resource systems responsive to people;
- teaching problem-solving skills to people;

A number of examples of social work with children and families can be cited in these four areas.

Connecting people and resources

- helping a harassed mother of a handicapped child unravel the application process for a Domiciliary Care Allowance;
- helping a teenager with a drug problem to make contact with the appropriate drug services;
- helping local women gain access to a premises in which to hold support group meetings;
- helping a local playgroup gain the necessary grants from statutory bodies;
- helping an employed father whose wife is in hospital and who lacks family support to make child minding arrangements which avoid the need for the children to be received into care;
- referring a battered wife to the local refuge.

Creating new resources

- establishing a weekly support group for parents with handicapped children;
- setting in train the establishment of a day care service for pre-schoolers in a new community;
- setting up respite care schemes for mentally handicapped children in order to give their hard-pressed parents a break and the child a holiday with another, selected, family;
- establishing a toy library for handicapped and deprived children;
- lobbying successfully for the establishment of a local project to address, for example, unemployment, community development or juvenile delinquency issues;
- setting up a support-group for clients of social services (e.g. natural parents and relatives of children in care);
- establishing information sessions on health education issues;
- setting up a scheme to enable trained volunteers to reach out to families and parents in difficulty.

Making resource systems responsive to people

- influencing an agency to improve its techniques of reception and information-giving for its clients (e.g. what parents are told about the legal and practical implications of their children being received into care);

- prompting an agency to articulate a policy (e.g. on preparing children in its care for adult life) and to provide the resources necessary to implement it;
- convening meetings of all professional workers in a locality in order to discuss matters of common concern and to explore how all their services could be made more sensitive to local needs and conditions;
- arranging local sittings of clinics and other professional services (e.g. legal aid, ante- and post-natal care, social welfare information);
- setting up meetings in which representatives of local families can brief managers of various community services on current needs and difficulties;
- alerting agencies to the deterioration or emergence of social problems (e.g. drug problems, joy-riding, AIDS) at community level;
- enabling people to appeal administrative decisions that adversely affect their entitlement to services;
- drawing attention to bureaucratic procedures that hamper families in their attempt to secure welfare or other entitlements.

Teaching problem-solving skills

- coaching clients in the skills of negotiating on their own behalf with various bureaucracies about such problems as fuel or housing debts;
- teaching behavioural skills to parents to enable them to reduce and manage extreme tantrums and other difficult behaviour in their tearaway toddler;
- helping parents to find a way of resolving conflicts with adolescents, so that disagreements do not degenerate into explosive confrontations, with threats of ejection or walk-outs;
- setting up a personal development course for isolated and depressed young mothers with a view to enhancing their social skills and confidence;
- helping troubled adolescents find alternatives to physical means of resolving differences or disguising anxiety in situations of conflict in public;
- helping parents who fear that they will abuse their child to begin to identify stress triggers and to assist them in planning and rehearsing ways of defusing potential flash-points;
- participating in programmes to prepare youngsters in care for independent living on discharge;
- helping a child in care to devise a 'cover story' that allows the child introduce his or herself and past in a plausible, yet discreet way in new social encounters and without revealing all the details about the circumstances of their being in care.

If social work practice is successful, then ideally it results in some real transfer of knowledge, skills and resources which goes beyond the resolution of an immediate difficulty. The client (in this case, child or family) is also endowed with additional and enduring assets for dealing with life by virtue of their contact with the social worker. This represents an ideal, an aspiration; in the real world, however, it must be recognised that such growth and development in the capacities of people in need do not necessarily ensue, and where they do, it rarely happens in an instant or magical way. Indeed, even if such change does occur it may be so slow and imperceptible as to be difficult to claim with any degree of confidence that the credit is due to social work intervention.

Social Work and Social Control
The above sample listing of social work activities is lacking in one important respect: it emphasises the more well-known, 'caring' functions of the work. But most caring contains substantial elements of control. Social workers may find themselves acting as 'soft cops', exercising social control over social minorities that society dubs 'troublesome'. In many instances, society requires social workers to intervene in the lives of children and families where either the fact, or the ultimate purpose, of the intervention is against the express wishes of some, or all, of the clients concerned. Arranging the compulsory removal of a child from parental care by court order can be a traumatic and stressful experience. So also can involvement with a youngster whose anti-social behaviour necessitates the social worker's co-operation in the child's compulsory detention in care. The exercise of social control may be less familiar and certainly less comfortable, but it is nonetheless an intrinsic part of the function of social workers.

The exercise of control that curbs civil liberties is at least transparent. But, because of the authority vested in their role by society, their employer, or even their clients, social workers can exercise control in a much more subtle and sometimes far-reaching way. The use of authoritative influence and persuasion, or the implicit — or explicit — threat of recourse to compulsion may induce compliance with the social workers' wishes in the difficult adolescent or the recalcitrant parent. But such control, especially when used in this covert way, can pose a professional challenge to social workers who are required by their professional code to emphasise the client's right to self-determination. The consequent dilemma is a compelling reminder of the point that social work is not some narrow technical set of activities, but rather a professional activity, conducted frequently in a welter of the deepest human emotions. Social work, therefore, requires of its practitioners great self-awareness, a firm grasp of professional values and ethics, and a skill and knowledge base which allows the worker to assess and intervene in relation to each situation in a manner tailored to that exact set of circumstances. The discipline of social work does not offer its practitioners 'off-the-shelf' solutions to difficulties. It is through the permanent struggle to reconcile the practical, emotional and ethical implications of each case that social workers preserve the professional vitality necessary to any therapeutic or constructive impact on the lives of their clients.

Community Care Social Work
Community care social work can pose great morale problems for social workers. The reasons for this include the unlimited potential demand for social work services in this field, especially in most working-class communities, the infinite scope of that demand, the inadequate numbers of social workers relative to the level of critically urgent need, the increasing alienation of the poor and powerless in society (which may manifest itself increasingly in open hostility to any exercise

of control over their lives) and the inevitably uneven success of social workers in tackling problems. Such problems are likely to be experienced most acutely in larger urban areas where there is increased social stress due to the impact of the national or local economic recession and the public fiscal crisis on pre-existing social deprivation.

As they advise clients who are searching for a solution to a greater difficulty, social workers must also partialise the problems they face. They may be forced to concentrate their service in certain specialist areas, despite being employed in the generic community care programmes. By dint of pressure of workload, especially in high-stress urban areas, they may have to confine their attentions to children and families. Often, they may only be able to deal with certain cases such as those of younger children who are judged to be at serious risk of physical or sexual abuse; to children who are in care; to the recruitment and support of foster parents; or to the provision of an adoption service to both natural mothers contemplating placing their child for adoption and prospective adoptive applicants.

This enforced narrowing of their role may not find great favour among social workers (especially among those outside community care). But a priority for children in need is at least in line with the first in a series of priorities set down for the emerging health board social work services in the early 1970s. At that time, it was seen as desirable that social workers should take over duties relating to health board commitments to deprived children. In addition, it was proposed that social workers should promote liaison and co-ordination between voluntary and statutory bodies in the welfare field. They might also attend to the needs of problem families, especially in urban areas, although concern was expressed that such problems could absorb an infinite number of caseworkers and that employing agencies must deploy social workers in the manner which in the long term would be most beneficial to the community (Department of Health, 1973).

The only official review to date of health board social work provision acknowledged the pressures that curb the range of services offered, whatever about the original intentions on the part of policy-makers or practitioners. The Department of Health (1985, p. 59) stated:

> Ideally, a social work service with a community base should provide a broad range of service, encompassing the elderly, the disabled and the young. However, in most areas the service is confined to families and child care. Indeed, in some areas this focus has been further concentrated on families with children at risk. This focus is not one of professional preference but is dictated by the pressure of demand coupled with staff restrictions. This prioritising has meant that not alone does community care not offer a comprehensive social work service, but in some areas is unable to offer a comprehensive child care service.

These limitations are likely to have been further aggravated by recent trends of increasing referrals of child abuse cases (see p. 65), together with the impact of regular rounds of cuts in spending imposed on health boards by government policy.

Child Abuse and Social Work

Child abuse is playing an increasingly dominant part in the workloads of community care social workers. Such work is very stressful for a number of reasons:

- the traumatic effect of recurring exposure to psychological or physical damage to children;
- the at least implicit physical threat to social workers from clients whose violent propensities towards family members may easily be transferred towards social workers whose intervention is often decidedly unwanted;
- the relentless increase in the numbers and apparent gravity of cases being referred to the social work services;
- the standstill, or in some cases the reduction (due to public service cutbacks), in the numbers of personnel and back-up services available, despite the remorseless increase in referrals;
- the complexity of the work in determining what precisely has happened, the risk of its recurrence and the correct steps in terms of protecting the child, while at the same time preserving where possible the integrity of the family in the longer run;
- the virtual absence of back-up services (commonplace in other countries), which can provide intensive treatment and support to families where abuse has occurred or is strongly suspected;
- the lack of adequate supervision and administrative supports in the management of child abuse work due to depleted resources despite ample evidence (from the British experience especially) of the importance of such support;
- the plight of social workers in the UK who have been subjected to criticism in the media and by statutory enquiries established to examine the circumstances surrounding the violent deaths of children on their caseload at the hands of parents or relatives;
- the widespread perception among social workers (and among fellow professionals) that they carry lead responsibility in the management of child abuse cases.

While it may be true that social workers are the community care field workers most likely to carry day-to-day responsibility for the management, monitoring and investigation of child abuse cases, the national guidelines on procedures in relation to child abuse make clear that it is the local Director of Community Care (who currently must be a doctor) who carries final responsibility for the conduct of such work. These guidelines, issued by the Department of Health (1987), also emphasise that 'inter-disciplinary and inter-agency work is an essential and integral element of the professional task of attempting to protect children from abuse' (ibid. p. 9).

The document (ibid.) emphasises the importance of the role of the public health nurse and the senior area medical officer in addition to that of the social worker and other disciplines. The position, therefore, is that social workers are not named as a group in any legislation relating to the protection of children from abuse, nor have they been assigned exclusive responsibility in relation to it. The multifaceted nature of child abuse means that anything other than an inter-disciplinary approach to the crisis and long-term management of child abuse cases is unthinkable.

The job description of social workers in community care embraces statutory functions which health boards have inherited or assumed in relation to child care

Figure 5: **Job description, Eastern Health Board social worker, community care**

1　To carry out the Board's statutory obligations in relation to children.

2　To engage in preventive work to avoid admission of children or others to institutional care unnecessarily.

3　To provide information and guidance for persons requiring services from the Health Board or other agencies.

4　To make available advice and guidance to voluntary agencies providing services for the handicapped and deprived and for those at health and social risk and to maintain liaison with those bodies.

1　Statutory obligations

  A　Adoption　　　　　(i)　Enquiries
  　　　　　　　　　(ii)　Assessment of applications
  　　　　　　　　　(iii)　Placement and supervision

  　　Adoption Acts 1952-88
  　　Health Boards are approved bodies for the making of arrangements for
  　　adoption in addition to the registered adoption societies.

  B　Fostering　　　　　(i)　Enquiries
  　　(long & short term)　(ii)　Assessment of applications
  　　　　　　　　　(iii)　Placement and supervision

  　　Health Act 1953. Boarding Out of Children Regulations. 1983

  C　Nursed-out children　(i)　Supervision of children placed by their parents
  　　　　　　　　　　　away from home
  　　　　　　　　　(ii)　Supervision of foster placements of other societies

  　　Children Acts 1908-89

  D　Admission to care　(i)　Admission to residential or foster care of children
  　　　　　　　　　　　whose parents are not in a position to care for them
  　　　　　　　　　　　either temporarily or permanently
  　　　　　　　　　(ii)　Follow-up work with each child
  　　　　　　　　　(iii)　Follow-up work with each child's family

  　　Health Act 1953 (secs. 55 & 56). Boarding Out of Children Regulations 1983

  E　Fit Persons Orders　(i)　Supervision of child's placement
  　　　　　　　　　(ii)　Follow-up work with child's parents

  　　Children Acts 1908-89 – voluntary commitment made to court

Source: Adapted from O. Garland *et al* (1981), *Social Work in the Eastern Health Board – Proposals for Change and Future Direction of Service.* Dublin: Authors, to reflect legal changes since publication in 1981

(see Figure 5). The implementation of measures in the Child Care Act 1991 will transform some of these functions into duties. However neither in the present nor proposed law are social workers assigned specific duties in the area of child care. It is important to stress also, of course, that social workers have a major role in relation to children outside of community care. This may include working with or for them in hospitals, in probation or in the mental handicap services, as well as in child guidance.

Community Workers

Community work can address an almost unlimited variety of issues. The brief of community workers may range from tackling illiteracy to rural underdevelopment, to social and economic regeneration in inner city areas, to the problems of single parent families in outer suburban estates, to alienation among young people or to health needs not met in specific populations.

Given this broad potential canvas, the precise role of individual community workers will be heavily influenced by his or her employer and the nature of the target group or community. The worker's own personal and professional assumptions and preferences will, of course, also heavily colour her practice.

Community work, as understood by most practitioners, involves attempts to enable people to improve some aspect of their living conditions. The community worker acts as a resource and catalyst in bringing people together. She helps them to identify common interests and concerns, and the means by which certain of their needs can be met; she also helps to mobilise resources from within the group/ community and from outside, which can move the group nearer to the attainment of its goals.

Many statutory bodies are attracted to employing community workers because their role is seen as lubricating relations between a bureaucracy and a local community. This tendency is heightened by the recent pattern of prefacing the title of almost every new initiative with 'community' — community policing, community playgroups, community training workshops, community schools, etc. The community label is seen, it seems, as conferring on the relevant service or programme an automatic relevance, credibility and 'street' acceptance. This process of lubrication, from the perspective of the statutory body, may involve anticipating and minimising sources of conflict between the body and locals, marketing new policies at local level or seeking to generate a local input (for example, through voluntary effort) which may reduce the cost of a service provided by the statutory body. This role of lubrication may conflict with an emphasis on empowerment and participation.

> If we are to make any progress in social planning and policy development, we must be clear not only about what community work is but also about what it is not. Community work, for instance, is not about manipulating people into subscribing to, and implementing, policies in the formulation of which they had no real part; it is not about reinforcing divisions by organising an 'us' to look after a 'them'; it is not about providing bread and circuses in the face of serious social problems (Ó Cinnéide, 1985).

The focus of community workers' efforts may be a locality, i.e. the people who share the experience of living in a given parish, town or neighbourhood. Alternatively, it may be an interest group sharing a common characteristic or experience other than a shared address, e.g. single parents, parents with disabled children or members of the travelling community.

The main employers of community workers are the health boards, or local voluntary bodies which receive ad hoc grant-aid towards salary costs, usually from a statutory source, such as the Combat Poverty Agency, health boards, FÁS or Vocational Education Committees.

Within the health boards, community workers may hold community worker posts or may be employed as project workers/leaders in neighbourhood youth, drug or other special projects. When community workers began to be appointed by the health boards in 1978, the Department of Health suggested the following functions for them:

- to assist in the identification of social need and develop a greater awareness of the social needs within the area;
- to advise on the priorities in meeting identified needs;
- to promote, maintain and develop the potential of voluntary groups promoting or providing social services and to help identify the support that they require from the statutory agencies;
- to develop and maintain liaison between these groups and the relevant statutory agencies and to help in the promotion and evaluation of standards and quality of services;
- to work with other officers providing health and social services in the area.

(Dept. of Health, 1985)

The first and second combat poverty programmes, during 1974-80 and 1985-89, have been influential in the development of community work practice based on local definitions of need (National Committee on Pilot Schemes to Combat Poverty, 1981; Barry, 1988). Kennedy and Kelleher (1989) analysed some of the lessons from the thirteen Integrated Rural Action Projects of the Second EC Poverty Programme (1985-89) (which have relevance in urban areas also). A community development worker, they contend, must act, within teams of people, both as a catalyst to open up new possibilities for action and change and as a broker/mediator between people/communities and resource holders/bureaucracies.

The activities undertaken by community workers therefore are many and varied. The following are examples of how they might serve the needs of children, young people and their families:

- the promotion of a local welfare rights service on an outer city estate, in which local people are trained to participate in the service;
- the running of adult education courses on community leadership training, personal development for women, assertiveness courses, parenting courses or literacy skills;
- the initiation and promotion of local resource centres with a focus on the needs of families;

- the launching and/or support of local development committees, geared to attracting additional resources for the community or interest group;
- the development of playgroups, nurseries, playschemes, summer projects, training schemes, youth centres or other local resources and facilities for young people;
- the promotion of health education activities;
- the promotion and support of community magazines;
- the support of local representative groups in their negotiations for resources with statutory bodies;
- the securing of practical services, such as typing, photocopying, printing and editing, to enable local groups to communicate their message to their constituencies.

Doctors

There are approximately 5,590 medical practitioners in Ireland or 15.8 per 10,000 population (Department of Health, 1989). These doctors work in a variety of specialisms, but doctors in four main areas (besides obstetrics) are likely to have extensive contact with children: paediatricians, child psychiatrists, general practitioners and public health doctors. Needless to say, children and adolescents are also likely to be encountered in many other medical specialisms.

Paediatrics

On 1987 figures, there were a total of 679 paediatric acute hospital beds in the country (Department of Health, 1989).

According to the World Health Organisation, paediatrics involves the diagnosis and treatment of sick children in hospital, as well as in the home and consulting room; and the preventive and social care of well children (cited in Comhairle na n-Ospidéal, 1979). The Irish Paediatric Association suggests that the functions of a paediatrician should include (ibid. p. 50):

- the promotion of optimum health in the child population, including care of the newborn;
- co-operation with teams established for the diagnosis and management of children with handicap;
- co-operation with community health teams in the operation of child health and school medical services, and
- the diagnosis and treatment of children referred for consultant opinion.

There are 56 consultant paediatrician posts established in Ireland, with 27 located in the Eastern Health Board region (see Table 10). This level of provision achieves a national ratio of one consultant paediatrician post to 18,300 population of children under 14 years. Regionally, this ratio varies from, 1:12,700 in the Eastern Health Board, to 1:38,500 in the South-East and 1:31,100 in the North-East (Comhairle na n-Ospidéal 1990, p. 15).

Table 10: **Number of paediatricians employed by Health Boards**

Health Board Area	Mid-West	South	East	Mid-lands	North-East	South-East	North-West	West	National
Establishment	3	7	27	2	3	3	4	7	56
No. of Vacant Posts	–	–	3	–	1	–	–	1	5
Ratio Consultant/ per 1000 population under 14 years	31.1	21.9	12.7	31.7	31.1	38.5	15.5	14.3	18.3
Distribution	5.4	12.5	48.2	3.6	5.4	5.4	7.1	12.5	

Source: Comhairle na n-Ospidéal, 1990, *Consultant Statistics as at 1/5/89*

Table 11: **Number of child psychiatrists employed by Health Boards**

Health Board Area	Mid-West	South	East	Mid-lands	North-East	South-East	North-West	West	National
Establishment	–	2	15	1	–	–	–	2	20
No. of Vacant Posts	–	–	–	–	–	–	–	–	–
Ratio Consultant/ per 1,000 population under 14 years	–	76.6	22.9	63.4	–	–	–	50.0	51.2
Distribution	–	10.0	75.0	5.0	–	–	–	10.0	

Source: Comhairle na n-Ospidéal, 1990, *Consultant Statistics as at 1/5/89*

Child Psychiatry

This sub-specialism of psychiatry is still in its infancy in Ireland. There are 20 consultant posts established, 15 of which are located in the Eastern Health Board region: there are two posts in the West, two in the South and one in the Midlands. The national ratio of provision is less meaningful, since four health boards have no consultant child psychiatrist posts within their region. However, the figure is one post per 51,200 child population and in the regions served this ranges from 1:22,900 in the Eastern region to 1:76,300 in the South (ibid.) See Table 11.

There are residential places specifically earmarked for children and young people with problems of psychiatric or emotional disturbance, or autism in three centres, two of which are in the Eastern Health Board region (St Paul's, Beaumont, and Warrenstown House, Blanchardstown) and one in the West (St Anne's, Galway). On 31 December 1987, there was a total of 51 children and young people in residence in these three centres (Department of Health, 1989, p. 41). Outside of the Eastern and Western Health Board areas children and adolescents must rely on adult services.

General Practitioners

For most children, the general practitioner represents the first point of contact with the health care system. The GP offers primary care by domiciliary and/or surgery consultation. Through his or her local knowledge of patients and their social context, the doctor is able to offer a degree of insight and continuity in the care provided that would not otherwise be available. The major exception to this pivotal role for the general practitioner is in the inner city areas where there is often an entrenched tradition of recourse to hospital casualty departments. This decision to short-circuit the GP may also have a pragmatic basis, since some families who are less organised and/or who move frequently may not have applied to secure themselves a named doctor in the Choice of Doctor [General Medical Services] Scheme.

It has been suggested that a general practitioner service should be characterised by the following features (Department of Health, 1984, p. 49):

- direct access by patients to the general practitioner's services;
- a close, personal relationship between the general practitioner and an identifiable and reasonably constant group of patients and families;
- continuity of care for that population;
- a holistic approach to the care of patients, taking full account of psychological, social and environmental factors influencing patients' health status;
- a concern with prevention and anticipatory care for that population, as well as effective response to illness;
- an ability to reach fully-rounded diagnoses, often under pressure, on the basis of special training for the conditions met in general practice.

General Medical Services

There are approximately 1,800 general practitioners in Ireland (Commission on Health Funding, 1989, p. 205). Of these, 1,538 general practitioners were participating in the Choice of Doctor Scheme under the General Medical Services in 1987 (Department of Health, 1989). This scheme offered coverage to 37.9 per cent of the general population in 1988 (ibid. 1989). It is provided under Section 358-9 of the Health Act 1970 and offers a free general practitioner, medical and surgical service to patients with full eligibility (i.e. people on low income, who qualify by a means test for the general medical service medical card, and their dependants). Each person covered by this scheme had an average of 6.45 consultations in 1987 (Commission on Health Funding, 1989, p. 208). Such consultations were four times more likely to occur in the doctor's surgery than in the patient's own home (Department of Health, 1987). The consultation rate varies by age group, with those in the 0-4 and 5-15 age groups being found to have annual consultation rates of 4.86 and 2.40 per annum for 1982 respectively (Department of Health, 1984).

Issues in the Development of GP services to Families and Children

Under the general medical services scheme as currently constituted, GPs maintain the relationship of independent contractors to the community care services. Under a new contract implemented in 1989, general practitioners transferred from being paid on a fee per item of service basis to a capitation fee per patient. This new fee is calculated on the basis of the patient's age, gender and distance from the GP. Crucially the new contract, unlike the one it replaced, also incorporates provisions for annual leave, sick leave, maternity leave and study leave, while preserving the GP's independent contractor status (Commission on Health Funding, 1989, pp 224-7).

A problem in collaboration between GPs and other community care professionals is that health board personnel serve a given catchment area, while the GP's focus is on a panel of patients who may be drawn from a number of catchment areas which together are served by a number of GPs. This dispersal of panel populations mean GPs must criss-cross these areas in a fairly random way. The panel system presents problems for the attachment of health board personnel to GP practices, as is commonly the case with nurses in the UK, and in some instances with social workers.

A further problem in the attachment of disciplines, such as social workers to GPs, is that the GPs outnumber most of these other disciplines under present staffing levels — in the case of community care social workers, by 4:1. Even if all these social workers were to be redeployed, such attachments could not achieve full coverage of all GP practices, not to mention attend to other duties that do not have a socio-medical content. These practical problems create very real obstacles to integrated primary health and social care.

One growing problem in the provision of general practitioner services is the burgeoning reliance on 'contractors' to provide cover out of hours for the doctor, who increasingly wishes to be free of work obligations at unsocial hours. Since medical emergencies, especially involving sick children, tend to occur at such times, attendance by, typically, a newly qualified doctor, unfamiliar with local and family routines and lacking the confidence and seasoned knowledge born of countless child examinations, is unsatisfactory, certainly from the perspective of anxious parents. This trend has also undoubtedly contributed to recourse to hospital casualty departments directly, since what they may seem to lack in intimacy or instant personal recognition they will make up for in the air of bustle and authority with which experienced nurses and senior doctors (if present) conduct their business.

Public Health Medical Officers

There are three grades of such officers in the health services: Director of Community Care, Senior Area Medical Officer, and Area Medical Officer (see Table 12). Currently, the Director of Community Care, who heads the Community Care Team, must be medically qualified. Generally appointments to the post of DCC have come from (Senior) Area Medical Officers. Higher training in community health or community medicine is now regarded as essential for appointment to these posts. The future objectives, deployment and structuring of public health services by doctors has been reviewed by a recent Working Party. The major proposal is to divide functions relating to public health from those relating to community care service management (currently merged in the DCC post), (Dept. of Health, 1990).

Table 12: **Survey of manpower in the Community Care Medical Team — 1 May, 1989 Complement of posts by health board and grade**

	DCC	*SAMO*	*AMO*	*Total*
Eastern	10	10	38	58
Midland	2	2	7	11
Mid Western	3	3	11	17
North Eastern	3	3	11	17
North Western	2	2	10	14
South Eastern	4	4	19	27
Southern	4	5	17	26
Western	3	3	19	25
Total	31	32	132	195

Source: Adapted from Dept. of Health, 1990.

Child Care Workers

Until the early 1970s, the large institutions that housed children in care were bleak places for the children and the adults who supervised them. Facilities were spartan and the large numbers of children were in the hands of a few untrained adults, who necessarily adopted a custodial rather than a therapeutic approach. These centres were starved of resources and apparently attracted little attention from government or from the central authorities of the religious orders that typically sponsored them. Such institutions constituted a residual part of the manifold functions of these religious orders whose mainstream concerns focused mostly around the management and staffing of schools and hospitals.

A variety of pressures, some from unlikely sources, suddenly forced improvements on a system which, while steadily shrinking, had remained otherwise impervious to change in more than half a century.

Economic growth, an air of confidence in the future and a more sensitive public conscience in relation to social problems characterised Ireland in the late 1960s. In 1968, in response to pressure (Tuairim, 1966) the Minister for Education, Donogh O'Malley, appointed the Kennedy Committee to review the state of these child care institutions. The Committee's recommendations emerged as the change prompted within religious orders by Vatican II had begun to gather momentum, especially in the female orders. The decline in recruitment of new vocations also coincided with this reappraisal of established ways. Two tangible changes ensued with the help of public funds: lay people began to be recruited and smaller, purpose-built centres began to replace the obsolete and impersonal buildings of earlier generations.

This decision to recruit lay personnel effectively introduced the discipline of child care to Ireland. The evolution of the discipline, with the trappings of formal training and a professional association now known as the Irish Association of Care Workers, paralleled the earlier development of its European counterpart of social pedagogy, which had grown out of the alms-giving of religious orders and Protestant altruism (Courtioux *et al*, 1985).

While the core of child care employment still lies in the residential centres within the health, education and justice systems, there has been a small, but significant, growth in the deployment of child care workers in day and community services — for example, in day nurseries, in work with youth and families at risk, and in work with the mentally handicapped. This expansion beyond the residential base mirrors similar and more marked developments in Europe. More and more child care workers in Ireland are likely to find employment outside residential centres as the number of places in these centres shrinks steadily (see p. 189).

The residential sector is in decline for economic and professional reasons. It involves high costs which both voluntary bodies and the public purse are either unwilling or unable to continue to bear. Its claim on resources is further undermined by increasing scepticism among social workers (the crucial gatekeepers to the sector) of the efficacy of residential placement.

Residential care is undoubtedly suffering the impact of a current bandwagon effect in favour of foster family care. Nevertheless, when the pendulum of fashion swings inevitably away from an almost blind faith in fostering, there is little doubt that a new balance will have been struck with a greater reliance on fostering and community services where previously residential placement had been almost the option of automatic recourse. The future for residential care must lie in a greater flexibility of operation in order to accommodate linkages with fostering and community-based arrangements. Child care workers have access to specific skills and knowledge of crucial importance in the management of difficult and disturbed behaviour in the context of a natural or foster family, or a school or day service. Residential units could, therefore, for instance, develop the capacity to offer respite care facilities and 'flying squad' support to natural or foster parents who may be 'burnt out' by sustained exposure to the raw turmoil and isolation of day-to-day caring.

The early challenges facing the child care discipline were the establishment of training opportunities and a national pattern of recognised pay and conditions. Over the years these have been gradually achieved, although not without setbacks. The influential one year, full-time training course which began at the School of Social Education in Kilkenny had to close largely because of the withdrawal of statutory funding. Training is now based on a variety of day-release and full-time structures with courses sited in certain Regional Technical Colleges (RTCs) and in the College of Catering within the Dublin Institute of Technology. These courses can lead to various awards accredited by the National Council for Educational Awards, viz. the (specialist) National Diploma in Child Care (Dublin and Waterford RTC) or the (generic) National Certificate in Social Studies (Cork, Sligo and Athlone RTCs). In all but one of these five courses (Athlone) students undertake practical work experience as part of their training.

Although continuing provision will be required for mature entrants to the workforce in child care, demand for basic training among existing workers has largely been satisfied. This, combined with the availability of European Social Fund support for training participation by school-leavers, has led to a shift in emphasis to this group. The prior requirement, of work experience in the field as a condition of entry to training, has had to be waived. This requirement offered some independent evidence of a candidate's commitment and suitability for admission to a field of practice where personal qualities are of paramount importance. It is not clear what effect the new arrangements will have on the future of the discipline.

For existing practitioners, the most urgent need in this area is for advanced training opportunities. Their absence creates serious problems not only at the level of the individual practitioner, but also in terms of the future of the discipline as a whole. The gap in training provision has had three serious repercussions. Firstly, it has created a morale problem for the discipline due to the fact that the qualifications now available to practitioners are not sufficient to entitle even the most able award-holders to compete (without a degree) for teaching posts on the training courses. Secondly, it has limited the claim the discipline can make on senior posts, especially in the newly developing services. This is a matter of concern even more because it deprives these services at a critical level of the vital and practical perspective that child care practitioners can bring to their work with children in difficulty. And thirdly, there has been a steady drain on the discipline, as many of its most able members, unwilling to endure the frustration of stunted career chances and narrow responsibilities which they foresee within their original discipline, defect to training for field social work. Clearly, this trend, if unchecked, has serious implications for the quality of service to a client group which so crucially depends on the charisma and calibre of their daily caretakers.

One American textbook on the task of residential child care is entitled *The Other Twenty-three Hours* (Treischman, 1969). This neatly sums up the remit of the child care worker. Outside of one hour of psychotherapy a day, which was a tradition in the better-resourced American centres, the care and management of the child remains the primary responsibility of the child care worker. It falls to him or her to structure the child's day, to cope with the child's moods, to tackle tantrums, to cajole and persuade. Ultimately, the worker must ensure that the child conforms to the rules of the setting, does not bully staff or other children, and contributes a reasonable share to house-keeping. This may mean having to spend hours with a sobbing child following a tantrum apparently triggered by a reminder to wash the dishes in line with the children's chores roster, but which actually has more to do with the fact that that day the child had a fight in school or failed to get a promised phone call from his or her parent. During the tantrum, one or two workers may have had to restrain the child, so that he could experience physically the psychological limits he craves but which have been inconsistently or not applied by adults in earlier years. There must also be of course many moments of fun and tenderness, too, if the child is not to perceive the worker merely in a policing role.

Children in residential care are often damaged, physically and/or psychologically. They may have been physically or sexually abused, they may have been neglected in terms of health or nutrition, they may have been left for long periods untended, they may have been moved from 'Billy to Jack' as their parent(s) made ad hoc arrangements to off-load their care onto a shifting variety of relatives, neighbours or friends. This lack of intimacy, warmth and constancy can scar a child psychologically and make it very difficult for him to get close to or trust his peers, let alone any adults. Experience may have taught the child that other people are without value or unworthy of trust. Consequently, it is often impossible for the child to feel safe or secure in the company of others. Sadly, the child has learned that new people, new relationships and new experiences invariably constitute a threat; the habitual response by the child is to defend or distance himself from such danger. This defensive posture presents quite a challenge to the child care worker who must patiently seek to engage the child by harnessing his/her personal qualities and therapeutic knowledge. The worker must expect to encounter hostility, anger and rejection, especially as their relationship becomes meaningful to the child. The relationship at this point becomes enmeshed in a complex pattern of transference, projection and countertransference, processes which Freud identified as occurring inevitably in therapeutic relationships of any significance. Interpreting the meaning of behaviour within a relationship of this depth is one of the most important — and demanding — aspects of the child care worker's task. Often the detached view of a colleague is required in order to help clarify what is going on.

All of this should serve to illustrate that child care is not merely the effortless or instinctive replication of a quasi-parent/child relationship, nor the kindly wiping of noses and bottoms. Child care workers are often irritated by superficial comments that their work requires little more than commonsense and 'the milk of human kindness'. These qualities are a necessary but not sufficient part of what a competent and effective child care worker must bring to helping children and, increasingly, their families. The child care worker enacts therapeutic relationships with a multiplicity of children and joins with co-workers in creating a therapeutic environment (within and beyond the physical confines of the centre) where the children, as a group and individually, can be helped to address their problems. In all of this, workers must resist becoming over-involved and so lose vital detachment; yet, they cannot remain aloof or indifferent. The discipline of child care is deceptively demanding of its practitioners, in terms of their knowledge, skill, integrity and stamina. Increasingly, the complex problems presented by youngsters will require of child care workers an ability to apply skills and methods from within a variety of theoretical frameworks (behavioural, group work, family therapy, etc.) (see Whittaker, 1979).

Home-helps

Section 61 of the Health Act 1970 empowered health boards to provide a home-help service to people who are sick or disabled (or their dependants), to women in receipt of maternity care or to anybody who, but for the service, would have to be maintained away from their own home.

In 1972, the Minister for Health asked health boards to use the powers given them by this section, thus paving the way for the beginnings of the service on a national basis. In the circular to the boards in connection with this development, the Department of Health recommended that priority be given to the needs of families and also to the elderly.

Home-helps contribute to the practical running of a home by undertaking 'in a companionable, caring way, normal household duties, e.g. laying fires, making a light meal, cleaning the house, making beds, getting messages' (Department of Health, 1973) where it is not possible for a member of the household to do so. Their work will normally require them to visit the relevant household a number of times a week, perhaps daily. In some instances, it may be necessary for them to attend on a full-time basis to the needs, for example, of a young family.

In suggesting a priority for families in the new service, the Department (ibid.) gave examples of circumstances where such assistance might be appropriate:

- where a mother is in receipt of maternity care;
- where a widower is in employment and his children would otherwise have to be received into care;
- where children had been abandoned by one parent and the provision of a home help would enable the other parent to work and the children to remain at home.

Clearly, home-help services can similarly benefit families where parents are affected by physical or mental illness, or by a chronic disability or problem.

While the original intention was that the service should give a primary focus to families with children, in practice they have made up a minor part of the total number of beneficiaries. Table 13 indicates the number of beneficiaries (i.e. individuals or families) in receipt of the service in 1987 and the proportion of total beneficiaries who are non-elderly. This frustration of initial intentions would appear to be due to two factors: the heavy reliance on part-time home-helps, 7,904 compared to 112 full-timers in 1987, and the particular challenge of delivering a home-help service to families. Families with special needs make special demands which only a full-time home-help might have developed the capacity to satisfy.

Part-timers have achieved their dominance partly for reasons, no doubt, of economy but also because neighbours can be more easily recruited as part-timers for a specific recipient, thus avoiding the costs to the employer in terms of travelling time and expenses normally incurred by a full-timer. The original, 1972 Departmental circular acknowledged that families could require the service on a full-time basis, yet the numbers of full-timers clearly limits the capacity of the service to respond to families.

The other factor inhibiting the response of the home-help service to the needs of families is the complexity of their problems which may prove to be beyond the capacity or endurance of the personnel available. The task of replacing an ill, disabled, inadequate or absent parent should not be underestimated. The home-help is a stranger entering the intimate core of the family's world. In some instances, this transition may prove relatively smooth. In others, the home-help may serve as a reminder to all concerned of the often painful deficits in the family which precipitated his or her arrival. Thus, home-helps in families require a competence and a level of sensitivity, tolerance and tact that goes beyond the cheerful completion of household chores.

Table 13: **Home-help service 1987**

Health Board	No. of home help organisers	No. of home helps* employed full-time	No. of home helps* employed part-time	No. of beneficiaries	% of beneficiaries who are not elderly
Eastern	77[1]	–	2,965	4,389	29.8
Midland	2	13	323	463	33.9
Mid-Western	6[2]	–	784	1,845	36.3
North Eastern	–	5	684	838	13.5
North Western	7[3]	32	330	979	14.3
South Eastern	4	7	630	766	12.3
Southern	4	–	1,450	1,681	10.1
Western	3	55	738	1,729	12.3
Total	101	112	7,904	12,021	

* Includes those employed directly by the health board and those employed by voluntary agencies which receive grants from health boards to provide a home-help service
1 Includes 37 part-time organisers
2 Includes 2 part-time organisers
3 Includes 1 part-time organiser

Source: Derived from Dept. of Health (1988), *The Years Ahead — a Policy for the Elderly,* Report of the Working Party on Services for the Elderly, p. 205

In recognition of this, the Task Force on Child Care Services (1981) recommended that home-help services for families with deprived children should be provided by trained personnel as an integral part of a general child care system and separate from the service to other groups. There has been no response to this recommendation at a national policy level, although there are isolated examples of relevant initiatives.

In Ballymun, the local home-help organiser — a nun — instigated training courses to prepare local women for employment as home-helps. This training has been most successful in boosting the confidence of people who themselves have known a good deal of adversity in their lives. It has also set a precedent for comparable developments elsewhere. Interestingly, Ballymun is an example of a district where a high proportion of the home-help service is devoted to the needs of families.

In a small number of community care areas, 'home-makers' have been employed in what appears to be a local response to the problems encountered in the application of the home-help service in its present form to the needs of families. The post of home-maker seems intended to offer families the resource of a person with home-management skills who can impart those skills to families which might benefit from them.

While it is impossible to estimate the level of actual need for the home-help service (or an appropriate variant) among families under stress, it is safe to assume that the patchy and marginal level of present provision falls far short of what is required. Prospects for development are gloomy, since the momentum of growth in the service seen during the 1970s has largely been dissipated. Spending now stands at approximately £6.5 million per annum (Department of Health, 1989) and seems unlikely to grow in real terms. The original administrative patchwork remains, with services being managed by a home-help organiser who may be employed directly by the health board or by a voluntary body which is grant-aided for this purpose. The original circular provided for this diversity of arrangements, although a review of community care services questioned its desirability in terms of the long-term interests of the service (INBUCON, 1982).

This same review highlighted a conundrum at the heart of the service. While it remains the Cinderella of the community care system in terms of its modest allocation and vulnerability to further cutbacks, the home-help service is highly regarded by fellow-field staff and is seen as pivotal in any implementation of a full-blooded community alternative to institutional care. The problem for the service is that it seems to enjoy much goodwill but little clout. It lacks the prestige and visibility associated with more 'flashy' parts of the health and social services. Critically it is funded on a discretionary rather than a mandatory basis and serves a politically mute constituency.

Psychologists

Clinical psychologists have an important role to play in the operation and development of children's services. However, the potential of this role may remain unfulfilled because of the relative paucity of their numbers and the failure to date to establish a psychological service geared to the needs of the primary schools sector.

The introduction of child psychologists to Ireland can be traced to an initiative in 1952 by the Department of Health and the World Health Organisation to fill what was seen as a gap in Irish mental health services. Until then, there had been no clinical psychologists practising in any of the social services. The first appointments were in the area of child guidance (McKenna, 1986).

Currently, within the health service, psychologists tend to be located mainly in the psychiatric and mental handicap services, with a smaller number in community care. It is difficult to calculate how many psychologists work exclusively or largely with children, although it seems safe to assume that those in community care and mental handicap would have considerable involvement. In terms of psychiatry, only those assigned to child guidance or child or adolescent psychiatry would ordinarily deal with children, although presumably adult psychiatric services may pick up some adolescent problems especially where no specific provision for adolescents exists.

What kind of children are referred to psychologists? A national survey of first-time referrals of children to psychologists was undertaken during one month in 1980 (McConkey and O'Connell, 1982). Coverage was quite comprehensive, with 93% of relevant agencies participating and survey forms being returned for 95% of children known to have been seen. Boys made up a disproportionate 69% of children referred. Referral was most often for educational/intellectual assessment, although with pre-schoolers developmental assessment was the most common reason. Seven in ten (69.6%) of the children were in the 5-12 age range, with the peak rate of referral at age 7. In terms of direct follow-up by the psychologists, they

> hoped to see 18% of the children on a regular basis, but such intent varied markedly according to the children's needs. For example, the psychologists planned to be regularly involved with 44% of children needing developmental intervention, 34% of those with personality/behaviour problems and 30% of those cases in which family factors were important.

The widespread perception of psychologists as largely administrators of various forms of psychological testing is one which causes much irritation and frustration to practitioners. It is true that their extensive training equips them thoroughly for this role, but their work embraces much more than merely generating individual sets of psychological data. They can also advise on or participate in the detailed planning and execution of appropriate programmes of intervention in a variety of areas, including educational development, behaviour modification, social skills and interpersonal relationships.

Clinical psychologists also possess significant research competence by virtue of their training. In addition, many are interested in developing skills in direct therapy and counselling with clients and families on an ongoing basis, so that face-to-face contact goes well beyond simply an assessment session. The more traditional mould is also being broken by psychologists who have become active in the delivery of community services alongside colleagues from other disciplines and by a role in consultation to staff teams in fields such as residential child care. Thus, a current profile of psychological practice must include reference to activities such as therapy, research and community service, over and above more traditional testing.

Detailed information on the deployment of psychologists in Ireland is limited. There are 94 psychologists in posts funded by the health services, 36 of whom are employed directly by the health boards, with the remainder working in voluntary agencies in areas such as mental handicap (Dáil Debates, 26 November 1987). Earlier data would suggest that a majority of health service psychologists work in psychiatry (including those in child psychiatry). A total of 58 psychologists was reported to be working in this area, with the heaviest concentrations in the Eastern and Western Health Board regions (Department of Health, 1985).

See also chapter on Education (p. 76) for a discussion of the role of the psychologist in the school system.

Community Welfare Officers

Community Welfare Officers have essentially three functions as members of the community care teams. The first is to administer the Supplementary Welfare Allowance Scheme which health boards operate on an agency basis on behalf of the Dept. of Social Welfare. Secondly, they undertake means testing activities to determine eligibility for various health service entitlements, e.g. general medical services medical card. Thirdly they offer an information and advice service on matters relating to income support and welfare rights generally. There are 407 community welfare officers employed by the health boards, 39 of whom hold supervisory posts (Association of Community Welfare Officers, 1989, p. 13).

The Supplementary Welfare Allowance (SWA) Scheme represents a vital safety net to individuals and families who are unable to provide the necessities of life from other sources. The rates of payment are modest (even by the standards of state income maintenance payments generally) and both they and details of the scheme's administrative and procedural arrangements have been subject to criticism (Independent Poverty Action Movement, 1986). Entitlement to payment is subject to application, and to investigation of the applicant's circumstances by the Community Welfare Officer.

Supplementary Welfare is a lifeline to a substantial number of children. At the end of March 1988, there were 25,375 child dependants of adult recipients of supplementary welfare payments (of whom there were 13,736 children in 11,353 family units depending entirely on supplementary welfare (Dept. of Social Welfare, 1989, p. 37).

Supplementary Welfare Allowances comprise two forms of payment: basic allowance and supplements. Applicants who are working full time, or who are in full-time education, or who are involved in a trade dispute will not normally qualify (although a striker may claim on behalf of dependants). The basic allowance is payable where a person has no other means. If a person is entitled to another form of allowance, the basic SWA allowance may be paid until payment of the other allowance comes through.

Where the basic allowance or other forms of income prove insufficient to meet basic needs, supplementary payments may be made, at the discretion of the health board concerned. Such special needs may include rent or mortgage interest, heating needs, exceptional heating expenses due to ill health, or special diet due to a health condition (such as diabetes, kidney failure or coeliac disease). While these supplements would normally be payable on a regular basis, other supplements to meet exceptional need may be paid on a once-off basis. These single payments may be made in respect of needs such as bedding or other essential household equipment, or funeral expenses. Where applicable, health boards may arrange to make such exceptional payments in kind. Families which are in receipt of supplementary welfare or other health board or social welfare allowances can apply under the SWA scheme for assistance towards the cost of footwear during the winter.

HEALTH AND SOCIAL SERVICES DIRECTED AT CHILDREN AND FAMILIES

Health care for Mothers and Infants

Health boards are obliged to provide free to all low and middle income mothers 'medical, surgical and midwifery services' in respect of ante-natal and maternity care (S. 62 Health Act 1970). In addition health boards are also obliged to provide free 'medical, surgical and nursing services' for children born to mothers entitled to services under Section 62 up to the age of six weeks. These obligations are discharged by the Maternity and Infant Care Scheme which provides for the supply of general practitioner services ante-natally (minimum of six consultations, attendance at confinement, and post-natal check-ups for mother — and at the discretion of the GP for the baby) up to six weeks.

A survey in 1980 of all births in a given week found take-up of the scheme was confined to 65.6 per cent of eligible mothers (ranging from 38 per cent in the Eastern Health Board to 92.4 per cent in the North Western Health Board (Dept. of Health, 1982). Non-take up should not be equated with the absence of ante-natal or maternity care since mothers may refer themselves directly to hospital (ibid. p. 22) which is certainly a strong tradition in the Dublin maternity hospitals.

In reviewing the services for scheme users and non-users it was found that 96 per cent of babies were examined within four days of birth as required. However, 3 per cent of mothers did not know if the check had occurred and 1 per cent said their baby had not been examined (ibid. p. 26). In relation to the prescribed six week check, 23 per cent of children had not been examined, even by 10 to 12 weeks after discharge from hospital (ibid). This shortcoming was most likely to affect infants of low income mothers where one in three (33 per cent) were found not to have been so examined (ibid. pp 69-72). Similarly 27 per cent of mothers had had no post-natal check-up by 10 to 12 weeks and this again was most likely with low income mothers (43 per cent of whom had not been checked). Limitations were also revealed about the dissemination of information in relation to family planning. Almost half of the mothers (48 per cent) had had no discussion about it with any of the professionals involved. Of these, 39 per cent (48 per cent in the case of low income mothers) would have liked such discussion (ibid. pp 73-5). Almost half (45 per cent) of the mothers had not had a visit from a public health nurse in the first week after discharge from hospital (a pattern which it was speculated was due to faulty liaison between hospital and community services) (ibid. p. 26).

Pre-school Child Health Services

Developmental Paediatric Clinics

In the early 1970s the Department of Health proposed that health boards should establish a comprehensive developmental paediatric examination service. This service was to discharge a responsibility imposed on health boards by the S. 66 (1) of the Health Act 1970 which required the boards to provide a health examination and treatment service to children under 6 years. Initially the service was to be confined to centres of population of more than 5,000 (although it has never been extended). The service is intended to monitor the developmental progress of children by scheduled checks at 6-10 months, 12-18 months and at 24 months. In 1988, 77 per cent of eligible children, i.e. those of the appropriate age in towns of more than 5,000 people, attended for their first such examination. However, since this represented only 60.1 per cent of all children in the relevant age cohort in the State, it is not clear how this level of coverage satisfies the explicit legal obligation on health boards to provide a health examination and treatment service for *all* children. The rate of non-attendance is explained by the non-appearance of eligible children and the effective disfranchisement of most children from rural areas or smaller population centres. The importance of such a service can be gauged by the fact that one in four children (28 per cent) examined at the six month stage required further attention; at the checks at 12 and 24 months the corresponding proportions were 22 and 27 per cent respectively (derived from Dept. of Health, 1990, pp 28-9).

School Health Service

Health boards are obliged by S. 66(2) of the Health Act 1970 to provide a free health examination and treatment service to all national school pupils. The present policy is to undertake a comprehensive examination of all new entrants to national schools and selective further examinations of older children where indicated. In 1984, 74 per cent of all new entrants were examined and one in three (35 per cent) of these required further attention (O'Connor, 1987). A total of 112,745 children or one in five (22 per cent) of all national school children were examined under this scheme in 1988 (Dept. of Health 1990).

Child Guidance

Child guidance clinics were a concept imported into Europe from the United States in the 1920s. They have had an important influence on child welfare provision on this side of the Atlantic since then. Child guidance clinics (now sometimes known as family guidance clinics or child and family centres) were conceived to address (on an out patient basis) behavioural, emotional and mental health problems of the growing child and adolescent.

There are two core features to the work of these clinics. Firstly, they function through a multi-disciplinary team composed of, at least, a psychiatrist, a psychologist and a social worker; the team may also include representatives of other disciplines, e.g. a speech therapist, a play therapist or a child care worker. The second core feature of these clinics is a focus on the family unit to which the child belongs. The problems or symptoms with which the child presents are addressed in their own right, but only in the wider context of the child's family.

In several ways, child guidance practice anticipated many of the insights later promulgated by the specialism of family therapy (which, indeed, it helped spawn). Child guidance recognises that often the symptoms of a child serve some function within a family and/or are maintained or reinforced by patterns of behaviour by the parents or other family members. For that reason, parents are a focus in child guidance intervention. This can be a source of some tension between parents and therapists, since the parent typically will expect the spotlight to be on the child rather than on themselves.

Traditionally, a psychiatrist has led the child guidance team and as such has retained clinical control, thereby determining the division of labour under which the team members approach their work. Commonly, the child would be seen by the psychiatrist, while the social worker would see the parents; the psychologist would be responsible for administering psychological tests. The incorporation of new techniques, such as behaviour modification and family therapy, has challenged such rigid patterns of demarcation. There are now calls for the precise division of labour to be renegotiated for each individual case, according to the needs of the referral and the interests and expertise of the team members. Looking to the future, Rutter (1986), himself a towering figure in child psychiatry, has observed:

> It must be expected, and welcomed, that psychologists and social workers will often work as autonomous clinicians. I believe that interdisciplinary clinics should continue because there is much to be gained from consultation and co-operation between disciplines, but I do not see that as necessarily, or even usually, involving all members of the team in each case.

The effectiveness of child guidance intervention is often strongly questioned in terms of the results achieved, especially in the context of the resources invested in it relative to other forms of intervention. One aspect of practice that causes concern to professional colleagues is the typical child guidance response to non-appearance of new referrals or the non-return of families for subsequent appointments. Non-compliance with the referral or appointment arrangements, and with the require-ments set down for the clients between interviews are frequently used by clinic teams as measures of client-motivation to seek and use help. Yet many child welfare workers would argue forcibly that the most telling evidence of a referred family's problems may often be that very lack of motivation. According to its critics, child guidance should devote its considerable professional resources to devising interventions which succeed in sparking and retaining motivation, rather than using the rather predictable absence or oscillation of motivation as a pretext for professional withdrawal.

Child guidance has also been criticised for a too-narrow clinical pre-occupation with a few children at the expense of many whose lives could be influenced by attention to their wider social systems, such as schools (Tizard, 1973). The same critic — a leading British psychologist — also commented on what he saw as the lack of attention in child guidance to research and the paucity of evidence about its effectiveness.

In evaluating such criticism, it is important not to throw the baby out with the bathwater. While there may well be legitimate grounds for criticising the priorities, deployment or efficacy of aspects of the existing child guidance services, there is undoubtedly a need within the wider child welfare system for such concentrations of expertise in work with troubled children. The question is clearly not whether such clusters of excellence should exist, but how best these valuable resources can be mobilised and deployed to have the optimal effect on the lives of children in need.

Partly to take account of such criticisms and partly in recognition of the more recent proliferation of front-line workers who have contact with children and families under stress, clinics may now devote some time to liaison and consultancy functions, in which they advise and support other professionals in order that more cases can be handled at the primary-care level. In this way, the resources and expertise of the clinical team are spread more widely and perhaps with greater impact on more families and children. It has been noted that this broader preven-tive role can embrace a range of front-line services, including schools, residential units for children, adoption and fostering services, hospitals, courts and health education programmes. All of these may benefit from such a consultative advisory and liaison service (Department of Health, 1985). Thus, primary-care workers may be enabled to contain problems which might otherwise have escalated were they to have awaited referral to a further service.

Giving front-line workers resources to cope with problems is also consistent with the concept of normalisation, which holds that as far as possible problems should be dealt with within mainstream services. This is because referral to specialist programmes is seen as differentiating people from the norm and can generate the risk of stigma, with consequent social isolation, thereby seriously aggravating the original basis for referral. If the need for further referral is avoided, it also eliminates the aforementioned problem faced by such services as child guidance, i.e. of securing the client's interest and commitment to using the service.

This more outward-looking, less clinical and more community-oriented approach to the practice of child guidance has received striking endorsement from a watershed research project conducted in Newcastle-upon-Tyne (Kolvin *et al*, 1981). From an initial screening of 4,300 school children, 574 children at junior level (screened as 'at risk') and senior level (screened as 'maladjusted') were randomly allocated to treatment and control groups. The children in the treatment groups were subjected to one of four different regimes, each of which was carefully structured and prepared, viz. behaviour modification (senior), nurture work (junior and senior) and group therapy/playgroups (senior/junior). The results were enlightening (ibid. p. 300):

> ... with regard to time, it was particularly interesting to find that outcome and improvement continued to gain ground in effective therapies, even when treatment had finished. We have suggested that direct therapy [with child rather than an adult] may be more effective than indirect ... Shorter term treatments (group therapy, play-groups and behaviour modification) were seen to have the best outcome. Our results suggested that it is type rather than amount of treatment that is a critical factor in intervention ... Those therapies (group therapy, playgroups and behaviour modification) that have given the most promising results have done so in the shortest possible time.

These findings vindicate the researchers' belief that the school was a logical site in which to deliver mental health services to children and that a child guidance team through their professional support could provide a vital back-up function to teachers.

Kolvin *et al* (ibid. p. 329) concluded that:

> while there will certainly need to be modifications to the traditional child guidance approach, the concept of the core team of mental health professionals who work regularly together and who can deliver a high level of expertise in community settings is one that must be preserved if the findings of our study are to be applied effectively. The reason for this is that personnel in schools will need back-up teams, both for training and for continued professional and emotional support.

Child Guidance in Ireland

Child guidance services remain underdeveloped in Ireland. Many parts of the country lack local services. The effects of this shortfall in service are all the more keenly felt because of the absence of a national psychological service for schools at primary level. The position at secondary level is better in that there are guidance counsellor posts in the schools and the Department of Education employs a team of psychologists with the status of Inspectors of Guidance Counselling who are available to support teaching staffs (see pp 75-6).

Three health boards (the Eastern, Southern and Western) have full-time services, provided directly or by a voluntary agency on a contracted-out basis. The Eastern and Western boards also have residential facilities as part of their service. The Midland Health Board has its own child psychiatrist and provides a partial (out-patient) service with the assistance of social workers and psychologists from the community care programme. The remaining four health boards (Mid-Western, North-Eastern, North-Western and South-Eastern) do not have any child guidance service of their own. Insofar as any facility exists for the assistance of disturbed or mentally ill children in these regions, it is through referral to clinics in other regions or the part-time visiting services of child psychiatrists (see p. 115) from outside the region (Department of Health 1985, pp 178-182).

While this level of provision may be disappointing, it should be judged against the fact that there was only one full clinic functioning in the country as late as the 1950s (Commission of Inquiry on Mental Illness, 1966). Recently, it has been recommended in a national review of psychiatric provision that each health board should have at least one child guidance team to provide its own local service (Department of Health, 1985, p. 95).

In those regions without a full-scale service, provision may be confined to initial assessments of children's problems. Those assessments may have to take place in unsuitable locations, such as the local adult psychiatric hospital, and are effectively conducted in a vacuum since in most instances there exists no practical means by which to implement comprehensively any set of treatment recommendations.

O'Connor (1987) has commented on the shortcomings of present provision in child guidance, especially in the light of referrals to child guidance clinics/ psychologists, which enjoy the lowest rate of take-up of any service to which children may be referred from the school medical service. She reports (ibid. p. 67):

> It is not clear that the present service, which has evolved in the absence of a school psychological service, is adequate or appropriate. The present health board provision should be evaluated. It is probable that if an educationally oriented psychological service were integrated into the school system to a greater extent, take-up would be greater. The present situation is conducive to referral for psychological assessment when the need may be for advice on classroom management. Apart from the expenses involved in the frequent use of sessional assessments, the present arrangements militate against an overall assessment of the needs of particular areas, schools or population groups.

The case for a rationalisation of various clinical assessment/treatment services for children has also been floated in an earlier Irish study of child referrals to psychologists (O'Connell and McConkey, 1982). The problems created by the lack of a psychological service to primary schools has long been a source of frustration and concern to the Psychological Society of Ireland (Psychological Society of Ireland, 1981). (See section on Education, p. 76).

Adoption

Legal adoption was introduced to Irish jurisdiction in 1953 following an energetic campaign for its introduction (see Whyte, 1980). Since then, a total of 35,981 persons have benefited from this facility. The system of adoption is governed by the Adoption Acts 1952-88, and is operated largely by adoption societies in conjunction with the statutory Adoption Board. Adoption Board (1989) and Shatter (1986) provide details and discussion of the legal aspects of adoption.

Who can be adopted?
Any person up to the age of 21 who is born illegitimate, or who is orphaned, or in the case of a legitimate child whose adoption has been authorised by the High Court under the terms of the Adoption Act 1988, may be adopted. In the case of an illegitimate child, the natural mother must give her consent in a two-stage procedure. Only where she has given an initial consent and then behaves unreasonably in relation to the withholding or withdrawal of consent can dispensation with the mother's consent be sought (in the High Court under the Adoption Act 1974).

Who can adopt?
In the normal course of events, it is only a married couple who may adopt; exceptions include a widow, the natural mother, the natural father or a relative of the child (on the mother's side, in the case of an illegitimate child). A widower may only adopt if his wife dies after the couple have applied for an Adoption Order to the Adoption Board and the couple had the care of a child prior to the wife's death.

Who can place a child for adoption?
Adoption Societies and Health Boards: There are currently 19 registered adoption societies which, in addition to health boards, have powers to make arrangements in relation to adoption. Their work entails counselling pregnant women who are contemplating adoption, advising and selecting prospective adoptive parents, and making arrangements for the care of children prior to placement for adoption. In most instances, these societies are voluntary and are usually denominational in character. Some societies are run in association with a health board, and in two cases societies are fully staffed by health board personnel.

The Natural Mother: It is illegal for a private individual, other than the natural mother, to place a child for adoption. The natural mother may place her child with a relative, a choice which accounted for 6.0% of all adoption orders made in 1988. She may choose to adopt the child with her husband (having married after the child's birth) (27.4% of adoption orders in 1988); she may also choose to place the child directly with a non-relative (3.8% of orders made in 1988). (The Adoption Board, 1989). The natural mother may also adopt her child herself although no orders were made for such cases in 1988.

There is some concern that a mother may be susceptible to special pressure at a vulnerable period in her life and that the option of private placement by her with a non-relative should be closed. This would protect her own and her child's interests,

Figure 6: **Number of adoption orders 1953-88**

Adoption orders made:

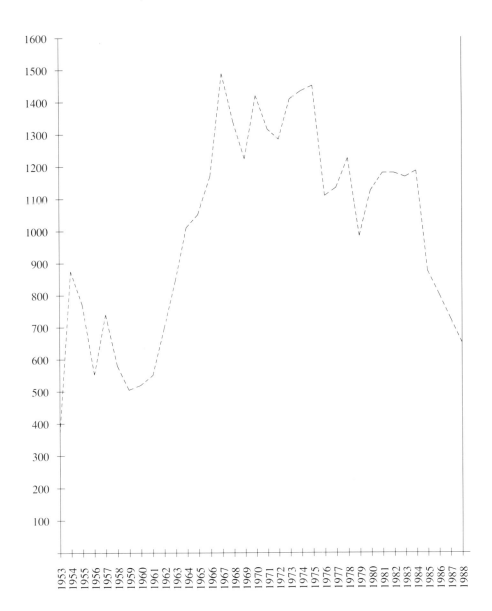

Source: derived from Adoption Board (1989)

and eliminate a possible loophole for unscrupulous behaviour by couples who may have been turned down for adoption on grounds of suitability through the normal channels (Department of Health, 1984).

How is an Adoption Order obtained?
When a child is placed by a registered society, health board or natural mother with a couple, that couple must apply to the Adoption Board for an Adoption Order. This effects the complete legal transfer of all parental rights and responsibilities in respect of the child concerned from the natural mother to the adoptive parents. The child will acquire the surname of his or her new family and for the purposes of succession is treated as if born to the adoptive parents.

How is the welfare of children protected?
Because of the monumental nature of the decisions being taken in the field of adoption, and the lifetime implications of those decisions for all concerned, it is essential that practices and decisions conform to the highest standards in terms of both legal detail and professional practice and knowledge. The greatest burden of responsibility in this regard rests with the societies, although it is the Adoption Board that must approve the initial registration of the societies. It is also the Board's responsibility to satisfy itself that a child's interests are secured by the making of an adoption order in respect of the child in favour of a specific set of applicants.

Adoption societies receive grant-aid from the Department of Health towards their running costs, in particular towards the costs of employing qualified social workers. Social workers undertake much of the direct counselling and vetting work on behalf of the society's placement committee, which would make final placement decisions on consideration of the social worker's advice.

Adoption Board
The Adoption Board is made up of a Chairman (who must have legal training) and six voluntary members (one of whom serves as Vice-Chairman and who must also be legally qualified). The Board is appointed by the Minister for Health and has five-yearly terms of office. It has available to it the services of a number of welfare officers (social workers) seconded to it from the Probation and Welfare Service of the Department of Justice. This latter arrangement has been inherited from the time when the Department of Justice was responsible for the adoption system, before its transfer in 1983 to the Department of Health.

Statistical overview
Two in every three (63.9%) of adoption orders in 1988 were made in respect of children under 2 years of age. In the case of non-relative adoptions, 92.4% of orders were for children under 2 years. In family adoptions the age profile was different, with over half (49.8%) of the children in respect of whom orders had been made falling into the 5-10 years age group. Age at the making of the adoption order is different to the child's age at placement. It is considered good practice to minimise any delay in placement once a mother has given consent to adoption. This is because the earlier the child joins what is intended to be his or her

permanent family, the earlier what are believed to be the crucial psychological processes of attachment and bonding can begin between them. In 1988, 44.4% of the children placed with non-relatives were less than 2 months old at the time of placement. Nine out of ten (90.7%) of all such children were placed within 6 months of age (ibid).

Trends in Adoption
The number of babies being placed for adoption has fallen steadily in recent years. This is reflected in the decline in the numbers of adoption orders made, from the most recent peak of 1,443 in 1975 to 649 in 1988. The decline in placement with non-relatives, (the conventional form of adoption) is even more marked than these figures reveal. This is because the numbers of family adoptions increased in relative and absolute terms during this period. Family adoptions refer to adoptions by the natural mother, by relatives or, most commonly, by the natural mother and her husband. In the last instance, the couple has married after the birth of the child; their decision to adopt confers legal advantages on the child otherwise denied to him or her. In 1975, family adoptions accounted for 126 adoption orders made, or 8.7% of the total. In 1988, they accounted for 217, or 33.4% of the total.

This decline in conventional adoption — the placement of fit infants with non-relatives — reflects earlier trends in other Western countries. These have contributed to an extension in the categories of children considered suitable or eligible for adoption. In Ireland, this trend is also evident with the passage of the Adoption Act 1988 which extends the possibility of adoption to legitimate children in certain very specific circumstances. Previously adoption had been confined to children who were illegitimate or orphaned.

The Irish adoption system has seen a number of important developments in the past decade:

- Responsibility for adoption has been transferred to the Department of Health which carries lead responsibility for other aspects of child care. Thus, the adoption system can be more easily integrated into the overall child care service.

- Increasingly, adoption societies are employing qualified workers to assist them in their work and grant-aid has been made to facilitate this.

- A major review of the system has been undertaken (Department of Health, 1984). The passage of the Adoption Act 1988 (see above) extended the scope of adoption and is a first and major step in giving effect to the many important recommendations of this review committee.

- The Adoption Board has had members appointed whose professional background is more likely to prepare them for the many difficulties and dilemmas upon which the Board is asked to adjudicate. In addition, the greatly improved quality of the Board's annual reports suggests that it now regards itself in a more pivotal role in relation to the overall operation of the system.

- A decline in the number of adoption orders (see Figure 6) and in the use of traditional adoption i.e. for the transfer of children from their mothers to non-relatives (strangers) (see above).

Inter-country Adoption

Looking to the future, a particular challenge facing the Irish adoption system is that of inter-country adoption. Inter-country adoption entails the placement of babies or children, usually from third world countries, in Western adoptive families. The demand for these placements in the West has been fuelled by families anxious to adopt but unable to find suitable or eligible children in their home country. During 1990 media coverage of the plight of children incarcerated in appalling conditions within orphanages by the ill-fated Ceaucescu regime in Romania, has caused a surge of interest in Ireland among families wanting to adopt these children. In response to the legal, social and ethical issues raised by such inter-country adoptions. An Taoiseach announced in the Dáil in December 1990 that the government was preparing legislation to deal with such matters. At the time of going to press, the legislation — the Adoption Act 1991 — had passed into law. (For a helpful discussion, from an Irish perspective, of the professional and ethical issues raised by inter-country adoption, see McCabe 1990).

Day Care

Traditionally, day care has been taken to mean care for pre-school children outside their own family. More recently, abroad, the concept has been extended to include provision for schoolchildren after school hours.

In most Western countries there is a network of state provided, supported or regulated day care available to families. While coverage may not be comprehensive, the extent of provision is substantial. The impetus for provision derives from four sources:
(1) the late (by Irish standards) school entry age in many countries;
(2) a commitment to removing child care responsibilities as an obstacle to participation by mothers (and fathers) in the labour force;
(3) a belief in the educational and social value of day care as a supplement to the child's normal family experience;
(4) a belief in the capacity of day care experiences to compensate for adverse home and social circumstances.

Day care can take many forms (see Figure 7). The range of direct providers is also varied. In the private sector, these may range from a company providing a network of services to an individual housewife who is child-minding in her own home as a means of supplementing the family income. In the public sector, agencies within the educational or personal social services areas may run services directly and/or support or regulate the provision of the voluntary sector. Employers may also make provision of this kind for their workforce as a fringe benefit, or more likely, to secure continuity in their staffing arrangements.

The extent to which day care should be available is a point of major controversy on both ideological and psychological grounds. Attitudes to the question of day care provision are likely to reflect wider ideas about the relationship between society and the family. For some, day care gives practical effect to the rights of

Figure 7: **Day care types**

Full-time day care
    Day nurseries (public, voluntary and private sectors)
    Workplace creches
    Private childminder/family day care
    Day fostering (family day care organised by a health board)

Part-time day care (daily or less frequent)
    Child minding facilities — community centres, public place (shopping centres etc.)
    Playgroups (private sector, community)
    Nursery/pre-school/kindergarten
    Mother and toddler groups

---

women to participate in society irrespective of their family status. For others, it is seen as undermining the fundamental obligations conferred on parents and more especially women towards their children. People in this camp may see day care as an unacceptable, tangible expression of collectivist political ideas or of the unwarranted encroachment of the State.

On the more specific question of its impact on child development, the debate continues within the field of psychology. Inevitably, arguments are enlisted when convenient for the wider ideological debate surrounding day care. This has made detached consideration of the issue difficult. Concerns from within the discipline of psychology relate to the effects on the child's cognitive and emotional development of separation from the mother (figure) and to the impact of multiple caretakers (as may be the case in group care settings). In general, the research evidence seems to support a favourable view of the effects of day care subject to certain conditions about its quality (Rutter, 1986). There has also been renewed optimism about the potential of specialised programmes of day care to achieve enduring improvements in children's social and educational progress, even where they remain exposed to serious social disadvantage (Clarke and Clarke, 1986).

Day Care in Ireland
In the Irish context, public policy has taken a fairly clear, minimalist position on the public provision of day care. Official estimates in the mid 1980s suggest that there were 20,000 children attending 1,400-1,500 centres (Department of Health, 1986), although only one-fifth or so of these centres are in receipt of any State support. (It should also be noted that these official estimates of the total number of places may now be too low — see below under Playgroups.) The State has still not assumed a role in the regulation of provision, although it has acquired powers to do so in the provisions of the Child Care Act 1991. In addition, a substantial report on the child care requirements of working parents has produced little or no visible follow-up (Working Party on Child Care Facilities for Working Parents, 1983). There have, however, been ideological and practical reasons for this reticence and apparent vacuum.

Ideologically, many of the key decision-makers (usually middle-aged and male) have little feeling for a development which is alien to their likely personal view, that the place for mothers and children is in the family home. This ideological position is conveniently reinforced by the costs of day care provision. In the current climate of public finances, arguments for the extension of public provision based on feminist or enhanced child development considerations have carried little weight. As a consequence, demand motivated by these factors must normally resort to the private sector.

An idiosyncrasy of the Irish educational system may also have dampened potential demand for a more comprehensive provision of day care. Ironically, despite the modesty of public sector day care provision and the ideological anti-pathy to its extension, the rate of participation by Irish 4 to 6 year olds in out-of-home provision is relatively high. The key to this lies in the very high proportion of children entering school before the official entry age of 6–55.7% of 4 year olds and 99.7% of 5 year olds (Department of Education, 1990). Irish children start school two and sometimes three years earlier than their European peers. Thus the mainstream school system absorbs much of a demand which is served by nursery schools and kindergartens in other countries, e.g. in France 80% of 3 year olds and 98% of 5 year olds attend State-run nursery schools (Thayer 1988, p. 30), (although whether this early school entry is a cause or effect of the relative under-provision of day care in Ireland is a point worthy of further reflection).

In the light of the above factors, public policy and intervention have largely been confined to deprived children. While it was the Department of Education that took the first initiative in this area, with the important Rutland Street Pre-school experiment of 1969, the Department of Health has emerged as essentially the only public agency willing to contribute (through the health boards) to provision of this kind. (In Dublin City, Dublin Corporation has also grant-aided the development of networks of playgroups as a contribution to community development.)

The Department of Health, through the health boards, has evolved a system of assistance to day care facilities geared to supporting families at risk by providing respite care and/or to offering compensatory experiences to children whose home circumstances may be inimical to their social, emotional or educational development.

> Health boards provide grants towards the operating costs of centres, e.g. creches, playgroups, catering for children of families in need of special support. They may also support the establishment of such day centres by providing suitable centres or making a grant towards equipment (Ireland, 1986, p. 286).

The categories of children normally provided for are:

- children of single parent families;
- children whose mothers have been deserted or widowed and have to find employment through economic necessity;
- children of parents who, because of illness or similar circumstances, are unable to cope with the children at home without special support.

The great bulk of provision tends to be sponsored by voluntary bodies, such as social service centres, the ISPCC, Barnardo's or local committees. The sponsoring bodies of the nurseries and playgroups which qualify must apply annually for grant-aid towards a proportion of their running costs. There is no set formula for the calculation of such grants and the sums for individual centres may be quite modest. The total expenditure by health boards on day care centres in 1985 was £1.12 million (Department of Health, 1990). The number of centres benefiting from this support has grown over the years, from 31 in 1975 to 274 (serving 7,263 children) in 1987. The centres received an average annual grant in 1987 of £4,666, or £154 per child per annum.

These national figures mask a wide variation in the degree of support, and are further distorted by more generous grant-aid of day nursery provision in the Eastern Health Board region. Nationally, grants to individual day care centres (nurseries and playgroups) ranged from a low of £666 per centre, or £20 per child per annum, in the North Eastern Health Board to £15,828 per centre, or £440 per child per annum, in the Eastern Health Board (ibid).

The gradual engagement of the Department of Health in this area, first in the role of funding and then in the role of regulation, is due to a number of influences. There was, for example, the emergence of day care facilities in the voluntary sector and the example set by the Eastern Health Board in the early 1970s in offering financial assistance to selected centres in its region. Then, there was the impact of the Rutland Street project, begun in 1969, and comparable initiatives abroad which sought to establish day care as an essential contribution to combating the effects of poverty among children. The converging recommendations, especially on the question of regulation of centres, of successive official reports played a part; these reports include the Commission on the Status of Women (1972), Task Force on Child Care Services (1981) and Working Party on Child Care Facilities for Working Parents (1983). Finally, the Department's own conviction that day care represented a feasible form of preventive child care — economically and operationally — seems a major factor in the development of the service.

From the Department's vantagepoint, day care had many attractions. Costs to the health service were relatively low, grants could be spread widely and, by mobilising the obvious grassroot commitment, funds invested could be converted easily at local level into immediate, useful and visible activity on behalf of deprived children.

On the question of regulatory powers, the Department finally set up a committee in 1983 to advise it on the content of possible regulations. The committee made recommendations on compulsory registration for services operating on a full day basis, staffing ratios, training requirements for personnel, the administration of the proposed system of registration and the importance of parent and community involvement in the operation of centres (Department of Health, 1985). The Child Care Act 1991 contains provisions to allow for the regulation and supervision of various aspects of 'pre-school services'.

Day Nurseries
In a study of eleven State-supported day nurseries in the Eastern Health Board region, Hayes (1983) found opening hours varied from six to ten hours per day. Five nurseries opened for less than eight hours, which meant that they were unable to meet the needs of a parent working full time. Only one nursery was open

throughout the year, with most taking at least six weeks (and in one case, ten weeks) holidays over the year. These periods of closure would also seriously affect working parents, or children for whom full day care was considered as the last alternative before admission to full-time care. In most nurseries, children were in the age group 2-5 and at least some had been referred by social services (all, in the case of six nurseries).

Hayes found 'a service that, in the majority of cases, contained, rather than stretched, the children attending'. She concedes that her findings suggest that the service provided is 'successful in achieving the short-term goals of offering a stable and secure environment to children, while relieving parents of stress'. In her view, the service fails to reach its full effectiveness due to a variety of problems. She found a lack of clarity about the role of both service and staff, resulting in an emphasis on care at the expense of more educational and developmental work which might benefit the children attending in important ways. With some more structured daily programmes, children might gain a great deal more from their day care experience. She also found problems in relation to funding and an absence of minimum standards, of guidelines for good practice and of advisory support to staff. Furthermore, she found a need for greater emphasis on parental involvement as a means of maximising the benefit of the nursery care for children.

Playgroups

Playgroups provide pre-school children with an opportunity for supervised and social play. Some 20,774 children (mostly 3-5 year olds) attend a total of 1,514 playgroups in Ireland (Irish Pre-School Playgroups Association, 1990). Each playgroup is usually open for a period of two to three hours per day. Barnardo's Irish Division (1985) found that 'while the home provides the first play environment, the pre-school playgroup, in providing play facilities in a group setting, answers the child's need for a gradual, gentle transition from the home to the school environment'.

The majority of playgroups tend to be run on a business basis from private homes or the like. The remaining 15.2% of playgroups are community playgroups (Irish Pre-School Playgroups Association, 1990). This usually means they are run under the auspices of a local committee or voluntary body and are geared to serving the needs of a local area on a non-profit making basis and to encouraging parental involvement. Barnardo's, (1985, p. 49) reported:

> A community playgroup which is set up, organised and run by parents themselves for their children provides all the advantages of a playgroup, plus the additional benefits of enabling parents to identify and meet the needs of their own children, to increase their own parenting skills by approaching their child and other children in a new way and by working together with other parents to form a nucleus for community development. This aspect has proven particularly important in new and/or disadvantaged housing estates or areas.

It has been suggested that this self-help ethos for playgroups is founded on essentially middle-class assumptions and is inappropriate in working-class districts. Full-time mothers from such areas may lack the energy or skills to run such activities and as Finch (1983) stated, 'if they want pre-school provision to provide a very necessary break from their child, they are hardly likely to welcome the suggestion that they should run it themselves'. This point is echoed in some remarks made to researchers on playgroups in Tallaght (Murphy-Lawless, Redmond & Ungruh, 1989).

If women in disadvantaged areas are to persist in their involvement in community playgroups, they are likely to depend heavily on external support for practical assistance in securing resources for their venture and for encouragement in the face of conflict or adversity. Advisors to community playgroups have played an impressive role in the stimulation and development of such facilities in a number of districts in Dublin (Ballymun, Tallaght, Blanchardstown and various parts of the inner city). Barnardo's (1987) suggested that the adviser's role could include calling meetings of interested parents to establish or maintain a playgroup, weekly visits to existing groups, liaison with relevant outside bodies where necessary on behalf of a playgroup, the organisation of adult education classes as a basis for training of parents involved, attention to committee matters, such as the resolution of conflict or funding matters, and the management of a toy library which can serve the needs of playgroups and perhaps the children in their own homes.

When a community playgroup is established, a playgroup leader is appointed or elected. He or she may be paid a modest stipend. A rota of mothers to help the leader will usually require each mother to assist once a fortnight in order to ensure two helpers for the leader each day. Barnardo's (1985) found that:

> The regime of a typical playgroup consists of a period of free play, during which the leader and helpers may encourage the children to work on specific pieces of equipment. Then there is a period when the children are seated at small tables and a snack, usually milk and biscuits, is served, under supervision, by the child monitors for the day. The leader, or if appropriate one of the parents, takes a short group session in which the children are taught songs or are read to. They are collected by a parent or friend at the end of the session and the leader and helpers clear up for the next playgroup session or user of the premises.

Consumer Views

Parental satisfaction might seem a useful gauge of the adequacy of existing provision. By this criterion, Irish playgroups seem successful, although evidence from some American research suggests that parent-users of different kinds of day care provision are likely to overrate the quality of facilities (Browne, 1984).

In Dublin's inner city and in Tallaght, interviews by Barnardo's researchers (1985) elicited generally favourable feedback from mothers on their perceptions of, and reactions to, the community playgroup services supported by the organisation. In Cork, parents in seven pre-schools were asked for their views on the service (O'Sullivan, 1983). An overwhelming majority saw these facilities as meeting a local need (97.3%) and would recommend their local pre-school to a prospective user (97.9%). There was considerable satisfaction and identification with the pre-school and participation in its work. This seemed (on the basis of teacher assessments) to be positively associated with educational attainment in parents and with the levels of interest in education in the family home, as manifested by child centred activities on the part of parents at home.

O'Sullivan's findings produce interesting echoes of Finch's point (1983) about the middle-class ethos of much pre-school provision. Thus, perhaps those parents with more middle-class practices/aspirations seemed most likely to identify with the Cork pre-schools. The degree of parental identification was also enhanced by the image these pre-schools conveyed. As O'Sullivan (1983, p. 290) noted:

> Because of the use of non-traditional and non-institutional locations, parents had not to cope with the problems of boundary maintenance associated with State schools. There was nothing of the forbidden areas, closed doors or classroom privacy, so typical in accounts of school culture, which serve to curtail the access of non-professionals. Parents freely entered the classroom when delivering or collecting their children, to meet the teacher or to help . . . Parental participation was invited from the outset of the scheme and became an accepted element in the routine of the pre-school.

Talking to parents in Tallaght about their involvement with playgroups Murphy-Lawless *et al* (1989) also found favourable views on their benefits, which accrued not just to the children. As one parent observed (ibid. p. 45):

> You can learn so much from other parents, you know I think we're inclined to feel like people in authority know the answers and we tend to lose our own confidence and our own instincts!

Money problems may prevent families enjoying the benefits of playgroups. Some respondents noted how financial hardship means some parents had to spend the weekly fee of £2.50 on bread and milk instead of sending the child. Parents might be too proud to admit their difficulty (ibid. p. 44).

Irish Day Care — an Overview

Day care places in Ireland are a scarce commodity. The State plays a narrow role, supporting only a small number of full-time day nurseries, mostly in Dublin. It prefers to grant-aid a small proportion of the running costs of a variety of part-time provision, sponsored by various voluntary groups. State-supported places of any kind remain a minority of all day care places.

Reluctant to fund adequately, the State has also been reluctant to regulate. This has had implications not only for the quality of care which children are assured, but also for the working conditions of the women caring for them. Other symptoms of the residual status of the day care field include the problems of getting adequate data about what is actually going on and the relative weakness of attempts by the sector to organise itself. For a useful recent review of such issues, see McKenna (1988).

It seems likely that the quantity of day care places will expand in the coming years. What is less clear is whether there will be a commensurate improvement in the quality of provision. For those concerned with child welfare, the battle for the quality of day care for the pre-school child must be fought hard. Even if it is won, it will be important not to expect that day care alone can magically rescue or protect children from disadvantage in their current or subsequent social experience. Even the most sophisticated pre-school programmes cannot be expected to 'push against the river'. As Clarke and Clarke (1986) observed, 'Pre-school intervention programmes cannot, by themselves, be expected to have dramatic long-term effects in the absence of significant later reinforcers, including parental involvement' (ibid. p. 751).

142

Voluntary Bodies, Voluntary Effort and Children and Families

Historically, voluntary bodies have played a vital role in the development and provision of social services to children and families in Ireland. Until quite recently, State services played a relatively minor role, largely confining themselves to providing a modest legislative and regulatory framework. In the past, it was the religious orders or Protestant voluntary committees that ran schools for the poor, orphanages and hospitals. Organisations such as the ISPCC acted to protect children from neglect and violence. Societies like the St Vincent de Paul sought to provide some kind of financial safety net to poor families.

Traditionally, all these bodies have raised funds quietly from supporters and got on discreetly with the task they had set themselves. However, the climate within which such voluntary bodies operate today has changed dramatically. A number of reasons can be identified:

(1) There has been a change in attitude on the part of the Roman Catholic Church to the role of the State. In the 1960s and '70s, under the influence of Vatican II, there was a dramatic relaxation of Church opposition to a State role in social services. This opposition was most prominent in the celebrated Mother and Child Scheme controversy in 1951 (see Whyte, 1980). By 1972, however, a sub-committee of the Roman Catholic Bishops' Conference recommended a lead role for a government minister in relation to social policy as a whole, together with the establishment of a network of centres under the regional health boards to provide community-based 'personal social services on a family-oriented basis' (Kavanagh, 1972).

(2) Developments in the voluntary sector have been greatly influenced by the success of professionally trained workers in shaping much of the agenda. The 'professionalisation' of the social services has been one of the most striking trends in the social policy arena in the past 20 years. Trained social workers and child care workers have achieved a pre-eminence to the point where such qualifications are a condition of appointment to almost all front-line posts. Increasingly too, the credibility of management personnel depends on the extent of their direct experience and relevant qualifications.

This encroachment of professionalism undoubtedly will bring benefits. But in the case of voluntary organisations, it has often meant the diminution of services and the erosion of traditional autonomy. These voluntary organisations have been acquiescent in the face of a trend towards services delivered by trained full-time personnel, employed on conditions negotiated nationally (by statutory employers). This transition imposed heavy costs, even in the case of religious orders where there was some no-cost labour available for training. In the case of some agencies, many were forced to withdraw from the employment of full-time workers because of the prohibitive expense. In other cases, they came to rely almost completely on unpredictable grant-aid from health boards to pay staff salaries; thus, they found their autonomy and independence greatly compromised.

In the case of religious orders, many withdrew partially or completely from fields of work and/or arranged for their personnel to get training and/or began

143

to recruit trained lay staff. In many instances, the religious found themselves transformed from direct providers to managers of services.

Outside of the religious orders, the voluntary bodies that remained in existence or expanded, did so at the price of heavy reliance on State support, as well as extensive fund-raising from the general public. This creates the problem that policies may be dictated by what will generate the income necessary to sustain expenditure rather than by what service recipients actually require.

The only large-scale voluntary social service organisation to remain largely aloof from this trend of professionalisation is the Society of St Vincent de Paul. This body continues to work through the voluntary effort of its 11,000 members, North and South.

(3) The economic growth and development in the period 1963-74 facilitated a major expansion in the role of the State in welfare planning and provision. This period saw unprecedented State activity in the formulation of policy and the extension and development of a broad range of social services. The health boards were established and a choice of doctor (GP) scheme was introduced for low-income patients. Other innovations included free post-primary education, free school transport and considerable improvements in the range and value of income maintenance schemes under the Department of Social Welfare.

(4) A new and influential generation of voluntary bodies emerged, characterised by a single-issue focus, a campaigning dimension and often an emphasis on self-help principles. The growth of this new generation of voluntary bodies was influenced by a variety of factors. The ferment of social change in the 1960s was felt in Ireland as elsewhere. There was the influence of feminism, a growing awareness of social problems, such as family violence and the isolation of unmarried parents, and an impatience at existing responses, both in the statutory and voluntary sectors. There was also the impact of community development ideas and practice, and the influence of not-unrelated consumer movements in the marketplace. In the social services, all of this prompted a growing awareness of the therapeutic and democratic value of introducing greater involvement by service users partly as a means of ensuring greater accountability on the part of the organisation. Women's Aid (family violence) and Cherish (self-help for unmarried mothers) are examples of this new breed of voluntary body, which combined direct service with sometimes effective pressure group and public education activities.

(5) A number of bodies sprang up, with a co-ordinating role at local or national level, within the voluntary sector and/or between the voluntary and statutory sectors. At a national level, in the field of services to unmarried parents, mental handicap, the disabled generally and all voluntary effort, there has been a growth of co-ordinating mechanisms. Those involved would probably concede frustration at the stubbornly slow progress towards effective planning and support of services despite these mechanisms. Nevertheless, these bodies provide an important forum for the exchange of ideas and thinking, thereby influencing the development of practice and policy in many, often subtle, ways.

At a local level, there was a proliferation of social service councils and centres, inspired by the example of Kilkenny Social Services (Kennedy, 1981) and encouraged by the enthusiasm of the late Erskine Childers, when Minister for Health. Although a number of such councils remain (for example, in Clare, Sligo, Cork and Kilkenny), the concept has failed to realise the hopes invested in it originally. It has become clear that agencies of this kind cannot flourish without a core of exceptionally talented voluntary committee members and/or a 'sponsor', such as a local bishop or statutory administrator who is prepared to take the project under his or her wing. Effective fund-raising is also vital to success.

(6) Media interest in, and public awareness of, social problems are developments that are difficult to quantify, but there has undoubtedly been an explosion, and later perhaps a slight recession, in the level of interest in social problems. This media attention has offered an important platform to the interests of the poor and of others who feel in some way disfranchised in our society. The prospect of scrutiny by television, radio or print journalists also introduces an additional layer of accountability to the decisions of public servants and offers in this context some protection from arbitrary withdrawal of grant assistance to weaker voluntary bodies which may lack the necessary political clout to secure their funding.

Voluntary Sector and Child Welfare Services

The major forces in the voluntary sector in relation to children and families now comprise two larger voluntary agencies, church agencies (religious order and diocesan run) and a plethora of small and, for the most part, single-purpose services. The following brief profiles cover a selection of all of these.

National voluntary bodies

Society of St Vincent de Paul
The society has 10,933 voluntary members active in over 1,000 branches and spent over IR£8.5 million on its various activities in Ireland in 1989 (Society of St Vincent de Paul, 1989). The Irish society is affiliated to the international society which is active in 112 countries. 'No work of charity is foreign to the society' is one of the most favoured slogans within this Roman Catholic organisation. The other strong tradition of the society is the regular personal contact between volunteer members and those (regardless of belief) whom the organisation helps. Its work involving children and families in Ireland (thirty-two counties) includes the visiting of families in their homes; the offering of modest, though often vital, financial assistance to such families; the sponsorship of holiday homes, personal development courses for mothers, youth clubs, half-way housing for unmarried mothers, a neighbourhood based residential unit for children in care from Dublin's inner city, good as new clothing shops, and facilities for the travelling community. The society also sponsors research into social need from time to time, and generally seeks to influence social policy on the basis of the experience of its members.

Daughters of Charity of St Vincent de Paul
This congregation is the largest female religious order in the Roman Catholic tradition. It serves the poor and socially neglected and, in Ireland, its 300 representatives are active in the provision of schools, centres for the mentally handicapped, children's homes and community-based services to support families.

National professional voluntary organisation

The Irish Society for the Prevention of Cruelty to Children
This organisation has its origins in a branch of the (British) NSPCC founded here in 1889. Since 1956, however, the Irish body has been completely autonomous. Formerly, the society's work revolved around child protection undertaken by a corps of locally based uniformed inspectors, known colloquially as the 'cruelty men'. With the establishment of the health boards, and their gradual appointment of social workers with a brief which included child protection, the ISPCC reviewed its function. It decided to embrace a new preventive philosophy and currently it sponsors four family centres, ten therapeutic playschools, a playbus, a day nursery and a national holiday home. The society receives an average of 40 per cent funding from statutory sources for each of its projects, the rest of its costs being met by fundraising efforts (ISPCC, 1987).

During 1988, the society opened a new service, Childline, modelled on its British namesake. Childline offers a confidential telephone service to any child or young person who is in fear of abuse. This initiative has provoked controversy. Its critics believe the remoteness and anonymity of counsel by telephone prevents a sufficiently immediate and sensitive response to a child's plea for help. They also feel that the publicity surrounding the service may arouse exaggerated expectations of the range of help available. Some also fear that it signals a return by the ISPCC to a more traditional, and less preventive, role.

Regional/local professional voluntary organisations

Catholic Social Service Conference (Dublin)
The Conference was founded in 1941 and represents the social services arm of the Roman Catholic Archdiocese of Dublin. Its work has been expanding in recent years and embraces a range of activities relevant to the welfare of children and their families. It sponsors an emergency hostel for homeless children, a number of parish-based community resource centres on housing estates on the periphery of Dublin, and Centrecare, a centre city agency which offers advice, information and support to the homeless and rootless (and to emigrants through its emigrant advice arm). The Conference is also engaged in specialist work in the areas of drugs, AIDS, youth at risk and the travelling people (CSSC, 1988).

Clare Care — Clare Social Service Council
Founded in 1968, this agency operates, through 24 full-time staff and 1,000 volunteers, a range of services to children, families and others. Its services include social work, counselling, home-management support, adoption services, infor-

mation and support to single parents, parenting programmes, pre-school playgroups, playschemes, children's holidays, and services to people with problems of addiction. It receives much of its funding from the Mid-Western Health Board which has chosen to contract out to Clare Care the provision of many of its services in County Clare.

Barnardo's
Founded by a Dubliner, Dr Thomas Barnardo, the organisation's operation in the Republic has expanded in recent years and has become increasingly independent of the international organisation. Its work is still largely confined to the Eastern region but embraces an impressive range of activities: day nurseries, a children's bus, a playgroup advisory service, toy libraries, a neighbourhood resource centre, day foster care, a parents' advisory service, an adoption advice service, as well as youth work, community work and social work.

Single purpose organisation

Women's Aid
This organisation was founded in the mid-1970s to provide emergency accommodation and support to women victims of family violence. It also aimed to highlight the deficiencies in legal and social provision for such women and their children. Its resources include a purpose built shelter which is permanently overcrowded due to demand. Through its support work it helps women to clarify their intentions, and to plan and organise the practicalities of a new life on their own with the children, where no other course seems safe or reasonable. Since 1990, the hostel is managed by the Eastern Health Board, by agreement with the Council of Women's Aid.

Family Link
This modest organisation was founded by a group of workers in community and social services who were concerned at the lack of information and support which the parents of children in care often reported to them. Its main activity has been the production and dissemination of an information booklet (Boland et al, 1987), which has proven of value not only to parents but to professionals. In addition it has led to the establishment of a monthly information and support group in Dublin which is open to anyone related to children in care.

PART III:

WORKING WITH FAMILIES AND CHILDREN

Chapter 8

WORKING WITH FAMILIES
AND CHILDREN

In beginning their work with a child or a family, it is essential that professionals remember that their role carries powerful meanings for the client. In the client's eyes, the social worker or other professional has considerable power to influence decisions about the fate and destiny of the client and his or her family. The client may attribute meanings to the role and actions of the worker which may go far beyond what is actually intended. The client's attitudes will be coloured by previous contact with professionals and services, and by the attitudes current in his or her family or social network towards them. Perhaps the children of a relative or neighbour were taken into care in disputed circumstances, following what appeared to the people concerned as innocuous visits from a social worker. Subsequent contact with social workers is likely to be overshadowed by the fear that a repeat operation is the real agenda of the social worker despite all claims to the contrary. To have a social worker calling, or to be in contact with the psychiatric services in a particular community, may be a source of embarrassment, where the local custom is to sort out problems without the help, or interference, of strangers or officialdom.

It is important for professionals, therefore, to be sensitive to the often unspoken fears and anxieties which contact may arouse in clients. The clients may have very good reason, from personal or cultural experience, to interpret professional intentions sceptically. To engage clients successfully, it is necessary to start where they are. An essential stage in that process is trying to decipher the particular meanings for them of professional intervention, given their history and culture.

The client is likely to begin to engage fully in a relationship with a professional where he or she feels respected in a fundamental way, where his or her culture, values and personal experiences are accepted as real and meaningful irrespective of how they may diverge from the expectations of the professional. It is not necessary for the worker to approve of the adaptations and responses clients may have made to their particular personal circumstances. Indeed, it would be wrong for the worker to offer such approval where it patently was bogus. But it is necessary to acknowledge that generally clients have made choices in good faith in response to all the factors impinging on them, however inappropriate that decision may seem in the eyes of the professional.

Successful empathy by a professional with a client's circumstances will often require imagination and sensitivity in order to transcend social differences, which may include social class, age, gender, ethnic and cultural grouping, marital status and life experience. All of these factors represent potential barriers to an effective relationship, quite apart from the subtle chemistry of temperaments and personalities that facilitates or inhibits the general course of relationships.

The professional needs to be sensitive not only to decisive details in the culture, personal biography and family history of the client. She also needs to be alert to the precipitating circumstances that have resulted in their encounter at this, rather than any other, time. For some, the role of client will be familiar, for others new and uncomfortable. In many instances, a crisis in the client's life may force a search for help. The professional will need to be familiar with the patterns of coping that people commonly use in the face of crisis. While a crisis may seem, initially at least, overwhelming to the client, it also represents an opportunity to forge changes in perceptions and patterns of behaviour which may endure beyond the crisis and prevent its recurrence (O'Hagan, 1986).

In seeking fruitful contact between families and professionals, the following propositions or assumptions may prove helpful:

- Parenting is a complex and stressful task.
- Parents generally want to be good parents.
- Most parents experience serious difficulty some of the time.
- Some parents experience serious difficulty most of the time.
- Difficulties usually arise from an unfavourable interaction between personal (biographical, temperamental, marital) factors and environmental factors (inadequate economic and other resources).
- Every family has strengths and resources, which may often go unrecognised and untapped.
- Parents often experience professional intervention as haphazard, and/or disjointed, and/or impersonal, and/or patronising, and/or paternalistic, and/or blaming.
- Families will respond best to intervention which they experience as relevant and helpful and to workers, whom they feel like them and enjoy them.
- Successful families are not just those which subscribe to, or conform to, middle class values, of the kind espoused by most professionals.
- A relevant intervention in the lives of families will strive to:
    - start where the parents are;
    - engage their interest, understanding, co-operation and commitment;

- address personal and environmental sources of stress;
- be intelligible, practical and realistic;
- harmonise with and respect the past experiences, expectations, cultural customs and norms of the family.
- In relating to the family professionals should:
  - get to 'know' the family beyond the problems and symptoms;
  - see the family as an entity and the symptoms it presents as serving a definite function in the family's preservation;
  - look to the future rather than the past;
  - demonstrate trust;
  - seek opportunities to affirm and praise the family in its efforts to cope and survive;
  - seek to build confidence;
  - partialise problems and select most promising tasks for early attention;
  - negotiate rather than prescribe, and then articulate the ingredients of a plan or contract which allocates feasible tasks to family and worker, the execution of which are to be reviewed regularly at subsequent meetings;
  - ensure that any resulting steps to be followed are explained clearly and simply, with each side feeding back to the other in concrete terms their understanding of their allotted tasks;
  - avoid professional jargon or over-complicated language;
  - seek out resources in the family's wider kinship and community networks which might help supplement and perhaps ultimately replace the worker's efforts;
  - be prepared to 'reach out' to nurture the family's motivation to use and seek help, rather than require initial motivation as prima facie evidence of capacity to respond to the worker. (It is necessary to avoid colluding with, or enabling, any avoidance of responsibility on the part of the family, while recognising that shaky motivation is itself compelling proof of the family's need for help.);
  - give something of the worker's own self, so that the family can experience the worker's humanity as well as her professionalism;
  - take creative risks as appropriate;
  - have access to adequate professional support.

Prevention

Work to protect and support families and children can be classified as primary or secondary prevention. In the context of child welfare, primary prevention is taken to refer to those activities that reduce risks to the child and support the general coping and functioning of the family. This type of prevention seeks to prevent the actual occurrence of acute problems.

Secondary prevention, on the other hand, addresses problems where they have actually arisen and seeks to reduce their impact by, for instance, pre-empting the need for more serious intervention, such as compulsory reception into care. The goal of secondary prevention is to resolve the crisis in the life of the child or family, so that they may resume 'normal' living as soon as possible.

It is also possible to conceptualise work with families in a number of other ways. In each instance, a particular intervention can be located at some point along the relevant dimension or continuum between two opposing tendencies or poles.

Lay versus professional intervention
While there has been a dramatic professionalising of services to families, the role of lay (i.e. non-professional helpers) remains critically important. Besides the obvious point that family and kin carry the great bulk of caring responsibilities in society, it is also clear that within many different types of organisations lay volunteers continue to play a crucial role. The primacy of volunteers in the influential work of the Society of St Vincent de Paul is one example. The virtual explosion of self-help groups is another, where lay people sharing common troubles or characteristics offer each other peer support and solidarity. The momentum of this movement suggests that it fills a need which professional intervention has left unmet.

Emphasis on therapy versus adult education, community work approaches
It is probably true to say that therapy (i.e. approaches inspired by the traditions of psychoanalysis, psychotherapy, the case work tradition in social work and coun-selling) has had to make room for a model of intervention that understands the needs of individuals and families as deficits in the resources, social skills, social support networks and self-confidence of parents and families, rather than as resulting from particular manifestations of psychopathology in an individual parent or in the marital or family system. The emphasis in this newer approach is on resourcing and empowering families to tackle the stresses and strains in their lives, many of which are seen as entirely predictable consequences of social structures in modern society.

This model has been influenced by ideas from the practice of community development and of the adult education ideas of thinkers such as Paolo Freire (1972a; 1972b). In this tradition, the 'expert' tries to demystify techniques and share them with ordinary people, so that they may be used to awaken people's belief in themselves, their talents and their desire and energy for change in their own lives. It is the people who are seen as having the answers rather than the expert. The contribution of the 'expert' is to create opportunities in which people can explore questions and answers together around issues that they have identified as salient to their lives and prospects.

Emphasis on practical versus psychological support
Professional helping grew out of the traditions of practical charity and material assistance in areas such as housing and income support. An important contribution of professional training and practice was an acknowledgment of the importance of psychological and personality factors in human behaviour. In recent years, there may have been a slight swing-back of the pendulum as many professional helpers rediscover that no amount of insight or other fruits of psychological therapy will necessarily give a father a job in an area of 70 per cent unemployment, nor will it put food on the table for hungry children.

It is, of course, essential not to dismiss the great achievements of psychological approaches. But it is necessary to acknowledge that many variables (personal and environmental) influence a person's capacity to benefit from such therapy. It is now more likely that judiciously blended and individualised mixes of practical and psychological support will form the basis of future approaches.

Intervention with individual cases versus a group focus
Working through groups has become more widespread, a trend which has been prompted by two factors. Firstly, there has been greater appreciation of the practical and psychological value of group work and the possibility that more enduring benefits may result from group-based rather than individually based intervention. Secondly, the apparently universal problem in social services of constantly growing demand, faced by fixed or shrinking supplies of helping resources, renders group intervention more attractive since an obvious economy of scale is possible. More people can be seen in the same period of time and the skills and knowledge of the therapist or social worker can be supplemented by the insight and experience available within the group. It should be noted however that successful group work usually requires a lot of time in recruiting and sustaining the participation of individual members.

Contrasting these opposing tendencies inherent in work with children and families (and all social intervention) may be helpful at a conceptual level. Such distinctions are, however, rarely as clearly discernible in the real world. In practice, one tendency may gradually incorporate influences from its apparent opposite. An example is family therapy: it has been criticised for being excessively clinical in its orientation and for disappearing into spirals of ever-increasing jargon and mystification. While these features may be observable, it is also clear that the ideas of family therapy can be consistent, in principle at least, with the philosophy of community development. Family therapy aspires to help families examine the routines and assumptions of their lives so that they may discover for themselves ways of exerting more influence and choice over their daily round. Rather than accepting as inevitable the deeply ingrained patterns in their lives, the family may be enabled to tackle what previously seemed like intractable problems. Such therapy may free energy and build confidence. Families may be able to harness untapped reserves of their own creativity and power in order to reshape their destiny.

Where this happens, the work of the family therapist may differ from that of the community developer only in terms of the level of direct intervention — one deals with the family, the other with the community. Each may have an impact which can cause ripples in other systems or at other levels. For example, the woman who derives satisfaction, enjoyment and affirmation from her successful initiation as a member of the tenants' committee may become a more assertive and confident parent, and may be able to enjoy more her marriage and other friendships. Similarly, as a result of gains in family therapy a father may not only play a more active part in the parenting of his children, but may also have gained the confidence to participate effectively in community affairs.

Another example of the blurring of conceptual distinctions in practice is the teaching of behavioural techniques of child management to parents (Herbert, 1987). This successful marriage of elements from a clinical and adult education background can produce enduring gains in parents' coping and confidence and in child behaviour.

The lesson of these examples would seem to be that many of the most interesting and exciting programmes of intervention and support in relation to families are likely to be quite eclectic in their style and theoretical foundations. This is not a sign of woolliness, but more likely a logical response to the diversity of family needs and patterns.

A British specialist in the needs of families, De'Ath (1983, pp 33-4), has prescribed a series of elements which she suggests should constitute a framework for helping families in the future. To be supportive and helpful, such a framework needs to acknowledge and encompass:

- family diversity: a range of flexible measures to meet the specific needs of different types of families;
- a universal minimum income to ensure that a family's resources are adequate to meet the demands for an accepted minimum standard of living;
- a reassessment of employment patterns and obligations to give family life greater priority;
- the promotion of a family perspective in community health and of family involvement in the development of community resources and facilities;
- the promotion of self-confidence, self-esteem and self-reliance in the families to encourage them to make their own decisions and take responsibility for their own lives, providing help which gives them control over the situation rather than making them dependent;
- the development of personal and social skills in schools to help equip individuals with the knowledge to anticipate problems and the skills to cope with them, and to encourage a greater understanding of personal relationships.

Family Support: Techniques, Services and Projects

Lay intervention

Some of the most interesting initiatives in the development of support services to families in recent years have not involved 'high tech' clinical therapies. Rather, they have mobilised the energy and commitment of volunteers and of members of family networks to provide support to families through one-to-one relationships or through the leadership of support groups for parents. The contribution of the professionals, be they social workers, public health nurses or health visitors, is to support and supervise the volunteers.

Volunteers as 'Family Friends'
One of the best known initiatives in the area of family support is the British 'Home Start', which began in 1974 (Van der Eyken, 1982). Volunteers receive training and are matched to families who are experiencing, often quite serious, stress. These volunteers get supervision from a scheme organiser and have access to a

support group. The scheme aims to build the confidence of parents, in the expectation that this will produce a spin-off for the child in terms of more positive parenting. The volunteer is to encourage verbal and physical contact between mother and child, opportunities for play, the independence of mother and child, and the use by the mother of local resources. The first scheme in Leicester has been emulated successfully many times. Here in Ireland, one opened in 1989 in Blanchardstown with National Lottery funding for the full-time scheme organiser and organisational costs, and there are also a number of schemes in Northern Ireland.

'Newpin' is another British scheme, operating in South London as a home-visiting and befriending service, broadly corresponding with Home Start (Pound and Mills, 1985; Dowling, 1983). Newpin has a drop-in centre which participants are encouraged to use. The scheme relies on volunteers recruited from the local working-class community, in addition to a full-time organiser. It offers play facilities and group meetings.

Since 1982, Swedish social service law provides for 'contact persons' and 'contact families'. 'Contact persons' offer assistance and support to children, young people or adults in difficulty, through companionship, recreational trips or help in dealing with public authorities. 'Contact families' might help mind young children for a family for a weekend every three or four weeks. This purely voluntary (i.e. non-compulsory) mechanism has a preventive purpose and replaces earlier compulsory supervisory functions given to these lay people in legislation first enacted in 1902. People doing this contact work receive a nominal allowance, plus expenses (Gould, 1988, pp 77-98).

In the United States, child abuse programmes have included schemes to match volunteers to families where child abuse has been a problem. It has been suggested that volunteers who are older than the parents in their contact family may be in a position to 're-parent' the younger family, who in a sense are seen as being 'apprenticed' to the volunteer in what is intended to become a 'natural helping relationship' (Withey et al, 1980). One of these schemes, in Dallas, offers a comprehensive role to its volunteers, including activities in relation to public education (Rosenstein, 1978).

An American study (Ballew, 1985) examined the role of 'natural helpers' in the prevention of child abuse and neglect. Despite possible hazards, the author argued that such members of a family's network offer a potentially valuable source of support to the client and a supplement to professional intervention which may well be more enduring than that provided by professionals. It has also been suggested that natural helping networks can represent initially unlikely, but ultimately important, sources of information to professionals. In this way, culturally inept interventions can be avoided and the interest and concern of such natural helpers may be mobilised to assist people in need in local communities.

In Scotland, a volunteer scheme to ease the problems of isolation among single-parent families yielded real improvements in the families benefiting, when compared with a control group of such families which did not receive the service (Humphries, 1976).

In many of the schemes involving lay people as volunteers, there is not necessarily any attempt to match the volunteer visitor and the family visited in terms of culture and social class. There has been an interesting programme in the Dublin area in which experienced local mothers offer to visit first-time mothers within walking distance of their homes (Barker *et al*, 1987). In a four- year period, 500 'new' mothers benefited in the areas where this 'Community Mother' initiative was in operation. The experienced mothers are selected and trained by public health nurses, who themselves have trained in and operated the health education programme. The nurses relay the programme through the Community Mothers. The programme involves the use of non-directive techniques and a series of humorous cartoons, designed to stimulate discussion and reflection on health matters such as nutrition.

Leadership of Support Groups by Volunteers

There have been a number of initiatives in the development of local support groups for parents which rely on volunteer leadership. As in the case of one-to-one contact schemes, these volunteers have received training and have regular access to supervision and/or group support. In some cases, volunteer leaders may be recruited from among the ranks of group participants.

'Scope' is a Southampton-based scheme which runs a network of locally based support groups for parents. These groups are supplemented by home visits, a creche and toy library, facilities for short recuperative breaks for parents, training opportunities for volunteer group convenors and training in work with children for secondary school students and others interested (Poulton, 1982).

In London, the voluntary agency 'Cope' has promoted the operation of local activity and discussion-based groups for parents. The emphasis is on recruiting local talent to act as group leaders and also as play leaders (to provide care for the children while parents are absorbed in discussion). Dating back to the 1950s, these groups number more than forty (Cowan, 1982). At one phase in their development, some of these groups have been the subject of an EC-funded action research project (Knight *et al*, 1979).

'Chat' (Contact, Health and Teaching) is a network of post-natal support groups in an outer London borough. The first group emerged on the initiative of middle-class women, concerned to reduce social isolation among parents of young children. The 'Chat' network is reported to have grown to 28 groups and to have successfully involved working-class mothers in their own working-class or socially mixed groups, while achieving a high degree of attendance and enjoyment among group members (Hiskins, 1981).

In Ireland, a support group for isolated parents began with the help of a volunteer (who happened also to be a foster mother) in the Terenure/Harolds Cross area of Dublin. She undertook this work in conjunction with the local community care social work team.

Marriage Counselling

There is a strong tradition in Ireland of marriage counselling undertaken by volunteers. The two organisations engaged in this work broadly reflect familiar denominational divisions — the Catholic Marriage Advisory Council and the

Marriage Counselling Service. Besides offering remedial counselling where problems flare up in a relationship, both agencies are engaged in preventive work in the area of pre-marriage courses and in public education work through schools and other channels.

Community Information Centres
A significant innovation in the social service field in the past two decades has been the proliferation of a network of 80 community information centres staffed by trained volunteers. The development, training and information needs of these centres have been serviced by the National Social Service Board. An analysis of the work undertaken in one such centre — in Tallaght — has been published by Lavan (1981).

A role in the Juvenile Justice System
There is a tradition of involvement by volunteers in probation services in a number of countries. In Ireland, this was a feature in the 1940s (McCarthy, 1945). While the tradition may have lapsed here, it remains a significant feature of the service in other countries. In Sweden, for example, there are 8,000 volunteer lay supervisors attached to probation officers in order to assist them in their work, although most young people in trouble are processed under child welfare rather than probation provisions (Swedish Institute 1981).

In the celebrated Scottish system of juvenile justice, three lay volunteers decide cases where children or young people have been referred because of their own offences or because of a need for compulsory care or protection. This lay panel, which in each sitting must include both sexes, is advised by a Reporter (a full-time legal official). Hearings are conducted with the minimum of formality. This involvement of lay volunteers introduces important checks and balances into the decision making system, and also disseminates more widely through society greater understanding and support for the needs of young people in difficulty.

Professional Intervention with Emphasis on Counselling/Therapy
Social Casework
Social casework is the traditional method of social work. In its early form, it grew from the traditions of voluntary visiting and housing welfare work with the poor. It was also influenced strongly by psychoanalytic ideas. Like other institutions, social casework did not escape the cultural changes in Western society in the 1960s. More liberal thinking and greater preoccupation with broader political and philosophical issues meant that any casework with a dominant focus on individual psychopathology fell somewhat out of favour. Social work began to absorb influences from various growth therapies and from group work, community development and adult education.

Family therapy
Of the newer forms of therapy, family therapy has perhaps been the most influential in the helping services. There are many schools within the ambit of

family therapy but all share the ideas of:

- a focus on the family system as a unit for understanding dynamics and processes within the constituent and aggregate relationships which make up the family;
- a common preference to see the family together at least at some stage during the period of intervention;
- a calculation that interventions, in particular sub-systems (e.g. the marital relationship) should and will have an effect on other sub-systems within the family and possibly on other social systems to which the family relates;
- a heavy or almost total reliance on assessing here-and-now interactions in therapy sessions as a metaphor for divining and influencing the pattern of relationships within the family system.

Marital Therapy

Traditionally, marriage counselling or marital therapy has proceeded from a psychotherapeutic premise through which it was hoped that the marriage might be repaired as a result of the intervention. The more modern view takes the line that the partners might be enabled to make a clear decision about where their future lies in relation to each other. These newer approaches of mediation and conciliation are more influenced by legal and industrial relations models, which place less emphasis on healing (as in therapies) and more on the orderly administration of matters of mutual interest. Thus, the task is to enable the negotiations to be conducted in a low key, less-charged atmosphere. Focusing on the future often frees warring partners sufficiently to make more constructive use of these services than they might have been willing to make of more traditional counselling approaches. Many couples perceive the latter as more connected with raking over the past and re-opening old wounds.

Family Mediation

A development in services to couples in conflict is the pilot Family Mediation Service funded by the Department of Justice. It offers a mediation service — not a counselling or legal aid service. With the help of trained mediators who remain neutral, couples can be enabled to negotiate constructively the terms of their separation or future relationship. Typically the mediation aims to bring about agreement on questions relating to custody of/access to the children, maintenance, disposal of property etc.

Community Development/Adult Education Interventions

Interventions in this tradition differ from those in the clinical or therapeutic vein since they are more likely to assume capacity rather than incapacity on the part of the people towards whom the intervention is directed. Their focus has always been on identifying and building resources rather than searching out and treating pathology.

In addition, this tradition takes account of influences from systems theory and comparable thinking which, in this instance, emphasises the importance for the functioning of children and families in the context, or ecology, in which they find themselves. By strengthening the collective identity, social networks and resource stock of a family's community, it is believed that the family itself will benefit from this richer fabric of community life.

Many working-class families depend on public authorities for their housing. Traditionally, the response of local authorities has been to build large estates and then to allocate those vacant units to families on the waiting list. This often means that families are thrown together in an area new to them and far away from relatives and other supports. In addition to losing familiar contacts, they find themselves among strangers, often at a stage when the mother is tied down at home in the task of minding toddlers. Thus, her scope for maintaining links with her old networks or actively building new ones is limited by child-minding responsibilities, by the cost and inadequacy of public transport facilities (which tend to be sparse in such new areas) and perhaps also by her wavering self-confidence which can inhibit attempts at making new friendships or availing of new social outlets.

Community work in Ireland has strong rural roots, but it is in suburban working-class estates, as well as in run-down inner city areas, that much of today's community work is practised. Community work, despite its broad canvas in principle, is in practice often concerned with addressing the needs of children and families. It may be seeking to fill gaps in infrastructure left by a planning process which fails to co-ordinate the development of other facilities and services to complement the new housing stock.

Two studies document the problems of developing, mobilising and co-ordinating community resources over which people have a meaningful say. From Limerick, Counihan (1979), a social worker and a nun, describes efforts to identify and address community needs in what was to become the largest housing estate in the country — Southill. From Cork, Linehan (1984), a local curate, describes the rich variety of effort emanating from within a more established and more socially mixed community and the frustrations involved in trying to elicit coherent and sufficient responses to this indigenous activity from public bodies.

Community work (see pp 112-14, section on Community Worker) as a method need not be confined to communities or neighbourhoods. It can also be used to render services and institutions more accessible and responsive to the needs of those they serve. One Australian agency undertook a major shift of power within its family centre (Liffman, 1978). This sometimes difficult process has been written up in a challenging account of how formerly quite dependent clients finally assumed roles of power and influence in the direction of the agency. Closer to home, there has been an interesting experiment in the East End of London in which local people were employed to staff a family centre (Wilmott and Mayne, 1983).

Health Education
Parentcraft classes are increasingly offered by maternity hospitals to assist prospective parents to prepare or refresh themselves for their new role. There have also been attempts to offer support to prospective and new mothers at local community level. In Darndale, the ISPCC family centre has run a maternity group geared to the needs of women in the late months of pregnancy and the early

months after childbirth (Nic Giolla Choille, 1985). It grew out of a concern to improve attendance rates by local women at post-natal check-ups. It avoided presenting women who attended with a programmed set of classes, but instead offered the group meeting as an opportunity for the women to explore and define their own needs for information and support in relation to the experiences of pregnancy, childbirth and child-rearing. These maternity groups produced spin-offs for the agency as well, in that they spawned a family-planning group and groups for mothers and toddlers and for single mothers.

In Belfast, a campaign to increase the use of post-natal and baby clinic facilities used a community survey to elicit local perceptions and levels of knowledge of existing services (Kilpatrick and Mooney, 1987). A resulting publicity campaign deliberately used influential images and colours, the re-arranging and upgrading of previously drab clinic facilities and the offer of a cup of tea, all of which produced a threefold increase in the level of take-up of the service.

In France, the authorities encourage people to use ante-natal services by tying entitlement to children's allowance payments to attendance at such services.

In the Eastern Health Board region, a mobile health clinic has been delivering services to the travelling community since July 1985 (Committee to Monitor the Implementation of Government Policy on Travelling People, 1987). The take-up of services is impressive and members of the travelling community have collaborated in the production of a series of six videos which constitute part of the health education programme offered by the clinic.

Group Work and the Mental Health Needs of Women

Women are at greater risk of depression than men, according to Cullen and Morrissey (1987). One British study found that working-class women are five times more likely to be depressed than their middle-class counterparts (Brown, Ní Bhrolcháin and Harris, 1975). Another British study found that 39% of mothers with a child with a behavioural problem and 26% of mothers with 'normal' children were depressed (Richman, 1977). The same researcher found that 41% of mothers with two children under three living on a council housing estate were depressed (Richman, 1974). The problems of loneliness, isolation and depression were more marked among those mothers who were living in flats rather than in houses.

An Irish research study has found cases of depression in 17.9% of a random sample (n = 75) of inner city women (Cleary, 1985). The same study revealed a high degree of service-utilisation among the sample: over half the women (53.8%) had consulted professional services for psychiatric reasons at some time, while 33% were currently taking psychotropic drugs (40% had done so at some point in their lives). On the basis of her findings, Cleary suggested that the use of groups would be an appropriate intervention in these women's lives — both in the case of women with acute depression, and as a preventive measure for all women.

In this context, Cleary (ibid. p. 316) suggests that groups which allow a sharing of common problems and encourage assertiveness would be preferable to drug-based treatment. Ultimately, however, the answer lies in prevention rather than treatment. Women need a contemporary method to help them deal with contemporary problems and this should be based in their own community. Older networks of assistance, such as the extended family, are no longer available to many women. In a changing society, artificial support systems are required and this could be done by creating a network of community self-help groups for women.

Cleary also examined the origins of depression in a sample of patients attending a clinic for depression and concludes that depression (of the reactive type) can be seen as a learned 'response of helplessness' (p. 315).

Overall, Cleary's findings indicate that women who develop depression do so because their background has left them more vulnerable psychologically, less able to withstand assaults to their self-esteem and more likely to resort to a passive, or non-active, response to problems; this becomes their pattern when dealing with the issues of their lives (ibid, p. 315).

Support groups for women at community level may often prove to be support groups for mothers only, with a focus on domestic and child-care issues. This pre-occupation has been the subject of criticism (Morrissey, 1982). Perhaps taking account of this view, the ISPCC Family Centre in Cork has run a group for its female clients, who presumably are mothers also, on women's rather than mothers' issues (Nic Giolla Choille, 1984).

If women grow in self-esteem and in their capacity for assertiveness, this should diminish the risk of depression and the resulting gains should spill over into the various roles in their lives. Since children of depressed mothers carry a greater risk of developing depressive or other psychiatric symptoms themselves (Earls, 1987), it is clearly desirable, even purely from the child's perspective, that maternal depression be prevented or lifted. Remembering Cleary's view of the importance of developing self-confidence for women and also noting her finding that social isolation was more marked among the women who were depressed, it would seem to follow that personal development courses and support groups for women have an important contribution to make to their mental health and that ultimately in the case of mothers, such gains will be relayed to their children. In the Tallaght area of Dublin, Barnardo's have run two twice-weekly support groups, each with a different style reflecting the varying interests and priorities of the women participating (Mental Health Association of Ireland, 1987).

Also in Tallaght, there is an example of the use of personal development courses which are an increasingly common vehicle for raising self-esteem and widening the social networks of women previously absorbed in child rearing, often in daunting social and economic circumstances (ibid. pp 23-4). The opportunities, possibly for the first time, to discuss and reflect on personal concerns in a safe and sympathetic context, the enjoyment of shared activities and the invigorating experience of discovering solidarity with women in 'much the same boat' can be a potent force for growth in the lives of the people involved.

In 1987, the Combat Poverty Agency funded 18 local programmes throughout the country in which 355 women participated. These programmes attracted funding because they included in their aims and objectives some or all of the following: personal development, leadership development, development of group, and awareness of wider community needs and education. Typically, programmes were sited in communities with high social need and limited services. The context varied but there was an emphasis in all programmes on learning together in a relaxed atmosphere, with knowledge being drawn from within the group and from outside resources. A review of these programmes concluded that they had 'a substantial personal impact on those who participated' (McVeigh, 1988). This claim is strongly corroborated from the personal testimonies of participants in one such course in Dublin's north inner city (Nic Giollaphádraig, 1988).

Parenting Education

If parenting is a complex task and if the skills it demands are not necessarily available intuitively or innately to parents, then it follows that professionals may be able to help equip parents for the task. Preparation for parenthood obviously begins, unconsciously, in childhood experiences but increasingly, in the UK at least, formal educational provision at school and adult education level covers content of this nature (Pugh and De'Ath, 1984). Besides such a general preventive approach, it is possible to teach behaviour management skills to parents, to help them cope with the everyday difficulties that arise in child-rearing. Work of this kind has been done in Belfast (McAuley and McAuley, 1980) and in Leicester (Herbert, 1988).

In Ballymun, members of the local child guidance team have contributed to various local training courses on child development, including a five-session course at the request of a group of mothers with children in a particular playgroup. This latter experience proved rewarding — and challenging — for the professionals concerned and left one worker, at least, convinced of the value of such sharing of professional knowledge and skills (Scanlan, 1985).

In the field of mental handicap, impressive progress has been made by the St Michael's House agency in Dublin in providing programmes of education for parents with mentally handicapped children. An independent evaluation of a six-session programme found that mothers reported greater play and other activity among their children and more enthusiasm about their interaction all round with their child (McConkey, 1987).

Building Community Resources

Developing an infrastructure of supports for children and families at community level does not necessarily mean the provision of expensive buildings devoted exclusively to this purpose. In addition, such resources need not even be confined to fixed premises.

Playbus

The playbus is a concept which has been successfully employed by Barnardo's in the Dublin region. Two double decker buses are used as part of the Mobile Education Project to bring precious day care experience to children in areas where no such provision or facilities exist. By stimulating the interest and commitment of local parents, and by lending support, the playbus is intended to serve as a catalyst for the growth of a local playgroup with a permanent base of its own. The playbuses are also used to provide facilities on three halting/housing sites for children of the travelling community (M. Clarke, 1987; Barnardo's, 1979 and 1985).

Toy Library

Another example of an effective resource which is not necessarily confined to a fixed base is the toy library which is operated by Barnardo's in the Tallaght, Blanchardstown, the north and south inner city areas of Dublin, and with the traveller community in the Dublin region. The service first grew in the Tallaght area, where it began as a service to parents using the community playgroups. In Tallaght community playgroups, parent and toddler groups and families who have children with special needs (or where there are difficulties in the parent child relationship) may borrow from the toy library which is based in a local neighbourhood resource centre; in Blanchardstown the service is located in a health centre and is open to playgroups, infant and special classes, and families with pre-school children; in the inner city areas there is a toy lending service to community groups active in these areas.

In Tallaght and Blanchardstown, there is a weekly session where participating parents can meet each other or the organiser to discuss matters relating to their child's development generally. In Tallaght there is a limited mobile service operated from an estate car for families who for reasons of distance or other adversity are unable to attend the weekly sessions; some home visiting is also undertaken in Blanchardstown. Besides offering support and advice and the lending of toys, staff hope to remind parents that expensive toys are not necessary to their child's development and that often the most valuable play can arise from the imaginative use of everyday household items (Barnardo's, 1986).

Playschemes

Since the early seventies there has been a growing trend towards the organising of summer playschemes in local communities. These are meant to provide recreational opportunities for young people during school holidays and usually consist of a series of events, ranging from outings, through sports competitions, to activities based on arts and crafts as well as films and the possible mounting of concerts or the like. In some areas, local authorities may give grant aid towards the cost of full time staffing of the scheme, although more usually any grants that may be available will be payable towards a modest share of the running expenses. In all instances there is heavy reliance on the voluntary effort of local parents and older young people. Besides easing school holiday tedium and providing a constructive social outlet for children, these schemes can offer welcome relief to harassed parents and may help stimulate community identity and cohesion. The positive effects of a local playscheme instigated by staff of the ISPCC Family Centre, Wexford were commented on favourably by local residents who credited it with generating precious enthusiasm, confidence and identity among adults on the estate and offering important informal educational opportunities to local children (Nic Giolla Choille, 1983).

While playschemes or summer projects can yield many positive spin-offs and may even provide from their activists the nucleus of a committee for a local community group, their outcome is not necessarily always favourable. The success of such playschemes depends on the quality of interest within the local community and the degree of organisation and financial support available, especially in communities unversed in the mechanics of managing such a venture. There must also be a question as to whether parents have much surplus energy or even the confidence to undertake in large numbers the organisation and leadership roles demanded by the current model of playschemes. Despite a tradition of interesting scheme activities (with low participation fees) and financial and training support at an organisational level, Linehan reports problems of take up in a playscheme in the Cork suburb of Mayfield. He attributes these problems 'to financial constraints on families, and a climate of apathy, together with the problem of recruiting leaders' (D. Linehan, 1984).

Playgrounds

In the Dublin area there are a number of playcentres (supervised playgrounds) which are under the direct control of Dublin Corporation or run on an agency basis on its behalf by the Catholic Youth Council (the Archdiocesan youth service body). By and large these centres have not had a great deal of capital investment in recent times and certainly do not reflect the most modern thinking in relation to the development of playgrounds. In addition to playgrounds there are also a series of playlots (play areas) usually consisting of a modern supply of swings and other play furniture. Because of their unsupervised nature and their frequent location on the fringe of housing developments, these are often subject to vandalism. This 'tarmac and ironmongery' approach to play provision has been criticised not least on the grounds of lack of responsiveness to children's real play needs, the lack of attention to safety problems posed by the equipment and surfaces used and the quality of maintenance in the face of vandalism (S. Andrews and C. O'Connor, 1980). The authors of the only Irish book on play facilities compare Irish play facilities with the lively tradition of imaginative play provision in Denmark and argue strongly for a much broader conception of what really constitutes space for play:

> Parents and community groups must resist the temptation to accept the 'tarmac and ironmongery' eyesore as a valid play facility. It isn't. There are so many playground formats to choose from — the junk playground on the derelict site, the Danish style adventure playground, or the Swedish Playpark which incorporates playspace for both children and adults (ibid. p. 125).

Despite this advice, general play provision still conforms largely to the 'tarmac and ironmongery' style, but there have been more encouraging developments recently. There are some imaginatively designed playgrounds, provided by Dublin County Council or the Office of Public Works in the Dublin region, and one by private enterprise — the Trabolgan Holiday Centre in east Cork. All use high quality wooden designs and general layout to generate facilities which are extremely popular with consumers and their parents! It is to be hoped that such provision will be expanded, with special attention to the needs of children from low-income working class families. One other field where imaginative playgrounds have been developed is in the mental handicap services provided by, for instance, the St. John of God Brothers (ibid. pp 66-82).

Local Resource Centres

Local Centres

There has been a growing tendency to locate resource centres for families at local neighbourhood level. Local centres are more accessible for families and can serve as a convenient bridge between families and a range of services and resources which families may commonly need.

Broadly these centres share a number of common characteristics or intentions, viz.

- open access
- site within pram pushing distance of local catchment area
- broad preventive orientation
- non-stigmatising ethos
- multiple use
- prominence of group work/activities

These local centres can provide a convenient meeting point for local people with common concerns and a handy point of contact between various professional services and the local community. It may be the meeting place for a local mother and toddler group; it may house some of a local social worker or GPs clinics; it may be the venue of the local playgroup or a community advice or information service; it may host meetings of AA, of foster parents, of youth groups, or of adults with common pre-occupations — single parents, or parents with handicapped children.

These centres come in many shapes and sizes and in their development have anticipated or reflected the recommendations of the Task Force on Child Care Services. The Task Force suggested that the exact form a 'neighbourhood resource centre' would take would depend on local need and existing provision. Its function would be

> to mobilise community resources on behalf of children and their families and, by combining the resources of the community, voluntary organisations, [and the relevant statutory authorities] to maximise their impact on the wellbeing of children and families in the area (Task Force on Child Care Services, 1981, p. 145).

While it should help match families in need to the necessary resources and professional skills, it should also embrace non-stigmatising activities or services such as a toy library or launderette, so that families which are associated with the centre are not automatically labelling themselves as having serious problems. If this stigma were not prevented families might avoid contact to protect their reputation or might have their dwindling morale further undermined.

The rich diversity of provision which conforms broadly to this concept is due not only to differing local conditions, but also to factors such as premises, budget, sponsoring agency and its philosophy, and whether the centre has its own staff. Writing on comparable local family centres in the UK, Holman (1987) has distinguished between a neighbourhood model of provision and a community development model. Both have a local focus, but in the former the emphasis is on services provided directly by staff, whereas in the latter, the staff's role is much less direct and is concerned with stimulating locally led activities within the centre. In practice he concedes these distinctions may become blurred but it is probably helpful to consider his conceptualisation in the context of neighbourhood resource centres here.

A small number of centres are run directly by health boards and these tend to have two to four staff members of their own. In some other instances health boards may put a premises at the disposal of a voluntary group or committee. More commonly these centres are sponsored by voluntary bodies with or without the ongoing support of the local health board. In these cases centres may be staffed (usually on a modest scale). Alternatively, they may be run largely by voluntary labour under the auspices of a management committee which may have at least the part-time services of a community worker whose full-time brief extends to other matters in the community or to a much wider catchment area.

The nature of the premises used may vary. In a limited number of cases a purpose built premises may be provided by the local health board. One example of this would be a local Pre-school Family Centre opened by the Southern Health Board on the Mahon peninsula in Cork in 1983. Its operation is co-ordinated by a health board community worker and the activities it houses include playgroups, mother and toddler groups, youth groups, and keep fit classes. The Centre operated in close conjunction with a Family Development Project which is run on the Estate by the Little Sisters of the Assumption (P. Berwick and M. Burns (eds), 1984). In Granard, Co. Longford, the Midland Health Board has provided a purpose built premises and a grant towards the salary of a full-time community worker whose brief includes a role in the management of the resource centre which is intended to serve all age groups in the local community (Midland Health Board Community Care Programme 1987).

More typically health boards will undertake, or assist in, the adaptation of an existing premises for use as a resource centre. In Dublin, the Eastern Health Board has undertaken such conversion for centres it provides directly in Tallaght, Finglas and Ballymun. In Longford Town, the Midland Health Board entered into partnership with local voluntary bodies to assist in the refurbishment of a premise for use as a resource centre (ibid. p. 64). In Letterkenny, the North Western Health Board converted two adjoining local authority houses it had operated as a children's home to use as a neighbourhood resource centre.

Voluntary Bodies

In the voluntary sector, centres tend to be located in whatever empty space can be found, in temporary pre-fabricated buildings, e.g. centres provided by the Catholic Social Service Conference in Neilstown, Clondalkin, Fettercairn, Tallaght and Loughlinstown, or by the Daughters of Charity in Knocknaheeny in Cork; in a local authority flat, e.g. Barnardo's projects in Tallaght and Fatima Mansions, a large inner city local authority flat development in Dublin; in a local authority house, e.g. ISPCC Family Centres in Drogheda and Darndale, Dublin; or in a disused school, e.g. a Family Centre serving local communities in the south inner city of Dublin sponsored by the Mercy Congregation. One purpose built development under the auspices of a voluntary agency is the ISPCC Community Resource Centre in Tullamore (built with grant aid from the Midland Health Board and opened in 1986).

Selected examples from Centres operative at different times during the 1980s.

Eastern Health Board Family Drop-in Centre
St. Dominic's House
Tallaght
Dublin 24
Two health board social workers, part time worker supplied by Barnardo's, plus volunteers (including former users). Large old house, formerly used as old people's day centre. Drop-in facility; playgroups for various ages; parent and toddler groups; personal counselling; relaxation, arts and crafts, cookery and keep fit sessions; annual holiday. The centre has no budget of its own, and does some small fundraising (Mental Health Association of Ireland, 1987).

ISPCC Community Resource Centre
Arden View Estate
Tullamore
Co. Offaly
Purpose-built centre. Community playgroup; after-school project; mother and toddler groups; family support groups; adult education; local community groups. Centre's work co-ordinated by the society's local Children's Resource Organiser (ISPCC 1986).

North Western Health Board Family Resource Centre
Letterkenny
Community worker, social worker, two child care workers. Two adjoining local authority houses on estate. Youth Project — four groups for children aged 7-16; community development; mother and toddler group; single parent group; research on local community needs (Kenny, 1986).

Catholic Social Service Conference
Loughlinstown Resource Centre
Loughlinstown
Co. Dublin
A prefabricated building with five meetings rooms, it operates seven days a week and provides space for over 30 local groups. Activities start at 9.30am and continue to 10.00pm every evening. When the centre needed a new roof, it was the local people who organised it and raised £1,000 of the £3,500 needed. The rest was provided by CSSC (CSSC, 1988).

Parents Alone Resource Centre
Coolock
This is a community based resource to support lone parents funded by the second
EC programme to Combat Poverty. An annual review of its work reveals an
impressive range of activity:

> Establishment of a morning creche for children under 3 years of age; informal child
> care between parents; after-school creativity sessions; outings for parents and
> children; telephone, typing, photocopying available; a core of 12 volunteers, along
> with staff, deal with individual queries on housing, welfare, health, the law;
> Information display was held in a local shopping complex. During the year 120
> women availed of an individual counselling service; staff/volunteers accompanied
> women to court hearings. Drop-in sessions (informal groups) occurred regularly; a
> structured health education programme of a holistic nature was held during 1987 for
> eight-week period; a writing group was held; a parenting group was held; a magazine
> which included the women's writing was produced by the writing group (Barry et al,
> 1988, p. 12).

Practical Supports for Parents/Families under Strain

It is sometimes all too easy to lose sight of the fact that often what a family needs
is immediate and tangible practical help, rather than a course of high-powered
therapy. For the man whose wife is in hospital, who has no relatives nearby and
who cannot get leave from work, his most pressing need is assistance in securing
the care of his children during the day. For lone parents, perhaps at the end of their
tether due to the isolation and strain of the role, the availability of a reliable baby-
sitter twice a week may allow them to keep alive a social life and a life-line to the
adult world. For a mother fearful of over-reacting physically to the tantrums and
depredations of her toddler, the knowledge that a friendly voice and ear are no
further away than the end of a telephone may be the vital safety net which protects
her and her child from tragedy. For other parents, it may be important to know that
there is a 24-hour centre capable of coping with any emergency which may have
embroiled them. For the woman who is the victim of a spouse's violence, access to
legal aid and advice and a place in a refuge is likely to be of infinitely more
practical value than the intervention of a therapist, who strives to observe strict
neutrality as a therapeutic strategy in the face of the interpersonal violence.

Telephone Crisis line: The service provided by the Samaritans is probably the most
widely known of its kind. Within the field of child welfare specifically, the
voluntary group 'Parents under Stress' provides a crisis telephone service to
harassed parents who fear they may harm their children in the heat of the moment.
Also relevant to child care is the work of CURA, which was established by the
Catholic bishops to offer assistance to women worried about their pregnancy. Its
services include telephone advice and support, offered on a regional basis at hours
which vary but usually extend beyond normal office hours.

Following the precedent set by the UK charity Childline, the ISPCC established
a service of the same name in Ireland in 1988. Its inception was not without
controversy (see p. 146). Despite objections, the ISPCC pressed ahead with its

171

highly publicised service which is staffed by volunteers under professional supervision. The intention of the service is that any child experiencing or fearing abuse or neglect can phone for help and advice.

Emergency 24-hour service: Unlike in the UK, the Irish health board social work services do not provide an out-of-hours duty service to process emergencies. This gap in provision has been the basis of criticism (ISPCC, 1987), although it has been difficult to justify the diversion of precious existing or new resources to this use when so many vitally needed routine services are under-provided or do not even exist. As things stand, family emergencies must be contained within the family, or by neighbours or relatives, or must be processed either by the gardaí, the psychiatric services (where a psychiatric emergency is involved), a GP (or more likely an out-of-hours contracting service) or local clergy. The implementation of the Child Care Act 1991 is likely to herald the introduction of an out-of-hours cover service by health boards to deal with child care emergencies.

Domiciliary service: Intensive practical help in the family's own home may often be the most valuable form of assistance. A home help, there to prepare daily meals and do general housekeeping for school-going children, may enable a father to hold down his job while his wife is in hospital. For younger children, a child-care worker might stay overnight as part of a package of support designed to prevent the admission of a set of children to care. For a mother, buckling under the pressure of family life, regular extended visits by a home-maker or child-care worker may be a great boon: they may lend a much needed ear, help complete urgent chores and be able to make practical suggestions sensitively about how to minimise problems with children's behaviour, housekeeping or budgeting. With this kind of practical support, coaching and encouragement, a family's morale may be gradually transformed.

St Michael's House in Dublin is a mental handicap agency, which devised an imaginative scheme linked to a year's training funded by FÁS (the comprehensive statutory manpower agency). As part of the training in work with the mentally handicapped, trainees visit families with a mentally handicapped member (usually a child) once or twice a week over a period of eight months. The visits are timed to coincide with the mentally handicapped person's arrival home from day care and last until bedtime. The trainee may work with the handicapped child or the non-handicapped siblings, depending on the circumstances. Either way, the service succeeds in giving a much needed fillip to parents and families where the handicap may be causing considerable stress (St Michael's House, 1988).

In the United States, some child welfare agencies have recruited home-makers to act as emergency caretakers in cases where children have been left unsupervised in their homes. This may pre-empt the need for placement or at least allow a more planned response to be made to the problem (Brown, 1981). One US agency, in particular, has met with great success. 'Homebuilders' originated with a Catholic agency in Washington State in 1974. Its 'therapists' work with two selected families at a time, spending up to ten hours a week directly with each; the remaining time is divided between contact with other agencies and colleagues, and on paperwork. They work with families for whom all other forms of help have failed and are available on call on a 24-hour basis for the 4-6 weeks during which they work with each family. The programme provides intensive home-based family crisis intervention and education (Kaplan, 1986). Its goals are to prevent out-of-home placement of family members and to increase family resilience through immediate intervention that defuses the crisis, stabilises the family and teaches members new problem-resolution skills, so that they can avoid future crises. In the period 1975-84, 94% of children were still at home three months after their family's period of Homebuilders' intervention. This suggests an impressive rate of success for a programme which is now replicated widely throughout the US.

Respite care: In the field of mental handicap, there is a growing tradition of the successful use of short-term respite care to give parents a short break and their handicapped child a change of scenery. Since 1981, a number of Irish agencies have offered respite care in other families. Initiated under the title of 'Break Away', this scheme has been evaluated and seems to be firmly established to the mutual satisfaction of the different parties involved (Walsh, 1983 and 1986).

Besides this routine form of respite care, some agencies can offer crisis and relief care in residential units. The western region of the Brothers of Charity Mental Handicap service, for example, can offer six places in Roscommon (Brothers of Charity Services, 1988).

This concept of respite care has obvious relevance in the wider field of child welfare. With regular breathing space, children may be able to continue to live at home at least some of the time, if they and their parents have regular access to a reliable alternative care arrangement. In some families, an aunt or grandmother may offer a youngster asylum during a stormy period in family relations. In other instances, what is required is flexible, low-key and sensitive care which can absorb the child readily and return her home when the dust settles. The aim would be to preserve as many threads as possible in the child's life, such as remaining at the same school.

Services to meet selected needs

Work with physical abuse and neglect

While a great deal of professional time and angst in community care services is consumed by work with child abuse and neglect, there is actually little, if any, specialist provision available in Ireland to offer programmes of prevention, treatment or support to the families affected. Emergency care tends to be sought in a children's hospital where medical and technical expertise in the recording and interpretation of physical evidence is readily available. The great bulk of assessment and follow-up work will then fall on the already heavily burdened community care social workers, who often lack the time or resources which such families usually crave. Child guidance services, if available, may be in a position to supplement the efforts of the community care social worker. Clearly, mainstream support services (public health nurses, social workers, day nurseries — where available) can play a major part in meeting the needs of such families in crisis. Nevertheless, experience from elsewhere suggests that judiciously designed specialist provision may also have a part to play.

Comprehensive specialist services: In England and Wales in 1984, the NSPCC began to re-organise its services into 60 Child Protection Teams (Dale, 1986). The first of these was established in Rochdale with the close collaboration of the local authority's social services department (which, as in all of England and Wales, carries responsibility for the delivery of statutory personal social services including field social work). According to Dale (ibid.),

> The Rochdale Team has devised an impressively authoritative and coherent approach to working with families where child abuse is a problem. The approach relies on clear communication and the extensive use of contracts between all the parties involved, thorough and structured family assessments, gestalt and family therapy and network meetings involving family members and professionals in contact with the family.

In the Netherlands, there is an impressive array of child abuse services (Findlay, 1988), which differ in some interesting ways from those in Ireland. The system for processing child abuse referrals includes a 'confidential doctor' network on the assumption that people will be reluctant to make referrals openly. These doctors have the support of an administrator and a social worker, and are keen to secure the agreement of parents to programmes of intervention. Where this is not forthcoming, the case may be referred to the Bureau of Child Protection for compulsory intervention, although these powers do not seem to be widely used.

Residential programmes have also been devised to meet the needs of families where child abuse has arisen. Since 1972 the Triangel project in the Netherlands has offered a residential programme for families with various serious problems which, in some cases, may include child abuse (Van Rees, Oudendijk, Van Spanje, 1978). Its evolving approach includes massage and 'movement awareness therapy' which may consist of boxing, ball games, balancing exercises or therapeutic dance (Christopherson, 1980). A residential programme in Denver was run for three years, from 1974 to 1977 (McBogg et al, 1979). Claims have been made for gains made there in assessment, planning and rehabilitation which were attributed to the quality and intensity of the modelling and care enacted in the therapeutic environment. It was also conceded, however, that the residential dimension introduced further problems of dependency in the families and problems in maintaining detachment for the workers.

The Crisis Nursery at the New York Foundling Hospital for Parent and Child Development provides a three-pronged programme to families in crisis on a walk-in or referral basis: a 24-hour parent help-line, a 24-72 hour residential facility for children at imminent risk of maltreatment, and a counselling service. The Crisis Nursery seeks to offer a safe environment for children at risk of abuse; to serve as a non-punitive resource for their parents; and to connect families in crisis with community-based services so as to diminish further the possibility of maltreatment (Ceravolo, 1985).

There are also specialist day units which tackle problems of child abuse and neglect. In Belfast, for example, Barnardo's had a family centre which worked intensively on a contract basis with families referred because of serious difficulties in parent/child relationships (Birchall, 1986). One of the more interesting techniques employed was the video-recording of play sessions between child and parent. In some instances, the worker, who observed the session through a two-way mirror, might request the parent to behave in a particular way, e.g. to deprive the child of a toy for at least part of the session. Later, the worker and parent would review the video together and the worker helped the parent recount the feelings evoked by certain incidents and the session as a whole. By exploring earlier sources of similar feelings in the parent's life, worker and parent might come to a clearer understanding of influences on perceptions in the current parent/child relationship. The worker could also help the parent explore alternative courses of action at given moments and in this way coach the parent in the rehearsal of alternative strategies for managing the child's behaviour.

Again, in Northern Ireland, the health and social service boards have begun to develop a network of generously resourced family centres which offer a comprehensive programme of day care, group work and counselling, as well as coaching in practical child management and personal care skills. Families are referred to these centres by social workers usually because of concerns about the level of child care in the particular family. The Colin Family Centre, for example, has been established near the Poleglass Estate beyond West Belfast. Among its facilities are a number of apartments which can be used for work with individual families. Family routines, such as the preparation and eating of meals, can be re-enacted and the worker can be involved as a participant observer. The facilities and ethos of the centre allow service users to give as well as to receive. On one of the author's visits, a father was preparing lunch for those present, while a mother was thoroughly enjoying using the hairdressing facilities to do her key-worker's hair. It subsequently transpired that this latter session was one of the most productive in therapeutic terms in the course of the worker/family's whole relationship.

Intervention and child abuse

Child abuse cases are complex to deal with for a number of reasons:

- The intensity of feelings, including revulsion, guilt and anger which they are likely to evoke.
- The very real difficulty of establishing what has happened in the face of what is frequently ambiguous evidence. This often means that the correct course of professional intervention is not necessarily obvious or that a desired course of legal action is not necessarily feasible (viz. Did abuse actually occur or is the parents' denial the truth? Will the evidence support an application to a court for the compulsory removal of the child?)
- The challenge of preparing and presenting (perhaps under cross-examination) evidence to support an application for a court order for the care of the children.
- The struggle by a disparate group of professionals thrown together by the circumstances of the case to communicate and to collaborate effectively with each other. They are required to do this despite what may be formidable obstacles, such as the traditions of professional or agency autonomy (e.g. doctors unused to sharing information or decision-making powers in relation to one of their patients), or inter-agency, inter-professional or inter-personal tensions or rivalry.

- The stress the work generates. This is due, firstly, to the time these cases require, usually at the expense of other urgent work. Secondly, stress arises from the burden of moral responsibility imposed on isolated professionals in what may seem to them like 'playing God' in relation to the destinies of parents and children. It is not easy to exercise professional judgments which carry such enormous implications for the civil and human rights of the people involved.

- The ever-present fear for professionals of 'being caught out' — of a child on their caseload being killed or seriously injured, especially where they might have missed vital clues of the risk to which the child eventually succumbed. This is a particular problem for social workers in the UK where they have been hounded by the media (especially the popular press) for every failing in the management of child abuse cases. Undoubtedly, there have been some serious lapses, but one commentator in the quality British press has observed the imbalance of public responses to failings by social workers when compared to fatal errors by British surgeons and anaesthetists. In the same week, a report of an inquiry into social work failings in a child abuse case attracted strident media attention while news that 1,000 people die needlessly in operating theatres every year passed relatively unnoticed (Phillips, 1987). Fortunately, in Ireland we seem to have a more responsible media. Also, in the only document approximating to an official inquiry into the traumatic deaths of children on social workers' caseloads, there is a fairly clear and realistic official unwillingness to serve up professional scapegoats. The Department of Health's press release, issued in July 1982, reported on the handling by Eastern Health Board personnel of contact with two families in which two children died in 1981 (Government Information Service 1982).

Given the complexity of the work, it is clear that the agencies which employ social workers and the other professionals working at the frontline in these cases have a grave responsibility to ensure that their workers have access to clear and reasonable agency policies, adequate professional supervision, adequate support services to families, adequate specialist back-up (both legal and medical), and adequate clerical and administrative support for the convening and recording of case conferences and the follow-up of decisions arising.

The quality of intervention in child abuse depends, however, on the calibre of professional work by the practitioners directly involved as well as on the conditions under which the work is done. The Department of Health and Social Security for England and Wales published an analysis of eighteen reports of inquiry into the deaths of children there in the period 1973-81. It culls some hard-won lessons from the tragic evidence:

- The overall impression of practice given by the reports is one of much good work interspersed with numerous omissions, mistakes and misjudgments by different workers at different times. These failures can compound one another, producing a far more serious cumulative effect.

- Workers who might encounter child abuse must have the special knowledge, skills and experience to be able to recognise when it is taking place, or is likely to take place.

- Many allegations of abuse by members of the public turn out to be well founded. Such allegations should always be taken seriously and investigated urgently. The child or children must be seen.
- A major characteristic of many cases is the failure to bring together all available information and to use it in a structured, objective way, by carrying out full psycho-social and medical assessments. These require continuous re-examination and revision. The need for health monitoring is important, particularly in cases of neglect.
- A common cause of inappropriate or inadequate intervention is the lack of a clearly formulated plan of action. Decisions should always be explicit and objectives specified.
- It is important to see that decisions are carried out and their effectiveness kept under review.
- Effective communication and records are integral to good practice. Inadequate professional responses often stem from communicating and recording inaccurately or not at all, from failing actively to tap sources of information instead of 'waiting to be told', and from recording information in ways which make it difficult to use or collate (DHSS, 1982, p.69).

Figure 8. Assessing a parent's relationship with a child

> — when worker observes interaction between the parent and child
> How much physical contact is there (e.g. child sitting on parent's lap, being cuddled, having head patted, hair tousled)?
> How much eye contact is there when child is close or at a distance?
> How does parent address child, (tone of voice, appropriateness of parental demands, typical content of conversation between them)?
> How does parent react to child when the child does 'something wrong'?
>
> — when parent talks about child
> Do they have expectations for the child's behaviour/performance which are inappro priate considering the child's age?
> Do they compare the child unfavourably with others?
> Do they comment negatively on attributes which remind them of other people with whom they have had unhappy times (an estranged husband, a hated father, etc.)?
> Do they attribute malice to the child's intentions?

Professional Practice

In working with families in circumstances where physical abuse or neglect is suspected, it is important to come quickly to the point — to be honest in confronting concerns openly and directly, while as supportively as possible. It is especially unhelpful to 'hover' around the family, inventing excuses for contact. Any tension in the family and risk to children may be greatly aggravated as the family sees through the worker's all-too-transparent attempts to mask his or her own anxiety. Record-keeping is crucial, as is attention to detail. Sudden and unexplained interruptions in growth trends in height or weight may give vital signals about a child's current plight. A jigsaw of carefully documented minor incidents, when completed, may lend vital force to a court application for a care order. It is also crucial that professionals communicate with one another, attend case conferences at which they reach clearly enunciated conclusions, and discharge any obligations on them arising from conference decisions. The effectiveness of case conferences depends heavily not only on a full attendance but on capable chairing and efficiency in the recording and circulation of minutes. Effective decision making and assessment depends on the ability to judge the quality of parent-child relations (see Figure 8) and on adequate knowledge of the signs and symptoms of possible abuse (see Figure 9). Assessment is often the first step. A long programme of intervention in the lives of the child and parents is usually indicated, with perhaps, in some cases, permanent separation, especially where parents continue to deny the existence of abuse even in the face of overwhelming evidence or otherwise seem likely to repeat past abuse of the child.

Working with Child Sexual Abuse

Invariably, a veil of secrecy surrounds child sexual abuse. This is maintained often by fear induced in the victim by the perpetrator. Where abuse takes place within the family, there may also be the conscious, or unconscious, collusion of other family members in maintaining the secret. As in cases of physical abuse or neglect, professionals may have to invoke considerable legal force in order to prevent the recurrence of abuse. The sexual dimension, the implications for future family relationships and the humiliation for the different parties concerned places a great burden on the professionals involved.

A case may come to light through 'disclosure' by the child or through the suspicion of an adult. It is considered unusual for a child to fabricate an allegation of sexual abuse, since children usually lack the experience and language with which to do so. Given the adverse consequences of child sexual abuse, it is essential that disclosures or suspicions are investigated thoroughly. This process of inquiry should be undertaken by a multi-disciplinary team. The team's approach should include, firstly, sensitive interviewing of the victim (and also parents/family members) and, secondly, the assembly of physical and/or other corroborating evidence. Where abuse is confirmed legal remedies may be invoked in terms of prosecution of the perpetrator and/or the separation of victim and perpetrator in order to prevent any recurrence. While these investigation and assessment processes may consume much professional time and expertise, it is the long process of treatment which is likely to be crucial in helping the victim purge the worst psychological ill-effects of the history of abuse (see below).

The perpetrator engages not only in the abuse or betrayal of a child's sexuality, but also in the abuse of power and trust in the relationship between a trusted adult and a vulnerable child. Victims are usually threatened against revealing the fact of their abuse. Sometimes, therefore, disclosure may only occur accidentally. The history may emerge because of abuse-related physical injury, pregnancy, adverse changes in a child's behaviour, sociability or educational progress, sexually trans-mitted disease or sexually precocious behaviour on the part of the child. On the other hand, a child may consciously decide to tell an apparently sympathetic adult after plucking up the courage to seek protection from steadily increasing sexual demands or the risk of pregnancy or to save a younger sibling from a similar fate.

Figure 9: **Checklist to help identification and investigation of child abuse: physical and sexual**

No one indicator should be seen as conclusive in itself but must be seen in the context of a constellation of factors and consideration of the particular family and/or situation.

Suggestive features on history taking

1.1 *General Indices*
1. Parents' story at variance with clinical findings.
2. Repeated injury.
3. Visits to different hospitals or to different general practitioners.
4. Reluctance of parents to give information.
5. Lapse of time between injury and attendance at doctor's surgery or hospital.
6. Obvious familial discord, stress, etc.
7. Parents' refusal to give consent for investigation.
8. Nutritional deprivation.
9. Developmental delay.
10. Signs of physical neglect.
11. Poisoning.
    Poisoning may not always be accidental or due to carelessness.
12. A small number of cot deaths are non-accidental.
13. Persistent complaints of a gastro-intestinal or genital-urinary nature, e.g. vaginal bleeding or vaginal discharge, rectal bleeding or rectal discharge.

1.2 *Behavioural Indices*
All of these indicators can occur in other disorders where abuse has not been a factor.
1. Overly compliant behaviour.
2. Acting-out, aggressive behaviour.
3. Reluctance to be at home — seen in early arrival at school and/or leaving late with few, if any, absences.
4. Poor peer relationships or inability to make friends.
5. Lack of trust, particularly with significant others.
6. Non-participation in school and social activities.
7. Inability to concentrate in school.
8. Sudden drop in school performance.
9. Running away from home.
10. Sleep disturbances.
11. Regressive behaviour.
12. Withdrawal behaviour.
13. Suicidal feelings and self-destructive behaviour.
14. Depression.
15. 'Frozen gaze' i.e. wide-eyed immobilised expression of child who has learned not to cry because he will be subject to physical abuse.
16. Sudden onset of eating problems, particularly related to the start of puberty.

1.3 *Sexual Abuse Indices*
Although these symptoms are not necessarily indicative of child sexual abuse, if children exhibit extreme or combined symptoms from this list the possibility of sexual abuse should be considered and investigated.
1. Hints about sexual activity.
2. A sudden change towards uncharacteristic sexual play with peers or toys or with themselves, or sexually aggressive behaviour with others.
3. Detailed or age-inappropriate understanding of sexual behaviour (especially by young children).
4. Excessive fear of adults or displaying apprehension or withdrawn behaviour, or conversely very aggressive behaviour.
5. Excessive attachment to adults.
6. Inappropriate seductive behaviour.
7. Excessive fears of settling down at bedtime and/or being left alone.
8. Unusual reluctance to join in normal activities involving the removal of clothing e.g. swimming

Source: Dept. of Health (1987), *Child Abuse Guidelines* Dublin: Dept. of Health

In investigative interviews, it is important to establish a warm and accepting atmosphere. The venue for interviews should be neutral in the child's eyes and it may be necessary to conduct the investigation over more than one interview. It is important, especially in the early stages, to strike up a rapport with the child and to begin to win some trust. By stressing his or her previous contact with children who have had comparable experiences, the worker helps the child to proceed and aids their own credibility with the child. The interviewer should avoid leading questions and convey a belief in what the child is saying and should use the language of the child, while clarifying gently and patiently the precise meaning of terms used. Communication can be assisted by pointing to parts of the body and by the use of anatomically correct dolls (Shamroy, 1987). It may also be appropriate to have an ally of the child present during these interviews.

Furthermore, it is very important that adults respond sympathetically and without evident shock to any allegation. This may help to minimise the tendency common especially among young children of retracting initial complaints. When this happens, according to Damon *et al* (1987), 'it is critical that the interviewer not accept a child's denial as the final word.' The child may need time to test out the reliability of helping adults and overcome inhibitions due to the threats made by the perpetrator.

The information required about the abuse (most of which must be obtained directly from the child or adolescent) includes the following:

- what was the nature of the abuse, what activities did it involve?
- when and how did it begin?
- how did it develop over time (e.g. from kissing to fondling of genitals, or fondling outside clothes to eventual full intercourse)?
- how frequently did it occur?
- what other activities might have been attempted from time to time?
- where did the abuse take place?
- who else knows?
- why is the child disclosing the abuse now?

It has been suggested that sexual encounters between adults and children follow a common pattern. Sgroi *et al* (1982) found that the activity usually occurs in five phases: the engagement phase, the sexual interaction phase, the secrecy phase, the disclosure phase and often a suppression phase.

The perpetrator needs access to the child and therefore is likely to be someone known to, and trusted by, the child. The first encounter may be accidental and relatively innocent, but it may prompt the adult to create less accidental opportunities by perhaps offering the child inducements to compliance. As the pattern becomes more established, the perpetrator will threaten the child with dire consequences if their secret is divulged. Where disclosure occurs, a family may close ranks in order to suppress further discussion about the misdemeanour of the member(s). Where the perpetrator is not a family member, the family may still prefer to avoid further pain which, in their view, ongoing investigation or treatment entails.

In sexual abuse, families may contribute directly or indirectly to the episode of abuse. Obviously there is a direct role if a family member is the perpetrator. Where this is the parent, there has been a failure to protect, a failure to set limits (to the adult's own behaviour) and an abuse of power (ibid. p. 248). In extra and intra-familial abuse, parents may contribute by poor supervision, poor choice of surrogate caretakers or babysitters, inappropriate sleeping arrangements, or blurred role boundaries (e.g. children permitted to observe intimate parental sexual contact).

Where a case of child sexual abuse has been confirmed, the case should be referred to the Garda Síochána since a crime has been committed. The perpetrator and victim should be separated, preferably by the removal of the perpetrator, since to remove the child is a double penalty against the child — adding to her loss of innocence, the loss of home as well. This separation is important for a number of reasons (ibid. p.103). Firstly, it assures the physical safety of the child. Secondly, the child will not be subjected to direct pressure from the perpetrator to deny or recant the allegation. And thirdly, the perpetrator will be more likely to perceive that the intervenors believe that child sexual abuse has occurred and consider the situation to be serious, even if he or she denies the situation.

Work with families where incest had occurred will often require the use of authoritative intervention, leverage and outreach to induce compliance and involvement with a treatment programme. Workers must display strength and versatility in their style of intervention.

> Individual, dyad, couples and family therapy can all be used in some combination. Group therapy (for example, with fathers, or mothers, or parents, or adolescents) permits both peer support and confrontation — essential elements of treatment that are difficult to reproduce in individual therapy. Art therapies (including play therapy) will be invaluable, especially for the more damaged and less expressive family members (ibid).

In the end, the aim of intervention is to get family members to acknowledge responsibility, to ensure that the abuse stops, and to end the conditions which gave rise to the abuse.

Sexual abuse leaves a distressing legacy for the child or adolescent (Sarnacki Porter *et al*, 1982). They are likely to experience the 'damaged goods' syndrome, fearing the physical and social consequences of their abuse; guilt, fear and depression; low self-esteem linked with poor social skills. In addition, they are likely to experience repressed anger and hostility; impaired ability to trust; in the case of intra-familial abuse, blurred role boundaries and role confusion; pseudo-maturity coupled with failure to accomplish developmental tasks; and difficulties in achieving self-mastery and control (ibid. pp 109).

For the victim, the treatment is a lengthy and emotional process of re-building the child's ego (ibid. pp 128-9).

> To begin this strengthening process, the victim needs permission to accept the feelings of anger and hurt, so that these feelings may be expressed without experiencing further guilt. Victims often blame themselves for the sexual abuse, thus inhibiting the healthy attitude that they have a right to be angry and feel hurt .... The therapist should help victims to understand that the sexual abuse was not their fault and that they have a right to their own feelings.

Each child must be enabled to ventilate his or her feelings about the sexual trauma in terms of guilt and shame; positive and negative feelings towards the perpetrator;

in cases of abuse by a parent, positive and negative feelings towards the non-offending parent; feelings about the reaction of siblings; feelings about the reaction of peers, professionals and others in the community.

The child can also be helped to reflect on the effects of the legal system on their lives; the nature of parent/child relationships and intra-familial roles; the style of communication patterns within their family; and the conditions necessary for positive boy-girl relationships.

As the problem of child sexual abuse becomes more widely recognised, greater attention is being paid to programmes that alert children to the risks of abuse and that help them prepare to fend off and refuse unwanted and inappropriate advances from adults. It is important however that the children are not left with any message that they are responsible for whether or not abuse occurs.

The treatment of child sexual abuse demands great skill, delicacy and stamina on the part of the professionals involved. As in physical abuse or neglect, inter-professional collaboration and access to specialist support services are important. The amount of time absorbed by individual cases is staggering and for this reason alone it is not realistic in the absence of additional resources, to expect the main burden of this work to be borne by mainstream community care services.

Since 1988, two specialist child sexual abuse assessment units have been established in the Dublin area in Crumlin Children's Hospital and in Temple Street Children's Hospital. Both units are staffed by a multi-disciplinary team of two psychologists, two social workers and a child psychiatrist. These represent an important resource to community services and while geared to a role in assessment, they may conceivably become involved in some work in the area of treatment and prevention. Outside of the Dublin region, resources have been allocated by the Minister for Health to enable other health boards establish regional assessment services for child sexual abuse.

At the level of treatment resources are more limited. Child guidance clinics and rape crisis centres can offer a limited service but many professionals are concerned that a child who risks 'disclosure' may be betrayed not only by their abuser, but also by the services which fail to respond adequately and urgently to their treatment needs. Tackling the problem also requires attention to the treatment needs of perpetrators, since a combination of treatment and sanctions may successfully prevent the recurrence of abusive behaviour. Again, provision is limited, but there are initiatives under way from the Eastern Health Board forensic psychiatry service, the probation and welfare service in Arbour Hill Prison and the North Western Health Board.

PART IV:

CHILDREN IN CARE

Chapter 9

CHILDREN IN CARE — AN INTRODUCTION TO THE SYSTEM OF SERVICES

The number of children in health board care in Ireland in 1988 was 2,614, representing a rate of 2.12 per 1,000 children aged under 18 years (Department of Health, 1990; Central Statistics Office, 1987). The total number of children in care has increased by 9.81% in the period 1982-87 (Department of Health, 1986 and 1988). Taking a wider view, however, there has been a dramatic reduction in the population of children in public care, i.e. under the care of the Department of Education or the health authorities: in the twenty year period 1968-88, the numbers have fallen by over 2,000, from 4,834 in 1968 to 2,735 (2,614 in health board care and 121 in Department of Education care on committal/remand from courts for offences) (Department of Education, 1988; Committee on Reformatory and Industrial Schools, 1970).

Changes in the admission procedure have contributed to this downward trend. The availability of social workers within the health boards (since the early to mid-1970s) and the gradual shift to health boards of the responsibility for the maintenance of all children in care (other than those admitted through the juvenile justice system) has led to a streamlining of admission procedures. Previously, the admission process was largely controlled by the residential units themselves, which would decide unilaterally on the merits of referrals by such bodies as the courts, Garda Síochána, clergy or ISPCC inspectors. This system undoubtedly led to an excessive rate of admission and to a bias against foster care (which languished under a separate and remote arm of local government). While inevitably there remain subtle differences in approach by different social work teams, screening of referrals by trained professionals (and the availability, if even on a limited basis, of community based alternatives) has stemmed the flow for placement and has increased the chances that placements are confined and tailored to those most in need.

The risk of being in care varies by health board community care area and region. An analysis of the data on children in care in 1982 found that children in the Mid-Western Health Board region were twice as likely to be in care as children in the Western region and almost twice as likely as those in the North-Eastern or Midland regions. Children in the community care area of Tipperary North Riding (which includes part of Limerick city) were three times as likely to be in care as children in all but one of the other community care areas nationally (O'Higgins and Boyle, 1988). Such variations are difficult to explain, but they are probably due to the interaction of such factors as social conditions in the given area, the availability of day care and family support facilities (which might obviate the need for admission to care) and the decision-making style of the social workers concerned.

Of all children in care in 1988, two out of three (68.3%) were aged 7 or over and more than one in three (35.6%) was aged 12 or over. These are the age groups with a higher risk of being in care. In almost one in three cases (31.5%), the primary reason for admission to care was classified as being due to 'parent/parents unable to cope'. 'Neglect' accounted for 18.5% of admissions, while 'physical abuse' accounted for 8.0%, 'emotional abuse' 1.6%, and 'sexual abuse' 5.2%.

Since 1981 there has been a steady increase in the proportion of children in care on the basis of a court order. Between 1981 and 1988 (the latest year for which figures are available at the time of writing) the proportion had risen from 16.3% to 47.6%. The proportion of children in care on a compulsory basis varies considerably on a regional basis, ranging from 58.2% in the Eastern Health Board to 31% in the South-Eastern Health Board (Department of Health, 1990).

Foster Family Care

Children placed in foster care are cared for within a family rather than in a residential care setting. Usually, this family is not related to the child. In return for the care of the child, the family receives a boarding-out allowance from the health board which has placed the child.

To foster a child, families must first apply to their local health board. They will be invited to an information meeting and/or will receive a briefing visit from a social worker. If they wish to proceed with their application, they will attend a series of group discussions and/or be visited by a social worker on a number of occasions.

The purpose of these contacts is to enable the family to consider the likely impact on their lives of the arrival and presence of a foster child. The parents are helped to explore past experiences in their own families of origin and in the family of marriage which might assist or inhibit their adjustment to the role of foster parents. The social worker will lay great emphasis on the differences between parenting one's own children and parenting someone else's. Legally and emotionally, the child will never belong to the foster parents (since fostering is quite distinct from adoption, where the child becomes in law a child of the adoptive parents). This division of responsibility between parents, the emotional and behavioural reaction of the child to being fostered and to what led to his or her being fostered, together with the torn loyalties the child may experience in the relationship between the two families, indicate how fostering adds many complex layers to the already demanding task of 'ordinary' parenting. This complexity can be difficult to grasp properly in the first excitement of planning to foster a child.

There is a long tradition of fostering children in Ireland, dating back to life under the ancient Brehon Laws when fosterage was used as a means of forging links between powerful families. In adolescence, a youngster might be placed with another family in order to complete his education and to teach him the skills of a warrior. In this context, fostering had a political rather than a welfare function, since it bound clans together, thereby reducing the risk of conflict or hostility.

In later centuries, under English law, a form of fostering was adopted in Ireland, again largely to political effect. In 1715, George I authorised 'the minister and church wardens of every parish to bind out [foster], with the approbation of a justice of the peace, any child they find begging within their parish, or any other poor child, with the parents' consent, to any honest and substantial Protestant housekeeper or Protestant tradesman' (Powell, 1982). This provision clearly combined political and welfare functions, since the English authorities deemed Protestant families as politically reliable and thus could be safely expected to socialise poor (Catholic) youngsters into loyal citizenship.

The Irish Poor Law Amendment Act of 1862 laid the foundations of what is now the modern system of fostering in Ireland. It gave the boards of guardians which administered the Poor Law the power to 'board out' children up to five years of age outside the workhouse with families. This was done because of what was seen as the harmful effect of the workhouse environment on a child's development (Robins, 1980). The origins of modern-day social work in foster care can be traced to legislation in 1897 (Infant Life Protection Act) which gave powers to local authorities to appoint female inspectors who could visit and, if necessary, remove children placed in families.

The modern system of foster care is based on the Health Act of 1953 and the Boarding-out regulations of 1983. These require, *inter alia*; that:

- health boards place children in their care in foster care, unless there are clear reasons for not doing so;
- certain conditions be fulfilled before a child is placed with a family;
- a child must be visited in the foster home within one month of being placed there and at subsequent intervals of not more than six months;
- a health board must carry out a review of the 'health and well-being' of every foster child within two months of placement and at least every six months thereafter;
- health boards must pay for the child's maintenance, clothing and education, 'and for such other assistance of such children as it may consider reasonable'.

Foster parents receive a weekly allowance and a six-monthly clothing allowance. Long-term foster parents receive a supplement; further supplements may be payable at the discretion of the health boards where the child has special needs. Foster parents may also apply for any out-of-pocket expenses, which are repayable at the discretion of the board. In the case of the Eastern Health Board, short-term foster parents are paid at the rate £37.30 per week; day foster parents receive £4.20 a day and long-term foster parents are entitled to £142.50 per month, plus a clothing allowance of £115.00 payable in March and July (all amounts with effect from July 1990) (EHB Children Section, 1991). This author has shown that the value of weekly fostering allowances have declined in real terms since 1982 (Gilligan, 1990).

Trends in Fostering
In the period 1982-88, the proportion of children in care who are fostered has increased from 52% to 71% (Department of Health, 1986, 1990). There are important regional variations in the rate of fostering. According to the Department of Health (1990), rates range from a high of 94.2% in the North Western Health Board (which is responsible for 5.2% of all children in care) to 64.9% in the Eastern Health Board (which includes Dublin and is responsible for 37% of all children in care) and 52.2% in the South-Eastern Health Board (which accounts for 16.2% of all children in care).

The past fifteen years have witnessed a number of significant developments which augur well for the future of foster care, viz:

• the influence of the Poor Law origins of fostering, or boarding-out, has gradually been purged;
• the fostering system is now managed by professional social workers, according to internationally accepted standards of practice;
• placement is no longer closed in principle to older children, nor to sibling groups and children with various forms of disability, although the recruitment of suitable foster parents remains difficult;
• greater rigour is now applied in the selection of foster parents;
• group work and adult education techniques are increasingly employed in the training and support of foster parents;
• the media is increasingly being used for the purposes of recruitment and public education;
• the Irish Foster Care Association was established in 1982;
• new statutory regulations were introduced in 1983.

Residential Child Care

The residential child care system comprises children's homes and special schools. The stereotyped image of an orphanage is thankfully outdated and most of today's children's homes are no longer located in large, forbidding institutions. These older settings have been closed down over the past two decades and children in care now live in purpose-built houses or bungalows, usually accommodating between 8 and 20 children. These homes may be in the grounds of old institutions, but more often they are to be found in the surrounding locality. Since 1983, children's homes have been funded on the basis of an agreed annual budget by their local health board.

Essentially, the children's home sector is run by voluntary bodies, with only one in fifty (2%) places provided directly by health boards. Roman Catholic religious orders make up the major share of these voluntary bodies, accounting for more than four in every five (84.4%) of the 886 places nationally in Homes approved by the Minister for Health. Protestant voluntary bodies provide 7.4% of places and non-denominational and other bodies make up the remaining 6.2% of places (Department of Health, 1989).

The availability of residential care is uneven. Nine community care areas possess no residential facilities of their own. This problem of availability is unlikely to improve. In the period 1979-1987, the number of places in residential children's homes fell from 1,346 to 886. (Over a longer period the decline is even more marked: in 1968-69, there were approximately 3,348 residential places available within the Irish child care system.) In explaining this reduction, three factors suggest themselves: a declared preference for foster care in official policy, a general policy in more recent years within the health service of shifting care from institutional to community settings, and, finally, the withdrawal by many service-providers themselves. Many religious orders have opted out of this field of work, usually for one or more of the following reasons: a wish to concentrate on other activities; a shrinkage in their own numbers which prevents them from providing a sufficient staff presence through which to maintain their distinctive ethos; and the changing profile of youngsters in residential care, which poses radically different demands that some orders feel ill-equipped to meet.

Despite the fall in the absolute number of residential places and in the residential system's share of care provision overall, it is important not to lose sight of the considerable improvements achieved over the past two decades. The old institutions have been replaced, the quality of care the children receive no longer deserves the criticism levelled at it in the past (as in, for example, Arnold and Laskey, 1985); funding arrangements have improved; and responsibility for the system has been largely rationalised under the Department of Health. Training courses have been established and many staff have received at least basic training. Staff-to-child ratios have improved and now stand at one care staff member to 2.5 children. A survey in 1978 found a staffing ratio in the homes surveyed of one staff member to 4.5 children (Association of Workers with Children in Care, 1979). This change may have resulted more in an improvement in staff employment conditions rather than an increased level of service to children, although, undoubtedly, more satisfactory working conditions should lead to higher morale among staff, and in turn, lead to better quality care for the children. In the same period, there have also been improvements in real terms in pay levels for care staff.

The second type of residential child care facility is that of special schools (see p. 84). These centres have also seen remarkable change in recent years. Harsh conditions have been replaced by purpose-built or refurbished premises.

The Effects of being in Care

What are the effects of being in care for children? How does it affect their family? What kinds of care seem most helpful? These are vital questions for all who work in the child care field. But such questions are complex and do not yield ready or simple answers. Addressing these issues presents formidable methodological problems for both the practitioner and the researcher.

What measures are we to use about the effects of a care episode on a child or young person? Are we to ask the child and, if so, when — during the care episode or at some point later in his or her life? Are we to rely solely on these kinds of rating of client satisfaction? If not, how do we apply more objective measures? A child's progress can be measured over time — before, during and after care. But without controls, i.e. children who, except for the care experience, share as far as possible all the characteristics and experiences of their in-care 'partner', which in this context are obviously highly elusive, how can we know we are correctly attributing certain effects to the care episode?

In many senses, the acid test of care is whether the gains made during care continue afterwards, whether they endure or simply fade away. The difficulty in measuring this effect is that the longer the interval between discharge from care and the follow-up study, the greater the chance that some other life events have influenced crucially the progress of the person studied. A successful marriage, for example, may transform the life of a previously isolated and depressed graduate of care. It would be difficult to attribute this fortunate outcome to the young person's care experience.

This example highlights the problem — that care tends to get any of the blame going and little of the credit. Or at least that is how it may feel to those workers who struggle daily to offer care to youngsters. And yet, the evidence from the literature and research is not completely bleak about the achievements of care. (The paucity of Irish material forces a reliance here on largely international evidence.) It is probably true to say that the judgment of the literature is at best ambivalent about care. But this suggests that a pessimistic fatalism about the value of care or the possibility of bringing about change is not justified. Indeed, the needs of the children who depend on the care system impose a heavy moral responsibility on all involved, not only to avoid such pessimism but to use any knowledge available to build conscientiously the best system of care possible.

What follows is a selection of evidence about the impact of care not only on children, but also on their families. It includes the results of quantitative research, as well as quotations from practitioners and clients whose wisdom may bring issues to life more vividly.

The late Mia Kellmer Pringle (1974), who was a leading British authority on child care, wrote of the impact of being in care on the young child:

> However adverse a home, the child lives in familiar surroundings and is looked after, however inadequately, by familiar people. Being taken from it means the collapse of the world he has accepted as the only one he knows. The younger the child, the greater the distress at being removed to an unfamiliar environment. The more limited his understanding of verbal explanations, the greater is his likely bewilderment and the more difficult the task of restoring his sense of security; also he may feel it was his naughtiness which led to his being sent away (pp 133-4).

Noeleen Gorman (1985), a Belfast teenager who has grown up in care, wrote a prize-winning essay in *The Spectator* magazine on her experiences, part of which reads:

> I was taken into care early — not so early that I did not know what was going on. The welfare services had been alerted to my disastrous home by my primary school principal. Not that I was entirely aware that it was a disaster — how could I know, having nothing to compare it with? Perhaps this is one of the basic problems of child care: the child in question is not quite sure if it is his fault, his parents' fault or the authority's fault.

Besides this abiding uncertainty, the child may have to endure the guilt of divided loyalties. Gorman (ibid.) again recalls her experience:

> Anyone can see that we were in need of care — but looking back, I feel that the welfare services, once alerted, dealt with our case insensitively. We all appeared in court. I was made to stand in front of the judge, my parents on one side of me and my grandparents on the other. I was asked which I would prefer to live with. Can you imagine what it feels like to be asked to reject publicly two of the people with whom you have strong emotional ties? It was a piece of unnecessary cruelty and extra stress. In the event I chose my grandparents, but I cannot shake off the guilt that I turned my back on my parents, especially my father. It was of course, sensible, but no child should be put in such a situation.

Noeleen's experience may be atypical, but it should serve to remind us, nevertheless, that most children in care will experience such confusions of loyalty, albeit more privately.The process of being in care can undermine a child's sense of identity. Newson (1971) reminds us that it can mean that the child has

> no single person who shares his own most basic and important memories, no one to confirm whether these memories are in fact correct or figments of his imagination, no one to polish up a fading memory before it is too late. Such a deprivation seems so damaging that I am not at all sure that we can ever fully make up for it artificially.

Kahan (1979) summarises the views of a group of adults who had been meeting with her to reflect on their experiences of growing up in care:

> If children had to be in care, they felt that in as many ways as possible the continuity and wholeness of their lives should be safeguarded, not only for their own sake, but for the sake of their past as well as their present and future. What was it like when you were in that home, Dad? Andrew's children had asked him. It would have been very important to him and to them if he had been able to tell them about their grandparents, perhaps their great grandparents too (pp 34-5).

If children in care become cut off from the past, they may also become cut off from immediate happenings in their family. Gorman (1985) recounts poignantly her experience when she went into a children's home for what she was assured was a short-term stay when her granny became ill:

> Actually, my grandmother had cancer, and they didn't tell me that she was dead until the day afterwards. They thought they had broken it all very gently and that I had accepted the loss. Instead, I felt cheated: I should have been told immediately.

If the present and past are uncertain for the child in care, so also is the future. Children's homes may close, the child may be transferred, a foster home may break down, natural parents may fade from view or suddenly re-appear, favourite care staff may move on, a social worker whom the child has grown to trust may change jobs. As Kellmer Pringle (1974) puts it:

> Not only does the child in long-term care have no reliable past; equally devastating, he has no predictable future except that he will come out of care at the age of eighteen [sixteen officially here in Ireland, until the implementation of the relevant section of the Child Care Act 1991, unless the child is in full-time education].

Kadushin (1980, pp 382, 610) undertook a major review of the short-term effects on children of foster family care and group and institutional care. He found that if foster families are chosen carefully and given support, then foster family care 'is not injurious to the child's development'. He also observed that institutions for the dependent and neglected were 'neither as harmful as had been feared nor as helpful as had been hoped'.

In a review of long-term follow-up studies, Festinger (1983) observed, 'Overall, one might dare to say that over the more than 50 years spanned by these studies a majority of the adults from foster care [the American term for what Europeans mean by care] were functioning satisfactorily in their communities.' However, Festinger urges caution in relying too heavily on these studies because of their methodological flaws, inconsistent findings and the general lack of any comparison groups.

Tackling this problem herself, Festinger (ibid.) located and interviewed 227 adults who had been discharged from care in New York city in 1975. These were young people who had been in care continuously for at least the previous five years and were aged between 18 and 21 at the time of discharge. She checked the care histories of those she could not locate and found them broadly comparable to those she had been able to interview. On the basis of her findings, she compared the fate of those who had been in care with those of young people generally, and observed: 'How do the former foster children, now young adults, fare when compared with others of their age? Some fare a little better, some a little worse, but most are functioning in about the same way as others their age.'

Recent British evidence is not quite so consoling. Studies were undertaken to compare the functioning of mothers reared in care with mothers of similar social background who had remained at home during their childhood. Rutter et al (1983), for example, found that poor parenting was five times as common in the institution-reared group as in the general population comparison group reared by their own families, and overt parenting breakdown was confined to the 'ex-care' group.

This finding refers to women who have grown up in institutional care. But looking to another form of residential care, the evidence is possibly even bleaker. Rutter and Giller (1983) offer a pessimistic evaluation of the value of residential care in the 'treatment' of delinquency:

> Success rates following institutional treatment or care have generally been poor — at least as assessed by re-conviction rates, which have usually run at about 60-70 per cent. But, of course, that could be no more than a reflection of youths sent to institutions, just as also it could mean that most institutions are of poor quality or are inappropriately run . . . . The general picture is one of remarkably similar re-conviction

rates in the years following discharge, for institutions run on theoretically and practically different lines (pp 288-9).

So far, these observations have related to residential care. How do they compare with the outcome for other forms of care? Triseliotis and Russell (1984) compared current social functioning and perceptions of past care of three different groups drawn from respondents who had experienced adoption, residential care and foster care. Not surprisingly, given the social profile of most adoptive homes, only 9% of adoptees were currently experiencing severe financial and/or housing problems, compared with 35% of those in the residential category and 15% of those raised in foster care. Adoptees and those who had been fostered declared themselves satisfied with their experience to much the same degree (82% and 75% respectively), as opposed to 55% of those in the residential category. Only 15% of those in the residential care group were prepared to rate the quality of their relationships with their carers as 'very good', as compared with 45% of adoptees and, interestingly, an even higher 53% of those in foster care.

How is care perceived by those currently in the system as opposed to those who are looking back on it from the vantage point of adulthood? Rowe et al (1984), as part of a wider study of long-term foster care, interviewed 100 children who were being fostered long-term; 69 of these were at least 12 years old. Some of the findings are of particular interest, for example 76% of the children studied seemed well integrated in their foster home; 54% had some feeling of stigma or unease over their status, with girls being more often troubled over this than boys; and nearly one child in four feared not being able to remain in the foster home, usually because of their own behaviour, while a few wanted to leave.

What advice and insights does the literature offer about improving the operation of the care system? One recent major British study tends to corroborate previous findings. Between 1980 and 1983, the Dartington Social Research Unit traced the care careers of 450 children entering local authority care in the UK. The conclusions of the research project have been summarised:

* if a child remains in local authority care for longer than five weeks, it has a very strong chance (two out of three cases) of still being in care two years later;
* the maintenance of close contact with their families is the best indicator that a child will leave local authority care rapidly;
* children and adolescents, even if their chances of returning home are slim, function better psychologically, socially and educationally if they remain in regular contact with their own families (DHSS, 1985).

On the state of foster care, Rowe et al (1984) offer some trenchant criticisms:

In spite of many positive aspects, too many of the study placements had drifted from being short-term or indefinite into an undeclared permanency. Too often the children had neither true security nor access to knowledge of their origins. Work with natural parents was seriously deficient and, though foster parents were reasonably content with the support they received, social work input did not seem as effective as one would wish it to be. It was our very strong impression that, although many of the placements we studied were working well, they were doing so in spite of the system rather than because of it (p. 230).

Rowe et al (ibid.) go on to enunciate a whole series of recommendations for improvements in the fostering system. These are too detailed to recount here, but one point is especially relevant in the Irish context, where the extended family and the kinship network remain vibrant. The researchers found to their surprise that placements with relatives represented quite a success story:

> Unexpectedly, the data showed that children fostered by relatives seemed to be doing better in virtually all respects than those fostered by others. Social workers rated these homes highly . . . . The overall 'disturbance' rate in these [relative homes] was 17% compared with 30% of those in unrelated foster homes. The main difference was in the behaviour and adjustment of the teenagers. Children living with relatives showed less insecurity and were less troubled about their status (pp 187-8).

In relation to the residential care field, Whittaker (1985) summarises the evidence from research about what might be the elements of a more helpful practice and provision. His review leads him to make the case for a residential practice which is closely integrated with other services and which seeks maximum links with the family and community to which the child returns. He states,

> The most powerful determining factor of the child's post-discharge adjustment is the nature of the post-discharge environment. Central in this environment is, most generally, the family. Thus the extent of family support and the nature of familial relationships are crucial variables. Further, in light of this powerful factor, other factors such as pre-admission characteristics, characteristics measured while in residence, and specific treatment interventions are not strongly associated with post-discharge adjustment.

Reviewing the field of residential care with delinquents, Rutter and Giller (1983) make a similar point about the crucial influence of the environment to which the young person returns:

> The finding that the likelihood of re-conviction varies according to the characteristics of the environment to which the youth returns suggests that the lack of persistence of institutional effects is an indication that environments have effects, rather than that they do not. It is just that there tends to be very little continuity between institutional and community environments and hence very little carry-over from one to the other. The implication is that if we wish to see the benefits of good institutional experience persist, we need to pay equal attention to the environment to which the youth returns (p. 291).

Functions of the Care System: A Sociological View

Given that the international evidence about the value of care is at best ambivalent and at worst unfavourable, how can this perverse gap between good intentions and unhappy outcomes be explained?

To answer this question, it is necessary to ask another — What does the care system do? At one level this may seem a rather pointless question. Is it not clear, after all, that the care system represents the arrangements society makes to protect children whose parents have failed them or are unable through illness or whatever to provide adequately for them? Of course, this is true but it is by no means the whole story. If we fail to see that the care system may serve other functions in society, then we may fail to understand its true nature or the source of its contradictions.

It is suggested here that the care system may be as much about controlling people as about helping them. The care system may function to control wayward parents and their wayward offspring in order to preserve social order and to protect the wider community from contamination by similar social problems.

These ideas are explored further by suggesting that two models or ways of thinking have dominated approaches to child care practice and that these approaches may actually be heavily weighted towards controlling rather than helping, wayward families.

Traditional Missionary/Rescue Model of Child Care Provision

Modern child care in Ireland has grown out of the Poor Law system, under the British administration. The Poor Law represented a means by which the rich and powerful in earlier times sought to regulate and control the 'dangerous classes', as they were known. The aim was to ensure that any assistance offered was so minimal and demeaning as not to discourage a person from seeking a livelihood by themselves.

Concern was expressed at the effect of the workhouse environment on impressionable and vulnerable children and this led to the establishment of the boarding-out of children from the workhouse, the forerunner of what we know as fostering. The intention was to rescue children from the bad influence of their parents and their environment.

Thus, the early child care system sought to rescue children from unsavoury, unsanitary or unsafe social conditions. The system exercised social control in three ways. Firstly, it sanctioned failing parents. Secondly, it served as a warning to others. And thirdly, it acted quite openly as a means of transmitting new social and cultural values to these deprived children. In a sense the price of being helped for many children was the renunciation of their past, their parents and often their religion. This latter point serves to explain the denominational character of residential provision in many countries and the tensions surrounding cross-denominational care, which even now lie barely dormant. These denominational tensions were a powerful dynamic in the history of Irish child care and have shaped more than anything else perhaps our modern system (Robins, 1980).

Today, however, it is cultural rather than religious values that children may have to renounce in the child care system. For some children, being in care may involve conformity to values and behaviour quite foreign to their cultural experience. The children's home or foster home may be run according to middle-class values. Successful integration into the new setting may involve a subtle process of leaving behind old ways and the adoption of new standards and new behaviour. Working-class children may have to surrender the values of working-class culture in order to adapt to the cultural norms of their caretakers.

In Ireland, we seem to find it hard to acknowledge the significance of social class in our lives. But make no mistake, social class has an overwhelming influence on one's life chances and destiny, whether one uses infant mortality, general health, educational attainment or employment prospects as a measure. In each instance, working-class people score worse than their middle-class peers (see pp 19-27). The case made here is that social class differences exist in Ireland and that they exert powerful influences on people's lives. This may not be immediately obvious, but the fact that the goldfish cannot see the glass in its bowl does not mean that his life and choices are not circumscribed in a very absolute way. And so it is with social class, especially for the poor. While rural influences and the informality of social relations may disguise class differences in Ireland, they are actually more rigidly drawn here than in many other countries. It is more difficult here to move up from a lower to a higher social class (Whelan and Whelan, 1984; Breen *et al*, 1990).

Class differences are hard to see in Ireland also because of the homogeneity of the society in important respects. Race, religion, language bind people together. Leaving aside the Northern question, there are few political divisions; the political cleavages along class lines evident in other European societies are largely missing. The relative poverty of the country means that even the wealthy are few and in general are fairly discreet in their ostentation. Social class differences may thus be subtle in appearance rather than absent.

The main source of cultural differences in Ireland runs along class lines and along the urban/rural divide. When the comedian Brendan Grace jokes about 'Bottler' or about 'Culchies' and 'Jackeens', his humour is actually making a serious point. Cultural differences exist in our society and it is these that the comedian seeks to highlight for humorous effect. To acknowledge such differences is not to judge our society unfavourably; rather it is to get closer to the reality of modern Irish life.

For professional social workers these differences are of enormous importance, since, almost invariably, the professionals are drawn from one side of the social class divide. Usually, this divide is most obvious in terms of where people live. The poor live in their ghettoes and the middle classes in theirs "and n'er the twain shall meet". Contact between middle-class professionals and the poor communities generally involves car journeys by the professional into the working-class ghetto only for as long as is necessary to conduct the professional task. This leads to a form of what I have called 'hit and run professionalism' (Gilligan in Kelly, 1986). This pattern of contact breeds mutual suspicion and ultimately incomprehension between the two sides. Speaking of Belfast, where in many areas a handful of priests and nuns are the only professionals who actually live in the areas where they work, Dr Maurice Hayes has asked if it is any surprise that social workers and the like have come to be regarded as an army of occupation, especially when 'they come bearing care orders' (Kelly, 1986). It is suggested that the issues are no different in the other cities and large towns of the island.

What is to be done about this? Much can be learned from the radical changes in the practices of Irish missionaries in recent years. They, too, have had to face the challenge of moving from what appears to be their own better resourced culture to that of their hosts. Previously, missionaries sought to exercise control by transmitting their own values, cultural and religious, to the natives as a superior replacement for indigenous traditions. This approach has had many, what may now seem amusing outcomes, such as the teaching of Irish dancing to African and Asian children. (I have heard Victor Bannerjee, a leading Indian film actor, recollecting with fond amusement his being taught Irish dancing in the Christian

Brothers' College he was glad to have attended in New Delhi.) At one level, these may seem innocent and innocuous examples of over-enthusiasm on the part of the Irish religious; in terms of cultural arrogance and imperialism, they certainly pale by comparison with the behaviour of colonial administrations the world over.

Nevertheless, missionaries today see their role differently. The 'savage' is no longer to be tamed. Missionaries are more likely instead to marvel at and learn from cultures and people with whom they work. Paradoxically, in the light of missionary history, they would argue now that it is we in Ireland who have most to learn from contact with the Third World, if we can listen to its voice with sufficient humility and openness. Thus, respect and reciprocity now exemplify a relationship previously characterised by patronising paternalism, pity and the urge to control. The former attitude must surely be of greater mutual benefit than the latter.

Has this change in attitude relevance for practice in the modern child care system? It is strongly suggested that it has. A professionalism based on humility and the sharing of power, a professionalism that marvels at the endurance of families in the face of adversity, a professionalism that conveys respect and support to the families it meets and that learns in turn from those families is a professionalism that will itself endure, earn respect and maintain its relevance and authority. The challenge is to narrow the frequent gulf between the 'treatment environment' (clinic, therapeutic centre, school etc.) and the 'natural environment' (the neighbourhood and culture within which the child and family live out their lives) (Gilligan in Kelly, 1986).

Traditional Medical Treatment/Sterile Protection Model

Practice in child care is heavily influenced by another model or set of assumptions. This conforms to what might be called the traditional medical treatment model. Increasingly, medicine accepts an holistic view of the person it treats. No longer is the focus solely on the symptom presented. In order to appraise and treat symptoms, medicine now wants to understand the whole person carrying the symptom and their social world. Only then is sympathetic and effective treatment possible.

A practice that parallels the traditional medical model is still, however, influential in child care. In this model, there is a preoccupation with 'badness'. The child's problems are seen as stemming from an innate pathology or deficit, or from 'bad' parents or a 'bad' environment. The child needs to recover through a course of treatment — care — in a sterile environment — foster home/children's home — well insulated from the malign influences of parents and environment. With a course of the right treatment, the child can be built-up to achieve a level of resistance to the pathogenic forces in his life.

Unfortunately for this model, the child invariably succumbs to the effects of the 'diseases' which are endemic in his community on his return to that environment. This approach is bound to fail because immunity is achieved not by immersion in sterile conditions but by controlled exposure to the pathogenic or harmful forces.

This traditional model also fails to effect change and growth because it does not acknowledge social/structural factors in the causation of the child's problems. It fails because it takes children in isolation rather than seeking to help them in their social context — which, ironically, the approach has already acknowledged is very powerful. This approach fails because it does not understand that in order to influence a child's destiny, the forces that shape that destiny most directly — family, school, community and, ultimately, the wider society — must themselves also be addressed in an holistic way. Not only must they be addressed, they must also be closely integrated into any programme of intervention. The approach fails, too, because it undermines its own credibility by its basic fear and distrust of elements in the child's natural environment. How can parents truly co-operate with interventions which fundamentally discredit or discount them?

Taking the child in isolation diminishes the prospects of helpful intervention in another important way. It may collude with the child or young person's wish to deny painful elements in their heritage, elements which invariably hold the key to their future success or failure. Loppnow (1985), an American child care specialist, has commented on the importance of these issues for work with adolescents.

> Adolescents frequently believe that they are isolated and on their own in dealing with life's circumstances. In many instances, this perception has grown out of a history of deprivation, abuse and stressful family circumstances. The young person's response is often to cut off from family, which leaves him or her isolated, alienated and more at risk of being unable to resolve old misunderstandings, hurts and grievances. A prevalent theme in the literature regarding adolescent runaways, abuse of adolescents, and stress, depression and suicide among adolescents is the importance of the family and young person together as the focus of, and vehicle for, intervention. In the past, workers often believed young people needed help in separating from and giving up their neglectful or troubled families. Current knowledge suggests rather that young people need help differentiating from the troubled aspects of their heritages but remaining connected in whatever ways possible to those biological figures central to their identity and experience.

What, then, in summary are the implications of the two models discussed — the so-called Missionary/Cultural Rescue Model and the Traditional Medical Treatment/Sterile Protection Model? It has been argued here that both these approaches fail because they fundamentally blame or distrust the child and/or the family and/or the wider natural environment. The author contends that our practice as child welfare workers will only prosper when it respects rather than rejects all of these key elements and embraces them positively in a therapeutic partnership.

Working with Children in Care

Care Career

For many children, their careers in care are not necessarily a smooth and uninterrupted episode in the one setting, spanning all of their time in care. Often careers in care are punctuated by a series of moves between settings. Some children in long-term care may experience a short period of residential assessment, followed by onward placement in a residential unit and eventually placement in a foster home. In some instances, foster placements or residential placements may break down, necessitating yet another move. Children's homes may be forced to close due to shifts in the policies of public bodies or the sponsoring voluntary agency. Often children's homes set upper age limits and, in the past at least, may have regarded the onset of puberty as the ceiling for a stay by boys. Some children may manifest special educational or psychological needs which it is judged may best be met in another more specialised setting. Other children may experience a series of short admissions to care as intermittent family crises erupt. Disruption in these children's lives can be minimised if the child can return to the same care setting on each occasion, but in reality this may not be possible.

One of the pressing reasons for the decision to admit a child to care is presumably to supply that child with stability and the opportunity for meaningful relationships with reliable adults. What children in care may, in fact, encounter is the dislocation of possibly frequent, sudden and inadequately explained moves and the consequent fleeting exposure to a whole series of adults who play only a transient part in their lives. The lessons children may draw from all of this are — the unreliability of adults who profess to help and the fact that their parents, ironically, may be the only adult figures who remain constant.

A further hazard that children in care may experience is that of becoming lost in the system. Admitted originally for what was intended as a short stay, the time slips by, their social worker may change, disillusioned parents may fade from view, and return home suddenly seems very remote. By default, such children may face the prospect of growing up in care.

To highlight these anomalies in the care system is not to decry the sincerity and commitment of the many people who devote themselves to the welfare of children in care. Nor is it to imply that it is merely some perversity on their part that is preventing the immediate remedying of these difficulties. Doubtless, better decision-making and improved resources and policies could enhance the experience of care for many children. But the unavoidable reality is that no amount of good intentions will wish away the fact that the care system can prove a crude and ill-fitted response to the complex needs of individual children. To acknowledge this is not to dismiss the value of care: rather, it proves the case for careful assessment of a child's circumstances before admission and at regular intervals during the child's career in care. Only in this way can it be established that care is, and remains, the best option for meeting a given child's needs.

In growing recognition of the vulnerability and special needs of young people in care, there has been a slow but steady improvement in the quality of attention and decision-making directed towards young people before, during and after any sojourn in the care system.

Professional practice in relation to children in care can be divided into a number of categories, which reflect the stages through which a child will pass in his or her care career. These stages include pre-admission decisions, the admission process, support of the child in care and support of the child after care.

Pre-admission Decisions

Before the decision to admit a child to care is made and the choice of placement finalised, a number of questions must be answered. In particular, great thought must be given to whether admission to care represents the appropriate response to the child's circumstances.

(1) Should this child come into care now? Will admission to care protect the child or promote its welfare better than any other available measure? Are the problems sufficiently grave to suggest that care will actually improve the situation or at least prevent it deteriorating further? What is the parents' attitude? Can they offer alternatives? What is the child's view and preference? How realistic is the child's perception of the present circumstances and of the prospects offered by care? Can the child's need for care be met by the provision of care in the home by a home help, child care worker or other domiciliary care arrangement? Can neighbours or relatives offer care to the child in his or her own home or in their home?

(2) What is the purpose of the placement?

(3) What form of placement best serves this purpose?

(4) What is the planned length of placement?

The answers to these three questions can best be discussed together. Care may take different forms in order to serve a variety of purposes:

- planned short-term care, for example, where a mother is in hospital for a specified period;

- respite care, again for a specified period, to give a break to a family which is under serious stress, for example, due to grave illness or chronic disability in the family, or because of gross behavioural problems in a child;

- emergency care, for example, where a child is admitted suddenly because of parental desertion or because a serious instance of abuse or neglect has been provisionally diagnosed, requiring the child's immediate removal and protection;

- assessment, where a child's needs are unclear and a period of structured assessment outside of the normal home surroundings is deemed necessary in order to plan for the child's future;

- medium-term placement, where certain educational, health or behavioural objectives have been formulated for a child or where certain improvements in a family's circumstances are confidently expected and where these can be achieved within a specified period, thus facilitating the child's return home;

- indefinite care, where a child is placed in care until a change in home circumstances warrants his return home. In this situation, the prospects of improvement in the family's circumstances are not so strong as to justify plans for an early return; while they may be relatively slim, it is considered worthwhile to keep the chances alive for the moment;

- long-term care where the present circumstances indicate fairly unequivocally that a return home to the family on a full-time basis is not a realistic option. (Where the legal circumstances permit, a child in long-term fostering may be placed for adoption);

- bridging placement: where a child is in care, or when a young person is leaving care, a placement may be required which can support the young person in managing the transition between an earlier placement, which may have broken down or run its natural course, and new living arrangements in an alternative placement or in some form of sheltered or independent accommodation;

- contract placements for the care of adolescents where, for specified periods, the various parties to the placement contract to honour certain commitments during its course;

- shared care placement, where the child comes into care on a part-time basis to benefit from the structure of residential schooling or to avoid predictable flashpoints in a family's weekly routine. The family may be in all other respects quite capable of meeting satisfactorily the child's needs. Weekend heavy drinking might be a deeply ingrained pattern which, however undesirable, is not amenable to professional influence. If the child can be protected during this risk period by regular placement with another family or in a local residential unit, this imaginative compromise allows the child to preserve his or her place in an otherwise loving family which is the best, and only, one the child has. In the case of an older child, it may be possible to negotiate that the child uses the alternative placement if and when the child judges that serious trouble is brewing. In some ways, this replicates the informal understandings that may exist between children and relatives in extended families, where older married siblings, aunts, uncles or grandparents may provide a safe port of call to a child who wants to escape temporarily from serious strain and tension in the family home. This is not to advocate the accommodation of every adolescent whim or collusion with every adolescent tantrum. But it is to ensure that children and young people do not have to endure serious physical danger or excessive emotional strain when trouble erupts in their family, as it can do episodically in many families which live close to the brink of breakdown or disintegration.

(5) Which form of placement is most appropriate for this particular child now — foster care or residential care? The selection of an actual placement will be influenced by the purpose of the placement and by what is practical as well as what is desirable. There is a widely held view that fostering should be the option of first choice when considering placement decisions for children in care. It is held that fostering is better than residential care since it offers children the experience of family living. This is believed to be important because family life is seen as the laboratory where children and young people absorb and rehearse the relationship skills to be used in parenting and relationships in adult life. In longer term placements, children may be afforded the opportunity to form attachments, which attachment theory asserts are a crucial prerequisite for healthy psychological development and adult mental health. This may be more easily achieved in foster rather than residential care. It should be stressed however that residential care has an important role in relation to a variety of children, for example, children who do not want to be fostered, children in sibling groups who would have to be separated from each other if not in residential care, children with disturbed behaviour etc.

(6) Are there practical considerations that affect the choice of placement? The availability of vacant places in foster homes or children's homes will often be

a crucial factor in determining the choice of placement. Often there is the serious practical problem of finding a vacancy for a child needing care. In addition, location may be important: the possibility of enabling a child to stay in the same school and to maintain links in the neighbourhood may be an important consideration and may mean that a place in a local residential unit is preferable to a vacancy in a distant foster home. The attitude of the child and natural parent may also colour the final choice.

(7) Have the parent and child concerned had the opportunity to participate in an informed way in decision-making about the admission? Do they understand the terms being used, such as foster care or children's homes? Have they had a chance to express their doubts and anxieties? Are they offered exploratory visits to various settings? To what extent have they a real say? What are the constraints on this — does a shortage of available places effectively rule out choice or does agency policy or the worker's approach pre-empt a meaningful say for clients? What can be done to remove such obstacles? Involving parents is vitally important because only with their support and permission will most children do well in care. Otherwise loyalty to the natural parents may prevent the child putting down new 'roots'.

(8) Where siblings are being admitted to care, should they always be placed together, space permitting? Siblings placed together can provide each other with continuity and support, vital ingredients in the development of their identities which may not be available easily, if at all, from other sources. In their shared experience, they may better be able to absorb and make sense of what is happening to them and insulate themselves from the trauma of being in care. Keeping siblings together obviously is also consistent with the maintenance of blood ties which is important in most cultures. For children in care, close relations with siblings may help compensate for weakened relations with parents both in childhood and later in adulthood. In a comprehensive review of the issues, Hegar (1988) stresses the great value of siblings for children in care.

While the advantages of placement together may seem obvious, it should also be recognised that the needs of siblings must be assessed on an individual, as well as a group, basis and that in some instances it may be better for them to be deliberately placed apart. This is not intended to sunder or destroy the sibling relationship, but rather to prevent any replication of destructive patterns of relationships learned in the family of origin. An example of this may be a child who has adapted to the deficits in the family of origin by assuming a domineering or exploitative role in relation to the other siblings. Or a child may have assumed levels of responsibility for the welfare of younger children which are quite inappropriate for his or her age. To free a child of this pattern and to restore behaviour more appropriate to his or her age will be a necessary objective of placement in care. But this may only be achieved realistically if the over-responsible child is actually removed from daily contact with the other siblings. Another example where sibling separations might be considered is where one child may have been made a scapegoat by another sibling and may thus need separation for physical and psychological protection.

On a more pragmatic level, placements may have a better chance of survival if children with difficult behaviour are placed separately, since there are clearly limits to the degree of dislocation and stress that any one setting can absorb. In the long run, viable and enduring placements separately may be of more value for many children than a precarious and overstretched placement together.

Placing siblings separately need not diminish or threaten their collective sense of identity. This can be preserved so long as all the adults who are party to their placements appreciate the importance of regular physical and other contact as a means to sustaining their solidarity.

Ultimately, the decision to place siblings together or separately depends heavily on the individual needs of all the children concerned. Assessing those needs requires, like all aspects of the pre-admission process, as detailed a knowledge as possible of the individual children involved.

The Admission Process

Following the decision that admission is appropriate for a child at this time, considerable work must go into managing what is often a major, and potentially traumatic, transition in the life of the child and the family left behind. The setting receiving the child will also have to make adjustments. Children may have to move bedrooms and make other sacrifices in order to accommodate the newcomer in the children's home or the foster home. This is a visible example of the deeper disruption that the arrival and departure of children can cause in the life of the group or family concerned. Children in care are especially susceptible to the effects of these changes because they serve as often abrupt reminders of their own uncertain status and may evoke again painful and partly buried memories and apprehensions of their own.

Easing these transitions requires sensitivity to the demands being made on all concerned — the child, the child's family and the new caretakers. The foster parent or child care worker may also be apprehensive about the troubled reputation of a new child and the prospect of fresh turmoil in a group or family which has just begun to settle down after the last arrival.

The process of admission to care demands careful negotiation of its purpose. Trouble is needlessly stored up unless social workers and prospective caretakers alike can articulate clearly their expectations of the placement and can reach some kind of working agreement as to its purpose and likely duration. Detailed information will be needed about the child's personal history, including all relevant medical details and educational progress. It is also vital to know of the child's idiosyncrasies — the likes and dislikes, fears and preferences that all children manifest. Sensitivity to these will enable the child to settle in more easily and will transmit clearly to her in a concrete way that the new caretakers see, and will treat, her as an individual. What is the child's favourite food? Is the child used to sleeping with the door open or the light on? What injections has the child had? Have any allergies been discovered? These are the kind of questions that parents can answer, thus giving them some sense of playing a constructive role in what for them may be an otherwise painful, and possibly humiliating, experience.

The child, too, can be an important contributor to this process of information-gathering. Even a very young child may be able to tell of familiar routines and help identify important toys, photographs and other mementoes of home, all of which will contribute to the vital task of enabling the child preserve a meaningful thread between the past and the present. This thread may make it possible for the child to face the next day, and the future, with more confidence.

In the admission phase, parents and children must not be cast merely in the role of supplementary sources of personal information. They must be kept briefed on developments and accorded the courtesy (except in an extreme emergency) of a pre-placement visit to see the setting and meet the new caretakers. Seeing the reality may offer reassurance and help discard some of the wilder fantasies which may have been torturing child or parent. It is well to remember that most lay people are not familiar with the interior appearance or atmosphere of a modern children's home or foster home. Their impressions, especially in the case of residential care, are likely to owe more to gossip, rumour and historically outdated images promoted by the media.

Admission to care may be a response to a crisis in the lives of child and family. It is also likely to constitute a crisis in its own right. Under such stress, both child and parents are likely to find it hard to absorb key information and impressions without constant reinforcement. All helpers must be sensitive to the emotional overload that parents and child may experience and which may prevent their assimilation of information, even where such information seems straightforward and relatively innocuous to others less personally involved. This difficulty in absorbing critical information is not a sign of intellectual dimness; rather, it is a healthy sign of the operation of psychological defences which come into play at points of stress in people's lives in order to control the level of pressure to be dealt with at any one time. In conversations, it is worth asking people to repeat their understanding of what has been said in order to identify and clarify any misunderstandings. In addition, people may find it helpful if information is given in a written form which they can refer to later.

In a planned admission, it is important that the day of admission be carefully scheduled in advance. The structure of a previously agreed timetable can supplement the effects of pre-placement visits and familiar objects in minimising the insecurities that will inevitably surface for the child. It is especially important that the rituals surrounding the leaving of home and arrival at the new placement are handled with due care and that past and future significant figures are available to participate in marking the transition from old to new. Ideally, parents should be involved in the physical hand-over of the child, signifying to them and their child their continuing responsibility, even if they are not providing daily care. While it may be more painful for the adults, it is actually healthier for the child if he or she can begin to express the feelings of hurt, loss and anger which may be aroused by the separation from parents and fear of the unknown. Many children may be unable to release these feelings so easily and may present an exterior veneer of 'cool' indifference. This response can endure for a number of weeks until the mask begins to slip as the child feels more at home in the new setting. This 'honeymoon' period is well known to caretakers, who may regard its passing as a mixed blessing: it is scarcely consolation to them to know that the acting-out and other difficult behaviour they must now face may actually be a sign that they are beginning to mean something to the child concerned.

The social worker can be an especially important figure in the child's life during this period, since he or she represents, quite literally, a link between the past and the present and is likely to be seen as a powerful key to the child's future. For this reason, there needs to be close contact and appointments must be observed meticulously. Where an absolute emergency requires an appointment with a child to be postponed, the social worker should make sure to phone through an explanation to the child directly. (All of this obviously applies to a child old enough to appreciate the role of the social worker.)

Admission to care will entail a good deal of administration, especially on the part of the social worker. The details may differ slightly according to agency policy, but essentially the worker must ensure that parents have signed a 'reception into care' form — even where admission has been compulsory on foot of a court order. This form seeks parental permission for any medical attention that may be required when the parent is not contactable. It also requests information about the parents' financial circumstances.

Supporting the Child in Care
The effect of living in care and the support a child will require depend on a number of factors, including the child's age, the precipitating reason for admission, the expected duration of care, the level and quality of contact with parents, siblings and significant others, and the quality of fit between the child's needs and the setting in which the child finds himself

If the care episode is to be longer than a number of weeks, the child is likely to begin grappling with some quite painful material about his predicament. He may seek answers to questions such as: Who am I? Why am I different from other children who are not in care? Why am I in care? How do I explain being in care to other people? What will they think of me? To whom am I important? Where do I come from? Does anyone love me? Is all of this my own fault?

It is unlikely that the child will articulate these concerns coherently or widely. Children do not necessarily want literal answers; for many children, the issues are too loaded to be addressed head-on. They may search a long time before finding, if ever, an adult with whom it seems safe to broach such topics. Enabling these concerns to be aired demands alertness, sensitivity and skill on the part of the caretakers and social workers dealing with children.

Where an adult succeeds in engaging a child's trust, between them they can create a private world within which it is safe to touch on painful issues in the child's life. In this therapeutic relationship, the worker may introduce a variety of tools and media — dolls, puppets, drawing materials, sand and water — through which it is possible to create characters who are affected by similar concerns to the child. Both worker and child participate knowingly in the often unacknowledged deceit that the concern is literally about the pain of the doll or animal or whatever tool is being used, when in fact that character or third object represents a safe conductor for the feelings and anxieties being experienced by the child himself.

There is no particular mystique or secret technique involved in winning a child's confidence. Being reliable — following through on promises — is certainly an essential pre-requisite. Empathy with a child is also helped by the adult consciously recollecting the texture and detail of their own childhood and exploring their own memories, to give them some insight into the intensity of the child's feelings about issues such as rejection, separation or loss. Films, poetry, novels and short stories can be useful triggers or supplements to this process of recollection.

Adults should aim to 'be with' the child in a relaxed way, rather than feeling the need to be busy with, or 'talk to', the child. The task is serious, but it can only be accomplished with a lightness of touch and what must frequently be a spirit of fun. There may be quiet and poignant moments, but it is to be hoped that there will also be at least some 'crack' (in the Irish sense of lively conversation, banter and a good time), where the child gets the authentic message that the adult is really enjoying his company. Perhaps this is the most therapeutic and healing message a child can get from an adult.

Besides being helped to explore issues to do with identity and self-worth, the child in care has many other pre-occupations over and above those which may normally be the lot of children or adolescents. Children in care will often feel very isolated. For each child in the care system, it may be profitable to ask certain questions, such as: Does this child have any constant, predictable, stable adult figures in his life? Is the child being made a scapegoat by his peers, siblings, parents, teachers or caretakers? Can anything be done to break any cycles of isolation or ridicule that may be observed? What kind of relationship does the child have with his peers? Is the child being helped to come to terms with his sexuality? Has the child learned to gauge an appropriate degree of intimacy and self-disclosure on meeting relative newcomers to his life? Has the child been helped to develop a 'cover story' that will avoid the need to reveal details of his care career in even the most superficial new social contact? Is the young person learning to shoulder a fair share of the responsibilities involved in living with other people?

For the child in long-term care, it is vital that a great deal of attention is devoted to equipping her with survival skills for life on discharge from care. It is not sufficient for these to be the subject of some kind of belated crash course in the months preceding discharge. The whole programme of care in a young person's teenage years must be geared to the transmission and rehearsal of skills for independent living. Young people need the opportunity to acquire skills for:

- coping with loneliness;
- managing money and bills;
- dealing with officialdom (claiming welfare rights, contact with banks, electricity supply board, post office, hospitals, doctors);
- self-care (personal health and hygiene, laundry, cooking, budgeting for an adequate diet, housekeeping);
- handling sexuality;
- managing personal relationships;
- finding social outlets;
- job-hunting and relationships with employers and work colleagues.

Clearly, some children within ordinary families (mainly boys, it must be said) grow into adulthood without achieving this level of personal resourcefulness. But many families now expect sons and daughters to play a reasonable part in house-keeping. Thus they gradually acquire the skills of personal organisation necessary to manage laundry, money matters, shopping and budgeting. The cut and thrust of family life also prepares children for some of the emotional rough and tumble of the outside world.

Children in care, however, may lack such opportunities. In a residential child care unit, for example, food may be bought in bulk, clothes may be laundered centrally, and bills may be paid by some administrative mechanism removed from the daily life of the children. There may be very practical reasons for these features of residential life, but they prevent children's natural exposure to some of the realities of living in our modern world.

Thus, children in care may suffer a threefold disadvantage in the business of coping with independent living. Firstly, they have been deprived of the experience of growing up in their own family, which for most children is the laboratory where they prepare for adult life. Secondly, the institutional routines of residential care may not only fail to compensate for this, but may further aggravate the problem by insulating them from the complex trivia which comprise household and personal organisation. And finally, when launched into the world the young person may lack the supports and resources which immediate and extended family would automatically offer their young adult members. These may range from regular or emergency injections of cash to a place to seek asylum in the face of personal troubles or illness. The young person leaving care is less likely to have any such 'natural' safety net.

In the Irish context, discharge may occur as early as 16 years under present conditions, if the young person is not engaged in full-time education. This compares with the age of 18 in the UK; in Sweden, young people up to the age of 20 may be taken into care. It seems unrealistic to expect young people growing up in care to demonstrate a higher level of maturity and self-care than is expected of other children of the same age who have relatively untroubled upbringings. It would be considered extraordinary for families to send their 16-year olds out to cope in the world and yet this is what is expected of youngsters coming out of care. This anomaly is further compounded by the absence of explicit rights for them in the matter of accommodation or income support between the ages of 16 and 18, under the present law. (When the relevant sections of the Child Care Act 1991 are implemented young people will be able to remain in care until 18 years and may also be given help in after care.) These present deficiencies can have most unfortunate consequences, since problems leading to, and arising from, the history of care are likely to render young people less, rather than more, mature for their years. In some instances, this immaturity may be further complicated by mild degrees of mental illness or handicap.

Even where the task of preparation for independent living is accorded priority, its execution remains a daunting challenge. At the best of times, adolescents may not be especially receptive to the wisdom of their adult caretakers. Adolescents in care, however, may have additional reasons to be sceptical of adult advice.

Nevertheless, a combination of requiring minimum standards of personal self-care together with the use of group work and the adolescents' own ideas about their needs should help them begin their long, slow haul to reasonable competence for independent living.

Supporting Young People who have left Care

Building on preparation work done during the young person's time in care, caretakers and social workers together need to orchestrate the resources necessary to give the young person a realistic chance of beginning to make it on their own. In striking out for independence, he or she will need supports and a safety net, like all young people.

Loneliness, money and accommodation are probably the three most pressing problems experienced by young people after they leave care. But the problems they encounter will vary according to their individual circumstances. Thus a repertoire of resources needs to be available from which individually adapted packages of after care can be devised. There needs, for example, to be a continuum of accommodation possibilities, ranging from high support options (such as foster care or staffed accommodation) to flats rented on the open market from sympathetic landlords. This provision need not entail great costs, however, since the number of young people 'growing out' of the care system each year is unlikely to exceed one hundred, and not all of these would require their own sheltered or semi-independent accommodation.

After-care provision clearly requires practical services like money, accommodation, job-training and placement. But most of all, it requires personnel with the time, resources and mandate to construct and oversee the operation of the various packages of after care. The young person needs a named worker to refer to when in difficulty. Foster parents, landlords, employers, in fact all those who are involved with the young person, also need someone specific with whom to liaise.

Those unfamiliar with the deep personal and practical problems facing young people leaving care may regard this approach as cosseting such youngsters. But the reality is that if this effort is not invested, not only will many young lives be squandered, but a great deal of public money may eventually have to be spent on processing these young people through the penal and/or psychiatric systems. The streets of our cities and towns are unforgiving places, with magnetic powers to draw the lonely and vulnerable into their underworld of crime, vice and drugs. Clearly, a package of after-care is no guarantee of insulation against these pressures. But it does contain a great deal more hope and promise than the present vacuum in provision.

Care is clearly not just about maintenance and shelter. It is about the transmission of skills and values which will sustain young people when they are no longer in care. The greater the continuities between the care environment and the natural environment in which they will live, the smoother the transition can be. But all too often this transition will, in practice, prove difficult. Attention to this question is vital. We can learn much from the work of various schemes abroad which are wrestling with these very problems of vulnerable youngsters leaving the care system (Barth, 1986).

The Caretakers

The task of caretakers of children in care — foster parents or child care workers — has grown more complex and demanding over the years. Adoption, the greater availability of preventive services and shifts in thinking about the role of public care have produced great changes in the population of children in care. Fewer children today are reared from infancy in care. Increasingly, children come into long-term care only when family problems have deteriorated to the point where efforts at shoring up the family have had to be abandoned.

Children coming into long-term care are now likely to be older and to have been scarred by the troubles which culminated in their admission to care. The years they have spent at home will also mean in many cases that a significant relationship has developed between parent(s) and child, notwithstanding their common problems. Unlike the case of infants coming into care, it is generally not feasible (nor is it usually regarded as desirable) to see care as offering a fresh start in which links with the past are severed. Thus, caretakers are confronted not only with the practical day-to-day care required by any child; they must also expect to deal with acting-out and disturbed behaviour, a likely legacy of the problems which resulted in admission. In addition, they can expect to become enmeshed in the relationship between child and parent, which may be characterised on the child's part by a confusion of feelings, ranging from loyalty and love to a sense of rejection or ambivalence. The turmoil in the child evoked by these feelings, and by the status of being in care, may produce considerable stress for the caretaker who must try to absorb the 'flak'.

The work of caretakers is stressful not only because of these pressures. Their task is to use their personality as a therapeutic resource in the life of the child. This means that they must try to consider the meaning of their response to each incident involving the child in terms of his or her overall needs. They must not try to disguise the inevitably negative emotions such as anger which the child is likely to elicit with skill and tedious regularity. The child must experience the real consequences of their actions, but the caretaker is clearly constrained to respond in a controlled way. Responses that verge on bullying or resort to physical punishment (as opposed to restraint in violent incidents) are not acceptable.

The task of the caretaker is further complicated by the needs of others. In the case of residential child care, the worker has to be sensitive to the impact of one child's behaviour on the other children, and the staff, in the group. In the case of foster parents, they have to think of the needs of their own children, their marriage and where relevant other foster children in the home.

The effective care of troubled children demands considerable strengths on the part of the adults involved. They must possess a sufficient degree of self-awareness and self-control. They must combine this maturity with qualities of tolerance, persistence, diplomacy and tact, and most of all perhaps, inexhaustible good humour. It may well seem that only a saint could conform to these specifications! But although caretakers' personal qualities are vitally important, what is also crucial to their role is the degree of practical and psychological support available to them.

Supporting Child Care Workers

Conditions of employment play a crucial part in determining whether a child care worker can actually do the work intended. Good employment practices, which may be taken for granted among larger employers in the world of commerce, cannot be assumed in the social services. A precise and realistic job description, with accountability based on a clear reporting relationship, is important. So also are proper conditions of work, viz, arrangements in relation to annual and sick leave, the degree of staff input in the drafting of duty rosters, the adequacy of cover arrangements for staff absent on annual or sick leave, or on training. Often the unsocial hours of the job are further aggravated by the expectation that a worker's sense of moral responsibility will ensure that absent colleagues' duties are covered, often at short notice and usually entailing the working of extra shifts with no financial recompense. This kind of exploitation quickly corrodes a worker's idealism and can hasten demoralisation in what is often an already fairly thankless task.

It must be said, however, that the needs of children are not readily met in a manner compatible with conventional employment conditions. There is a tension between regular and social working hours and having staff available at the unsocial times when children are likely to be at their most needy, vulnerable or explosive. While the introduction of conditions based on the model of a 40-hour week has brought important and necessary improvements in the quality of life of child care staff, it has been at the high cost for children of a constantly changing set of care staff. 'Who's on today?' is likely to be one of the most repeated questions by children in residential centres. This problem of balancing the interests of adults and children has come more sharply into focus because of the steady withdrawal of religious personnel due to fewer vocations, redeployment and reappraisal of priorities. (Previously religious had worked extraordinary hours in the service of their vocation. This level of commitment had definite drawbacks, however. There was a high personal cost to many of the individuals involved and indirectly, presumably, to the children. The involvement of religious in the care system also served to disguise the real economic cost of providing such a service adequately. This seriously weakened the case for adequate staffing levels when the State had to assume responsibility for funding posts for which the religious were no longer available and where previously they had carried the duties at little, or more likely no, cost to the State.)

In addition to the practical support of fair conditions, child care staff need psychological support. They need assistance in distancing themselves from their work in order to interpret its effects on the children and themselves. Effective child care practice also requires the closest collaboration between adult caretakers. Damaged children can have an unrivalled capacity to divide staff groups. This tendency, coupled with the stress of the work can easily affect relationships between colleagues. Avoiding such difficulties requires a number of measures: especially careful and frank discussion in the staff team in order to prevent and resolve problems; professional supervision of their work by a senior practitioner; the opportunity of regular staff meetings to discuss the content and process of their work; access to consultancy support at regular intervals, as well as to in-service and other training opportunities.

Supporting Foster Parents

Foster parents are exposed to stresses which parallel, and to some extent, exceed those endured by child care staff. Foster parents face a range of problems which are undiluted by time out, by the separation of the care environment and personal home life, or by the immediate availability of support or advice from professional peers.

In residential care, the care environment is enacted by the staff while they are on duty; they leave this environment behind, at least physically, when they go off duty. For foster parents, however, the care environment is actually their own home and family. They have no escape. While they share the experience with their spouse and offspring, the role of foster parents is inherently more isolating than that of child care workers since there is not the same sense of belonging to a team.

There is the additional stress of coping with the 'fall out' from the placement on the foster parents' natural children and on the neighbours. Natural children may be suffering due to their parents' absorption in coping with the foster child. They may be subject to bullying, scapegoating or more subtle harassment from a foster child desperately competing for attention and testing the commitment of her new caretakers. Neighbours may not share the motivation and commitment of the foster parents and may dislike how the foster child, is generally 'lowering the tone of the place' with his newly patented and influential forms of depredation. Foster parents may require considerable reserves of diplomatic and mediating skills in order to preserve the peace all round. (It is important to note, of course, that these problems may be less severe with a younger child.)

Contact with natural parents is widely regarded as desirable for the child in care. Yet, for the foster parent, it may produce special pressures. Here again they have a sense of isolation as they cope alone with the behavioural manifestations of the child's anxiety in the anticipation, and the aftermath, of parental contact.

Fostering agencies (in Ireland, health boards) rely on social workers to offer support and ease the burden carried by foster parents. In the past, social workers felt obliged to be a comprehensive source of support and advice to foster parents, but in practice many strains have been found in their relationships. Despite the expectations of them and the importance of the task, social workers have not necessarily enjoyed complete success in delivering this support.

Orlin (1977, p. 21) lists some of the sources of potential conflict in the network of relationships surrounding foster parents:

- foster parents feel superior to natural parents;
- natural parents are resentful of and defensive towards foster parents;
- foster parents resent having an outsider, the social worker, tell them what rules to enforce in their own home. This is not the usual situation in natural parenting;
- foster parents believe their motives for taking a foster child are altruistic;
- the agency is alert for the non-altruistic motives of foster parents;
- all three participants — social worker, foster parent and natural parent — believe they know the child best and what is best for the child;
- the social worker relies on professional expertise as a claim to authority. The foster parents rest the legitimacy of their opinion on their knowledge of how to parent and on daily observation of the child;
- the foster child feels ambivalent towards all the adult actors.

There are ambiguities inherent in the relationship of the social worker with the foster parent. The same worker may have to balance all, or at least some, of these potentially conflicting roles:

* agency representative/inspector/assessor;
* advocate for the foster child;
* worker with the natural parent(s);
* confidant/adviser to the foster parents.

The social worker's role may seem compromised in the eyes of the foster parents for a number of reasons. Foster parents may find it difficult to seek or use support from a source whose sympathies or obligations seem to lie in other directions. In addition, social workers usually have not acted as foster parents themselves and may not even be parents. These deficits need not prevent good practice, but they deprive the worker of reliable experience with which to establish credibility and a realistic appreciation of the pressures of foster parenting. This inexperience, coupled with their frequent unfamiliarity with the detailed mechanics of behavioural management techniques, may deprive social workers of further relevance in the eyes of foster parents. They may thus be unable to offer specific and viable guidance in the management of difficult behaviour which may often be the most pressing problem in many placements.

Practical difficulties may also contribute to strained relations. From British evidence, some social workers have been reported as inefficient and as having failed to visit, communicate or consult adequately, thus leading to dissatisfaction among foster parents (Jones, 1975). Social workers may also change jobs regularly, thus discouraging foster parents from investing in their relationship with the worker (Shaw and Lebens, 1977).

It would be wrong to assume that all relations between social workers and foster parents are necessarily strained. It would be naive, however, to assume that the structural problems inherent in the relationship will not give rise to frequent difficulties. Perhaps the key to resolving these difficulties lies in a renewed conception of the social worker's role. In the past, the social worker has been given, or assumed, a great deal of responsibility for meeting all of the needs of the foster parents directly. The counselling and advice foster parents sought was to be administered directly by the social worker. The expectation was that the social worker would always have the answer, no matter what the question. This assumption gave rise to frustration on the part of foster parents and guilt on the part of social workers whenever it proved without foundation.

A new model of the role of social worker in fostering is now conceivable, in which the social worker has the role of orchestrator — orchestrating the placement and the resources necessary to sustain it. In this model, it is not essential that the social worker be the sole source of support or advice for the foster parent. Nor is it necessary that the social worker is an authority on behaviour modification, however useful that might be. What is necessary is that the social worker is aware of the available resources or support and advice that are relevant to foster parents and, where serious gaps exist, helps to fill them by the creation of new resources.

Social workers play a leading part in the establishment and maintenance of local support groups for foster parents. Regular meetings and the possibility of personal contacts between meetings can dramatically reduce the sense of isolation to which foster parents are vulnerable. The support of peers may also seem more pertinent and reassuring. In the case of advising on the management of difficult behaviour, the social worker's role may be to identify a psychologist or other specialist with an interest in this area, whom the foster parent can consult as necessary.

The social worker will retain regular contact with the foster parent and be alert to needs emerging at a practical and psychological level. The worker will endeavour to resolve practical difficulties, such as delays in payments or the issue of documentation, and will also seek to connect the foster parents to sources of support and training, such as support groups, consultants and training courses.

In this new model of practice, a more collegial style of relationship will emerge in which the social worker seeks to equip aspiring and practising foster parents for their role, by helping them identify their own needs, strengths, capacities and resource networks.

PART V:

FACING THE FUTURE

Chapter 10

FACING THE FUTURE

Principles to Guide Policy

A number of guiding principles are suggested here which might help a child care practice seeking to be relevant and effective face into the challenges of the final years of this millennium and the early years of the next.

Prevention

Prevention is a concept widely supported but perhaps not so widely understood. What does it mean in the context of child care: that no children shall experience poverty, or be abused, or be placed in care? First, one must distinguish between what might be desirable and what is attainable. For this author, the goal of prevention is to ensure that no clients of the child welfare system become isolated or alienated by virtue of their role as clients. Children in care may become cut off and isolated — from their own or any family; Jordan (1981) suggests that prevention is about not letting this happen. He lays particular stress on contact for the child with his or her family, which Millham *et al* (1986) remind us may turn out, for all its faults, to be the one constant thread in the child's career in care. If parents are to stay in touch, then we must seek to prevent the kind of stigma they often experience which is so vividly described by this American mother (quoted in Kelly, 1981):

> Your friends turn away from you when something like this happens. You may kill somebody, you may sexually abuse a child, you can murder somebody, you can rob a bank, you can even assassinate a president; there is always a group of people ready to support you. If you give up your children, you are worse than scum and nobody, but nobody, backs you up.

Normalisation

The price of being helped is too often being made to feel 'different'. For the weak and powerless clients of the child care system, such differences are frequently the foundation of stigma, which may produce further social isolation and aggravate the original problem. The price of being helped may also mean losing contact with the norms and rhythms of everyday life.

Normalisation aims to reduce these costs of being helped. In practice, it requires professionals to contain problems within mainstream services, seeking additional support resources as necessary, rather than hiving off the problems. This means schools not expelling difficult pupils or transferring them to special units. It means bringing the resources that would have been absorbed by the special unit into the school. Similarly, it means not transferring children from a children's home to a more specialist delinquency unit, because they have reached puberty, or because they have stolen a small sum of money from a caretaker's jacket, or because they have begun to smoke and play truant. Sadly, all of these are things which the author has seen occur. Ordinary families can contain such problems. Are they then really beyond the capacity of services specifically geared to providing professional care?

Cultural Sensitivity

Adherence to the principle of normalisation (above) will require professionals to understand the psychological and social meaning of their actions in the culture of the child with whom they are dealing. Reference has already been made to the gulf of mutual incomprehension that can exist between professionals and parents or children who have differing cultural backgrounds (pp 195-7). Class differences pose the greatest difficulty in this regard in Ireland, although we should also not overlook the special problems of the travelling community.

Perhaps we can learn something from the practice of Bradford Social Services Department in this area. Before taking any major care decisions about a child from the black community, they consult a panel of black community leaders which has been convened to advise on the likely meaning and implications within black culture of any decisions reached (Cheetham, 1986). Is there scope for similar consultations in Ireland, with community leaders in working-class ghettoes or in the travelling community?

Caring for the Caretakers

We must remember that without good quality caretakers (foster parents and child care workers) the phrase 'care' becomes an empty administrative category. Recruiting good people is difficult, so special attention must be paid to retaining them. The author is unaware of any research on this subject in Ireland, but a relatively high rate of defection seems to exist both from foster parenting and from face-to-face child care practice as a career.

Support and prestige are key ingredients in helping people feel good about their caring work. Financial rewards are important, too. The rates for foster parents at the moment are hardly calculated to attract many people; indeed they have fallen in value in real terms in recent years (Gilligan, 1990). To retain and motivate foster parents, not only must they be paid adequately but they must also get proper professional, administrative, peer and practical support. A weekend off now and again may make all the difference between a placement that survives or one that breaks down. In the mental handicap field, we have seen (p. 173) the success of respite care schemes in which specially recruited foster families give a break to the family of a mentally handicapped child as well as giving the child a change of scenery. Foster parents also need respite care or babysitting too. Perhaps residential settings can help in this.

What is often most challenging to foster parents is difficult behaviour on the part of a youngster. At such times, what is needed most is practical wisdom about how to reduce the youngster's propensity to such behaviour. Access to a practitioner with a thorough knowledge of the theory and practice of behaviour modification may represent a lifeline for the survival of such a placement. Again, residential settings may be an important source of such wisdom.

In the residential field, it goes without saying that staff should enjoy fair and social conditions of employment and have a written job description. The author would also attach great importance to staff support in the form of regular professional supervision, staff group meetings facilitated by an outside consultant and regular meetings of staff to plan and discuss the day-to-day running of the setting.

Finally, there is the fundamental question in the residential field of the crisis of confidence I see among practitioners and managers. One source of this is a feeling of relative powerlessness or inferiority on the part of the child care worker when faced with other professionals or administrators. There seems to be a structural source to this: to put it bluntly, one of the ways society puts a value on different vocations is the educational requirements for admission to the particular career. Higher entry requirements (with mature entry provision) and advanced training could transform the confidence and capacity of this discipline. This will become more crucial as the religious orders withdraw their management skills. If these higher standards have been implemented in the Garda Síochána and in psychiatric nursing, why not also in the care discipline? Ultimately, it seems desirable to seek common core training shared between field social workers and child care workers, with appropriate top-up specialisms added according to the student's work intentions.

Inclusive care/Localisation

Holman (1975) first made the useful distinction between 'inclusive' and 'exclusive' models of foster care. Inclusive care includes the natural parents in the fostering arrangements, in the sense that they are an active part of the picture. Exclusive care excludes or denies a role to the natural parents.

In keeping with his belief in minimising the gap between the natural and treatment environments (p. 197), the author contends that any form of care, even where it cannot be local, should strive to be as inclusive of elements in the natural environment as possible. To support this contention, the reader is referred to the research evidence summarised on p. 194, on outcomes in residential care, which supports the maximising of continuities between essentially the natural and treatment environments (Whittaker, 1985). There is also the compelling evidence of greater adjustment and earlier discharge from care of children who retain links with their parents. In a study of children in care in New York (Fanshel and Shinn, 1978), it was found that 86% of the children whose parents were good visitors were eventually discharged, compared to 41% of those whose parents were poor visitors. The researchers thus found a positive association between social worker input, parental contact and discharge to natural home. These findings are corroborated for the UK by the findings of the Dartington study, summarised on p. 193 (Millham *et al*, 1986).

The importance of continuities in the life of the child in care is also supported by the findings of two recent UK studies on foster care. Rowe *et al* (1984) found that fostering placements with relatives were more successful than those with non-relatives, while Berridge and Cleaver (1987) highlighted the importance of continuities in social networks for children in foster care:

> As we have seen with parent and sibling relationships and schooling, when certain aspects of children's lives are held constant, change in other areas is more easily endured.

This latter study of fostering breakdown found that placement with siblings and contact between natural parents and the child's social worker were associated with fewer breakdowns (ibid. pp 177-8). Continuation in the same school before and after placement seemed also to be important, although the findings were less clear on this point.

Clearly, the principle of inclusive care can be best applied in localised services. Localisation achieves the effect of narrowing the gap between the treatment environment and the natural environment. It means, for example, siting residential units close to where the resident children originate; at the moment, many community care areas have no residential unit of their own. Localisation also promotes generic rather than specialist services and so is compatible with the principle of normalisation.

There are some exciting examples of this inclusive care approach in practice in the Dublin area, such as the local residential units in the inner city, run by the Society of St Vincent de Paul (Gilligan, 1982) and by the Tabor Society. Their low-key approach has won the trust and respect of children, families, professionals and local people. Significantly, their image is largely devoid of any stigma. There is also the successful day-fostering scheme in Ballymun, managed by social workers of the Eastern Health Board. It has succeeded in harnessing local families to provide care for local children close to their homes as an alternative to the full-scale disruption of admission to a children's home miles away. Again, this approach is popular with the service users — and in addition is considerably cheaper than the previous alternatives.

Voluntariness/Minimum Intervention
These are two sides of the one coin. Interventions should avoid compulsion and a heavy hand as much as possible, in order to minimise the dislocation intervention causes in the lives of clients. There are further practical and ethical reasons for this.

Clients are likely to be more cooperative if they do not feel bullied into certain steps. Authentic cooperation is more likely to be an effective springboard to a successful outcome. With children, this means aiming to motivate them rather than imposing repressive sanctions, such as security, in order to elicit compliance. With parents, it means avoiding over-ready recourse to compulsory intervention. In a study of admission practices in two British local authorities, more contented parents and more satisfactory placements were found in the authority which resorted less often to the use of compulsory care orders (Packman *et al*, 1986). The sudden rise, here in Ireland, in the proportion of children in care on a compulsory basis from 20.8% in 1982 to 47.6% in 1988 (Department of Health, 1986, 1990) is a cause for concern in this context.

Participation/The right to Information

Social workers and child care workers may experience 'powerlessness' from time to time. There are, undoubtedly, circumstances in which this is real. Nevertheless, both types of worker appear very powerful in the eyes of their clients. An important way of minimising this power disparity is to ensure that clients are as well informed as possible about developments in their case.

A summary of a series of child care research projects in the UK reported on what clients valued most (DHSS, 1985):

> honesty, naturalness and reliability along with an ability to listen. Clients appreciated being kept informed, having their feelings understood and getting practical help as well as moral support. The social workers whose assistance was valued had a capacity to help parents retain their role as responsible, authority figures in relation to their children.

A useful Irish initiative in this regard is the publication by Family Link of an information booklet for parents and relatives with children in care (Boland *et al*, 1987). The response to date suggests that this has filled an important gap in information available to families — and professionals.

In the vital decision-making systems then, is there space for clients to be consulted, to voice their views, to participate in decisions? Given the, at best, uneven evidence about the success of their decisions, professionals can hardly claim that client participation will make matters any worse and there is always the chance that it will lead to better decisions and more satisfied clients — parents or children. In an American study of 370 children, Bush and Gordon (1982) found that

> children given a real say and choice about prospective placement proved to be 'significantly more satisfied with their placements' than children not given such opportunities.

Systematic Planning and Decision-making

Given the enormous import of the decisions taken in child care, it clearly behoves professionals to do all in their power to get it right and to avoid prevarication, woolly thinking and poor planning. A recurring finding of child care research is the needless drift of many children in the care system because they have faded from view. With greater alertness, children could be discharged or placed appropriately more quickly. Wasted time exacts a high price in a child's thwarted development. A relentless theme of recent inquiries in the UK into the handling of child welfare cases that went wrong is the importance of clear recording, clear inter-professional and inter-agency communication and cooperation, and the establishment and regular review of mechanisms to achieve these ends (Secretary of State for Social Services, 1988; Blom-Cooper, 1985; DHSS, 1982).

Avoiding False Dichotomies

The current resources of child care are thinly stretched and face infinite demand. Since this is the case, the field can ill afford the luxury of unnecessary divisions, divisions which are all too common.

Tensions between foster care and residential care, for example, are unhelpful. Both need each other and can and must co-exist constructively. It has been suggested that fostering can itself be seen as a form of residential care (Barclay Committee, 1982) and that, therefore, it is more helpful to see the two forms of care as part of a continuum of child care services rather than as polarised opposites (Berridge, 1985).

In the author's view, however, any notion that foster care will or can supplant residential care is wildly misguided, because it greatly exaggerates the capacity of foster care to absorb difficult children and adolescents, and it too readily assumes that all youngsters in care want to live in a family.

The tensions that can exist between social workers and residential child care workers may be understandable, but they are deeply frustrating when the enormity of the child care task requires all in the field to pull together. Many of the problems in these relationships arise from differences in training and work practices. It is essential that these are reviewed to maximise the potential for collaborative work.

Another common division is seen between the service-giver and service-recipient. Their respective roles may be unduly rigid: service-recipients may be able to give as well. Parker (1980) makes this point:

> Being 'in care', or being the parents of a child 'in care', is liable to cast people into semi-permanent positions of disadvantage . . . when, in any case, they are, or feel themselves to be, relatively disadvantaged in the first place. If their talents, skills and resources, however modest, can be recognised and used, then not only might there be marginally more resources but there might also be better services. Having one's resources recognised, valued and used is itself a common need.

The success in the UK of the National Association of Young People in Care (a self-help association for youngsters in care) and of the Parents' Aid movement (self-help for parents and relatives in care) provide ample proof of Parker's point. The success to date of the support group for parents and relatives with children in care in Dublin also supports Parker's case.

Care is clearly not just about maintenance and shelter. It is about the transmission of skills and values which will sustain young people when they are no longer in care. The greater the continuities between the care environment and the natural environment in which they will live, the smoother the transition can be. But all too often this transition will, in practice, prove difficult. Attention to this question is vital. We can learn much from the work of 'The Barnardo's 16+ Project' in London, which is one of a number of schemes wrestling with these very problems of vulnerable youngsters leaving the care system.

However threatening this concept of clients' rights may be to the beleaguered professional, it is important to remember that clients are 'fellow citizens' (British Association of Social Workers, 1975). Their citizenship and their clienthood entitle them to certain rights. When charters of specific rights have been articulated in respect of both parents and children as clients of the child care system, and when those sets of rights are given real credence in practice, then it will be possible to say that the child care system has truly come of age.

A CHILD-CENTRED SOCIETY?

Children are valued in Ireland — up to a point. Children can prompt admiring and interested conversation between total strangers on the street, in a shop, on a bus. There is little evident resentment of children in public places, and the explicit exclusion of children from events or places of entertainment is still relatively rare. Irish adults seem to hold more child-centred attitudes than their European counterparts. When asked whether parents should be prepared to make sacrifices for their children, even at the expense of their own wellbeing, three-quarters of Irish respondents (74%) thought they should, compared to less than two-thirds (64%) of respondents in all ten participating countries in the European Values Survey (Fogarty, Ryan and Lee, 1984, p. 201).

In assessing how child-centred a society is, obviously it is also necessary to consider children's and young people's perception of how valued they feel. What would be of especial interest would be research to elicit youngsters' subjective sense of belonging and attachment to their social networks. No work of this kind has been done here. Abroad, a Swedish study of children's living conditions in five countries revealed a surprising sense of detachment from their social networks among the Swedish children questioned. The samples of children from Spain, Algeria, Israel, Ethiopia and Sweden could reply 'often', 'sometimes' or 'never' to the statement 'I feel there is someone who likes me'. Of the Swedish children 11% answered 'never' and only 22% 'often'. For the children from the other countries hardly any said 'never' and 65-70% answered 'often' (Kalvesten and Odman, 1979).

While there has been no research directly comparable to the Swedish study in Ireland, there is some, albeit indirect, evidence that young people in Ireland may feel valued by adults close to them. In one survey of young people conducted for the National Youth Policy Committee in 1984, 88% of respondents believed that parents 'generally listened to the views of young people' and 65% thought this true of teachers, the next category of adults most frequently cited. Asked to identify categories of adults who 'generally understood young people' 84% referred to parents and 69% to teachers (Costello, 1985, p. 54). How these perceptions compare to those held by youngsters elsewhere is difficult to establish. In the European Values Study Irish young people responded as having greater confidence in the older generation than young people in all ten countries surveyed (Fogarty, Ryan and Lee *op cit*, p. 200).

All the evidence, however, does not necessarily justify a self-satisfied or complacent view of the sensitivity of Irish culture and society to the psychological needs of young people. One study of young people at second level schools in Cork (N = 1401) and in Lancashire and Yorkshire (n = 1496) compared the problems which they admitted to having. The researcher reported a 5% higher rate of problems reported by the Irish youngsters compared to their English peers. Worries about boy/girl issues were more noticeable in the Irish group. A possibly weaker sense of social belonging was also noted among the Irish youngsters. Overall the findings tempted the author to claim that Irish boys were less mature than Irish girls or any of the English children (Porteus, 1985, pp 465-478). Clearly only limited store can be placed on the results of a single study but the findings certainly provide food for thought.

Private Affection — Public Neglect
At a personal level it seems that Irish people are generally well disposed towards children both in principle and in practice. In observing Irish society, the paradox is the divergence between this private goodwill towards children and the relative inattention to their needs in the public sphere. Perhaps it is that children are taken a little for granted because they are not in short supply: the Irish birth rate remains easily the highest in the EC. Whatever the reason, private interest in children is not translated into generous public provision for them.

Child-centred provision in public policy in Ireland is more the exception than the rule. Compared with other countries our record in these areas is poor. Norway, for instance, was one of the first countries to introduce child protection legislation (1869) and reform of its illegitimacy laws (1915). It was the first country to appoint a children's ombudsman (1981). In Ireland we still rely on child protection legislation introduced under British rule over eighty years ago. More than twenty years of pressure by child welfare activists has still failed to deliver the implementation of legal and other reform. In the area of illegitimacy Ireland finally managed to reform its laws in 1987, but has no comparable office to that of children's ombudsman.

In the case of maternity and parental leave, mothers in employment in Ireland are entitled to fourteen weeks leave for each birth under the Maternity Protection of Employment Act 1981. In Germany, a mother is entitled to maternity leave until the child is six months old (Flamm, 1983, p. 69). In Sweden, either parent may take up a year's paid leave after the birth of a child. Up to six months of this may be saved for use at any time until the child reaches eight years. In addition, parents in employment are entitled to 60 days paid leave per child per year for the care of sick children (Swedish Institute, 1984, p. 2).

In the case of the age of criminal responsibility, in Ireland, it is possible to be charged with, and convicted of, a criminal offence at seven years of age. In this Ireland is markedly out of step with wider European practice. In Sweden the comparable age is 15 years, Denmark 15 years, Germany 14 years, Poland 13 years, Holland 12 years, England, Wales and Northern Ireland 10 years.

It is not only in the legal arena in Ireland that public provision for children falls down compared to other countries. Child-centred facilities in public places are scarce. In Finland, the railways provide carriages which consist exclusively of a playroom and nursery for the use of travellers with young children. In Danish banks, there are toys and a play-area for children. In Scandinavian Airlines System's timetables, passengers with young children are invited to give notice in advance of any special food requirements, which the company undertakes to satisfy. One finds no such provision in railways, banks or airline timetables in Ireland. Indeed, in many a restaurant or cafeteria, one is lucky to get a clean and safe high chair. Changing rooms for babies or toddlers are very rare in public places in Ireland, and parents usually have to make do with adult toilets. The needs of children are not seen as an obligation on commercial interests in, say, the catering industry. A similar neglect is evident in the public sector where, typically, in hospitals and public offices harassed parents with children must queue for long periods without any relief in the form of a playroom or play or creche facilities.

We have seen in section 2 that Irish children often face unfavourable material and social conditions. Children from disadavantaged backgrounds are less likely to be breast fed, more likely when older to have a deficient diet, to have poorer dental health, to be smaller, and to be more prone to psychiatric disturbance and drug abuse than their more socially favoured peers. In education, these youngsters face comparable disadvantage: they are more likely to be illiterate and to leave school without educational certification (one in three of working class school-leavers in Dublin compared to the national average of 20 per cent for boys and 17 per cent for girls). Children from disadvantaged backgrounds also have virtually no chance of reaching university — despite twenty years of free second-level education. Among the disadvantaged, certain sub-groups are especially at risk of additional problems: children of the unemployed, children of single parents, children of travellers, and children in families where violence is endemic.

Neglect Born of Economic Impotence or Political Indifference?
Many Irish children endure degrees and combinations of adversity unknown to many of their peers in other European countries. Part of their deprivation may be explained by the relative economic weakness of Ireland. Our gross domestic product per capita is approximately half that of France, Germany or Austria, one third that of Switzerland, and only higher than that of Portugal, Greece or Turkey (Eurostat 1988, p. 40). This economic weakness is further aggravated by high unemployment (at 17.0 per cent in 1989, second only to Spain — 17.1 per cent — and close to twice the average (8.9 per cent) for the twelve EC countries; Eurostat 1990), a high proportion of dependants in the population and a huge public sector debt. Thus government can claim itself to be hamstrung to some extent in terms of its freedom of action in the area of welfare provision. Critics, however, argue that welfare depends not only on the size of the economic cake but also on how it is divided.

Economic difficulties alone cannot excuse the relative lack of urgency attached to children's and youth issues in Irish society. Many measures would not require large additional spending. Despite comprising more than one-third of the population, the needs and interests of youngsters occupy relatively little discussion time in the Oireachtas. Political parties have few, if any, policies in relation to young people. Until the Taoiseach's recent announcement about new legislation, there has been a political silence about reform of the juvenile justice system (An Taoiseach 1991). The response to the problems of youth emigration remains feeble, as does the response to the problems of youth alienation in the working class ghettoes in our larger towns and cities.

Much of the public expenditure on youth matters now depends on funds from the National Lottery rather than on taxation. Since the lottery was conceived as providing for optional extras, this gives an idea of the priority attached to services tackling problems such as child sexual abuse and youth homelessness, which depend largely on the lottery. Since 1974, governments have acknowledged the need for an overhaul of children's legislation. In 1985, eleven years later, the first Bill aimed at achieving part of this appeared in the Dáil, but six years further on no legislation has yet reached the statute book. Compare this to the speed with which legislative matters relating to dogs, the sale of alcohol or financial affairs have been dealt with in recent years.

A Strategy for Change

If government and society did decide to give priority to children and youngsters what measures would be required to give this effect?

- a clear commitment in public policy to the needs and interests of the child-rearing family (in all its configurations);
- the provision for families, most especially those on low income, of realistic income support to assist them in the expense of rearing children;
- the placing on specific public authorities of an unambiguous duty to protect the interests of children;
- a complete revamping of legislation affecting children, with special reference to the areas of child protection and juvenile justice;
- the introduction of a properly resourced family court structure, with a judiciary trained and supported to deal with all children and family matters;
- the introduction of a child impact statement, which would require all new policy initiatives to be assessed for their likely or actual effects on children. Thus decisions, for instance, concerning environmental risk or physical planning would be subjected to this public test. Existing provisions affecting children could also be subjected regularly to a comparable review;
- the substantial improvement of the participation rates of poorer and deprived youngsters in the education system. In particular, the numbers leaving school without any certificate must be greatly reduced and access to places in third-level education by working class youth must be greatly improved;
- the placing of personal social services on a sound legislative, administrative and financial footing so as to ensure a sufficient level of trained personnel and services at community level;
- the establishment of a national children's council, with resources to promote monitoring, research and training in relation to the field of child and family welfare, and child protection

What is required is the determination of politicians to make these things happen.

Ireland had a children's allowance system (ahead of Britain) because of the determination of Seán Lemass. We have a 'free' education system at second level because of the commitment of Donough O'Malley. We have comprehensive succession legislation because of the legislative skill of Charles Haughey. We have a Supplementary Welfare System (warts and all) due to the conviction of Frank Cluskey. We have legislation to abolish the legal concept of illegitimacy — despite potentially powerful opposition — because of the determination of Nuala Fennell. Obviously the implementation of policy and legislation depends on more than ministerial flair. But the drive and vision of particular ministers are certainly essential ingredients in combating the typical inertia and resistance to change in areas of social concern.

The cause of children also needs active support from broadly based groups in society such as the teacher and other public sector trade unions, the Churches and the Irish Countrywomen's Association. Other pre-conditions for change are active and effective pressure groups and a responsible and alert media. Together these different elements could translate the undoubted latent goodwill for children's and family issues into a groundswell of support for concrete political action. Thus, reforming ministers could command a decisive political mandate for their approach.

Conditions for children in Ireland can begin to improve only if those who see the need for change turn up the political heat about children's issues, and identify clear priorities. For the author these priorities would be (i) the full implementation and adequate funding of all provisions in the Child Care Act 1991; (ii) the drafting and implementation of new juvenile justice legislation, (iii) the wholehearted implementation of the Commission on Social Welfare's recommendation in relation to the income support needs of child-rearing families on social welfare; and (iv) Ireland's ratification of the UN Convention on the Rights of the Child.

Chronology of Services, Legislation and Policy for Children in Ireland 1961-90

1961   Probation and Welfare Service established (with one officer serving Dublin Metropolitan area only)

1963   Juvenile Liaison Officer Scheme established within Garda Síochána

1964   Adoption Act 1964

1966   Tuairim Report *Some of Our Children* published

1967   'Free' post-primary education introduced by Donough O'Malley, Minister for Education

Kennedy Committee appointed to report on Reformatory and Industrial Schools

1968   Establishment of open centre, Shanganagh Castle, for 16-21 year old offenders by Dept. of Justice Prison Service

Irish Pre-school Playgroups Association founded

1969   Rutland Pre-school project established by Dept. of Education with the support of the Van Leer Foundation

Free Legal Advice Centres founded

1970   Kennedy Committee report published

1971   Health Boards established under the Health Act 1970

CARE, Campaign for the Care of Deprived Children, founded

Irish Association of Social Workers founded

Roman Catholic Bishops' Conference Council for Social Welfare established

National Social Service Council established

One year full-time course for workers in residential child care launched by the School of Social Education, Kilkenny, the first such professional training available in the state

1972   St. Lawrence's School, Finglas, opened. First purpose-built special school for boys in trouble. Funded by Dept. of Education and run by the De La Salle Brothers

Publication of what proved to be an influential manifesto for reform: *Children Deprived – The CARE Memorandum on Deprived Children and Children's Services in Ireland*

School leaving age raised to 15

Home Help service launched on a national basis with a brief which included the care of families in need

1973   Expansion of Probation and Welfare Service into a national service begins

Welfare Division established within the Department of Health

Handicapped Children's Allowance introduced

Cherish, the influential campaigning and support group for single mothers, is founded

1974   Government assigns a lead role to the Dept. of Health for child care services

Government appoints Task Force on Child Care Services to advise on reform and draft a new Children's Bill, within six months

Scoil Ard Mhuire in Lusk is opened as a special school for young offenders (replacing Daingean)

Adoption Act 1974

The promotion of a nationwide network of Community Information Centres is announced

Children First founded, to seek improvements in adoption and, later, foster care systems

1975   The Federation of Services for Unmarried Parents and their Children is founded

Interim Report of the Task Force on Child Care Services published

1976   Professional child care advisor appointed within the Dept. of Education

Adoption Act 1976

Dept. of Health issues what is to prove to be the first in a series of guidelines for professionals in the health services in relation to dealing with non-accidental injury/child abuse

1977   Supplementary Welfare Allowance Scheme replaces Home Assistance as a financial safety net for those on low income

Three pilot Youth Encounter Projects established in accordance with the recommendation of the *Interim Report of the Task Force on Child Care Services*

1978   Fostering Resource Group established by the Eastern Health Board

Amidst much controversy, Dept. of Justice opens Loughan House as a temporary Detention Centre for 12-16 year olds

Eastern Health Board opens Warrenstown House, a residential child psychiatric facility

1979   Child Care Division established within the Dept. of Health

Civil Legal Aid Scheme initiated

The Sixth Amendment of the Constitution secures, by referendum of the people, adoption orders against a particular technical legal challenge

1981   Task Force on Child Care Services publishes its final report

1982   Irish Foster Care Association founded

1983   Responsibility for the Adoption Board transferred from the Dept. of Justice to the Dept. of Health

Trinity House, Lusk opens as the first purpose-built secure unit for young offenders outside the prison service and Loughan House ceases to serve 12-16 year olds

Dept. of Health replaces capitation funding for residential care with a new system of annual budgets for individual centres

New regulations governing foster care replace 1954 regulations

Review Committee on Adoption Services appointed by the Minister for Health

Cuan Mhuire Assessment Unit for girls in trouble with the law opens (the first such facility in the state)

Criminal Justice (Community Service Act) provides for the courts to have available the disposition of community service for offenders aged 16 and over

Dept. of Health begins to collect statistics on non-accidental injury from the health boards on an annual basis

1984   *Report of Review Committee on Adoption* published

The National Youth Policy Committee, established in 1983, publishes its final report

1985   Scoil Ard Mhuire closes

Community Service Order Scheme implemented

The long awaited Child (Care and Protection) Bill is finally published

Dept. of Health convenes Working Party to advise on the revision of guidelines on child abuse and the coverage therein of child sexual abuse

Focus Point, the service for homeless young people and adults, opens

1986   Barnardo's creates a separate division for the Republic of Ireland

Catholic Social Service Conference of the Dublin Archdiocese opens a hostel for homeless children with statutory support and takes over the work of Hope Hostel which had run out of money and state support

1987   Dept. of Health issues revised guidelines on the management of child abuse

1988   Status of Children Act 1987 (which *inter alia* abolishes the concept of illegitimacy and counteracts discrimination against non-marital children) comes into force

Two Child Sexual Abuse Assessment Units are opened in Dublin and funds are provided for parallel developments in other regions

Adoption Act 1988 extends, somewhat, eligibility for adoption

Child Care Bill 1988 supersedes the Child (Care and Protection Bill) 1985

1989   With funding from the national lottery, Eastern Health Board establishes a Carer's Project to seek foster families who will be paid £100 per week per child or young person with special needs

Children Act 1989 restores the right of health boards to act as 'fit persons' under the Children Act 1908, a right which had been successfully challenged in an appeal to the Supreme Court

Judicial Separation and Family Law Reform Act 1989 is passed and implemented

Law Reform Commission publishes a *Consultation Paper on Child Sexual Abuse*

Barnardo's Republic of Ireland is formed as a separate company, independent of Barnardo's UK

1990   Child Care Bill 1988 passes all stages in Dáil Éireann

Law Reform Commission publishes its report, *Child Sexual Abuse*

An Taoiseach commits Ireland to ratifying the UN Convention on the Rights of the Child

Child Abduction and Enforcement of Custody Orders Bill 1990 is published by the Minister for Justice

An Taoiseach announces government's intention to introduce legislation on inter-country adoption

National Juvenile Liaison Office to be established within Garda Síochána

BIBLIOGRAPHY

Adoption Board, *Report of An Bord Uchtála* (The Adoption Board) 1988, Dublin: Stationery Office, p. 4, 1989

Adoption Board, *An Outline of Adoption Law and Procedure*, 1988

American Association of Mental Deficiency, cited in Trant (1980)

Anderson, H.R. *et al*, 'Recent trends in mortality associated with abuse of volatile substances in the UK'. *British Medical Journal*, Vol. 293, No. 6, December 1986, pp 1472-3.

Andrews, S. and O'Connor, C., *Space for Play*. Dublin: ISPCC, 1983

Archer, P., 'An evaluation of educational intervention programmes'. *Educational Disadvantage – Report of a Seminar*. Dublin: Irish National Teachers' Organisation, 1984

Arnold, M. and Laskey, H., *Children of the Poor Clares – The Story of an Irish Orphanage*. Belfast: Appletree Press, 1985

Association of Community Welfare Officers, 'Back to basics – discussion document on community welfare services'. *Welfare – Bulletin of the Association of Community Welfare Officers*, No. 11, 1989

Association of Workers with Children in Care, 'Final report of 1978 research project'. *AWCC Newsletter*, November 1979, pp 2-10

Augustinos, M., 'Developmental effects of child abuse: recent findings'. *Child Abuse and Neglect*, Vol. 2, 1987, pp 15-27

Ballew, J., 'Role of natural helpers in preventing child abuse and neglect'. *Social Work – Journal of the National Association of Social Workers* (USA), Vol. 30, No. 1, 1985, pp 37-41

Ballymun Community Coalition, *Ballymun: Its future can work*. Dublin: Ballymun Job Centre Project, Ballymun Community Coalition, 1986

Bamford, F. 'Spina bifida'. *From Asthma to Thalassaemia: Medical Conditions in Childhood*, S. Curtis (Ed). London: British Agencies for Adoption and Fostering, 1986

Bannon, M., Eustace, J. and O'Neill, M., *Urbanisation: Problems of growth and decay in Dublin*. Dublin: National Economic and Social Council (NESC), 1981

Barclay Committee, *Social Workers: Their Role and Tasks*. London: Bedford Square Press, 1982

Barker, W. *et al*, 'Early child development: The Dublin programme'. *Proceedings of the Twelfth World Conference on Health Education*, 1-6 September 1984. Dublin: Health Education Bureau, 1987, pp 134-7

Barnardo's, 'The Dublin Playbus'. *View*, No. 2, 1979

Barnardo's, *Working with Pre-School Children: The Development of Community Playgroups in Dublin 1 and Tallaght*. Dublin: Barnardo's, Irish Division, 1985

Barnardo's, *Services in Tallaght: Toy Library and Advisory Service*. Dublin: Barnardo's, 1986

Barnardo's, *Community Playgroups: Barnardo's Service for Families in Tallaght*. Dublin: Barnardo's, Irish Division, 1987

Barnes, G. and O'Gorman, N., 'Some medical and social features of delinquent boys'. *Journal of the Irish Medical Association*, Vol. 1, 1978, pp 19-22

Barry, B. (Ed), *Lofty Ideals – Tangible Results: Interim Report by the Projects in the Second European Programme to Combat Poverty*. Dublin: Combat Poverty Agency, 1988

Barry, J., Herity J. and Solan, J., *The Travellers' Health Status Study – Vital Statistics of Travelling People 1987*. Dublin: The Health Research Board, 1989

Barry, J. and Daly, L., *The Travellers' Health Status Study: Census of Travelling People*, November 1986. Dublin: Health Research Board, 1988

Barth, R., 'Emancipation services for adolescents in foster care', *Social Work*, May-June 1986, pp 165-171

Bennett, P. (Chair), *Good Practices in Mental Health*. Dublin: Mental Health Association of Ireland, 1987

Berridge, D., *Children's Homes*. Oxford: Basil Blackwell, 1985

Berridge, D. and Cleaver, H., *Foster Home Break-down*. Oxford: Basil Blackwell, 1987

Birchall, D., *Barnardo's Antrim Road Family Centre – The first five years, 1980-85*. Belfast: Barnardo's, Northern Ireland, 1986

Blom-Cooper, L. (Chair), *The Report of the Panel of Inquiry into the circumstances surrounding the death of Jasmine Beckford*. London: London Borough of Brent, 1985

Boland, G. *et al, Your Child in Care – Some questions and answers for families*. Dublin: Family Link, 1987

Bord na Gaeilge, personal communication to author, 25 August 1989

Breen, R., 'The sociology of youth unemployment'. *Administration*, Vol. 33, No. 2, 1985, p. 172

Breen, R. *et al, Understanding Contemporary Ireland: State, Clan and Development in the Republic of Ireland*. Basingstoke: Macmillan, 1990

British Association of Social Workers, *Clients are Fellow Citizens*. Birmingham: BASW, 1975

Brothers of Charity Services, *Brothers of Charity Services in Ireland: Report 1987*. Dublin: Brothers of Charity Services, 1988

Brown, G. and Harris, T., *Social Origins of Depression: A study of psychiatric disorder in women*. London: Tavistock, 1978

Brown, G., Ní Bhrolcháin, M. and Harris, T., 'Social class and psychiatric disturbance among women in an urban population'. *Sociology*, Vol. 9, 1975, pp 225-54

Brown, H., 'Effective use of caretakers as an effective alternative to placement'. *Treating Families in the Home An Alternative to Placement*. M. Bryce and J. Lloyd (Eds). Springfield, IL: Charles C. Thomas, 1981

Browne, A., 'The mixed economy of day care: consumer v. professional assessments'. *Journal of Social Policy*, Vol. 13, No. 3, 1984, pp 321-31

Burke, H., *The People and the Poor Law in 19th-century Ireland*. Littlehampton, West Sussex: Women's Educational Bureau, 1987

Bush, M. and Gordon, A., 'The case for involving children in child welfare decisions' *Social Work*, 27, 4, July 1982, pp 309-14

Callan, T. *et al, Poverty and the social welfare system in Ireland*. Dublin: Combat Poverty Agency, 1988

Carroll, L. *et al*, 'Retarded brain growth in Irish itinerants'. *Journal of the Irish Medical Association*, Vol. 67, No. 2, 1974, pp 33-6

Casey, M., *Domestic violence against women*. Dublin: Federation of Women's Refuges, 1987

Caul, B., *A Comparative Study of the Juvenile Justice Systems in Northern Ireland and the Republic of Ireland*. Unpublished PhD thesis, University of Dublin, Trinity College, 1985

Ceravolo, F., 'The crisis nursery – a metropolitan island of safety'. *A Handbook of Child Welfare – Context, Knowledge and Practice*, J. Laird and A. Hartman (Eds). New York: The Free Press, 1985

Cheetham, J., 'Reviewing black children in care: introductory note', Ch. 9 in Ahmed, S., Cheetham, J. and Small, J., *Social Work and Black Children and their Families*. London: Batsford, 1986

Christopherson, J., 'Child abuse in Holland'. *Community Care*, July 1980

Clancy, P., *Participation in higher education: A national survey*. Dublin: The Higher Education Authority, 1982

Clancy, P., *Who goes to college? A second national survey of participation in higher education*. Dublin: The Higher Education Authority, 1988

Clarke, A. and Clarke, A., 'Thirty years of child psychology'. *Journal of Child Psychology and Psychiatry*, Vol. 27, No. 6, pp 719-739, 1986

Clarke, M., 'Community pre-school services — the mobile education project'. Presentation to the 18th Annual Conference of the Psychological Society of Ireland, 12-15 November 1987. Dublin 1987

Cleary, A., 'A study of depression among women: implications for preventive mental health'. *Proceedings of the Twelfth World Conference on Health Education*, 1-6 September 1985. Dublin: Health Education Bureau, 1987, pp 313-16

Comhairle na n-Ospidéal, *Development of Paediatric Services*. Dublin: 1979

Comhairle na n-Ospidéal, *Consultant Manpower Statistics as at 1st May 1989* (Appendix A). Dublin: 1989

Commission of Inquiry on Mental Illness, *Report*. Dublin: Stationery Office, 1966

Commission on Health Funding, *Report of the Commission on Health Funding*. Dublin: Stationery Office, 1989, pp 208; 224-27

Commission on Social Welfare, *Report of the Commission on Social Welfare*. Dublin: Stationery Office, 1986

Commission on the Status of Women, *Report to Minister for Finance*, 1972

Committee to Monitor the Implementation of Government Policy on Travelling People, *First, Second* and *Third Reports*. Dublin, 1985, 1986 and 1987 respectively

Committee on Reformatory and Industrial Schools, *Report on the Reformatory and Industrial Schools System*. Dublin: Stationery Office, 1970

Connolly, J.A., 'Down's syndrome incidence: practical and theoretical considerations'. *Irish Medical Journal*, Vol. 70, 1977, pp 126-8

Connor, T., *Irish Youth in London, Survey 1985*. London: Action Group for Irish Youth, 1985

Cooney, T. and Torode, R. (Eds), *Report of the Child Sexual Abuse Working Party*. Dublin: Irish Council for Civil Liberties, 1989

Cooper, S., 'Annotation – the fetal alcohol syndrome'. *Journal of Child Psychology and Psychiatry*, Vol. 28, No. 2, 1987, pp 223-7

Corcoran, T., O'Connor, D. and Mullin, S., *The Transition from School to Work*. Dublin: Youth Employment Agency, 1986

Corrigan, D., 'Surveys and statistics on drug-taking in Ireland'. *Drug Questions – Local Answers (A training course)*, A. Dempsey, E. Donoghue and R. Gilligan (Eds). Dublin: Health Education Bureau, 1987

Council of Europe, *European Social Charter*, 1961

Council of Europe, *European Convention for the Protection of Human Rights and Fundamental Freedom*, 1950

Counihan, B., *Five Years a-Growing: A case study on community development in a new urban community, 1973-78*. Dublin: National Federation of Social Service Councils, 1979

Courtioux, M. *et al*, *Social Pedagogue in Europe – Living with Others as a Profession*. Zurich: FICE, 1985

Creedon, T., Corboy, A. and Kevany, J., 'Growth and development in travelling families'. *Journal of the Irish Medical Association*, Vol. 68, No. 19, 1975, pp 473-77

Cowan, J., *People Cope – Family Groups in Action*. London, COPE, 1982

CSO/Central Statistics Office, Census 1986: *Summary Population Report*. Dublin: Stationery Office, 1987

CSSC, *Dublin, Hard Facts – Future Hopes.* Dublin: Catholic Social Service Conference, 1988

CSO/Central Statistics Office, 1989: *Summary Population Report*, 2nd Series, p. 77. Dublin: Stationery Office

CSO/Central Statistics Office. *Emigration figures.* Personal communication, 16 Jan. 1990

Cullen, J.H. *et al*, 'Long-term unemployment: its role in complex vulnerabilities and their health consequences'. *Unemployment, Social Vulnerability and Health in Europe*, D. Schwefel, P-G. Svennson and H. Zoellner (Eds). Berlin: Springer Verlag, 1987a, p. 213

Cullen, J.H. *et al*, 'Unemployed youth and health: findings from the pilot phase of a longitudinal study'. *Social Science and Medicine*, Vol. 215, No. 2, 1987b

Cullen, M. and Morrissey, T., *Women and Health – Some current issues.* Dublin: Health Education Bureau, 1987

Dáil Debates, Minister for Justice, Vol. 359, No. 4, 6 June 1985

Dáil Debates, 26 November 1987

Dáil Debates, 2 December 1987

Dáil Debates, 27 January 1988

Dáil Debates, Minister for Education, 19 July 1989

Dale, P., *Dangerous Families – Assessment and Treatment of Child Abuse.* London: Tavistock Publications, 1986

Daly, P., *Final Report – Substance Abuse Enquiry.* Dublin: Social Work Department/Youth Development Programme, Community Care Area 3, Eastern Health Board, 1986

Damon, L., Todd, J. and MacFarlane, K., 'Treatment issues with sexually abused young children'. *Child Welfare*, Vol. LXVI, No. 2, 1987, pp 128-9

Darling, V., 'Social work in the Republic of Ireland', *Social Studies – Irish Journal of Sociology*, Vol. 1, No. 1, 1972, pp 28-37

Darling, V., *Adoption in Ireland*, Dublin: CARE, 1974

Darling, V., *And Baby makes Two.* Dublin: Federation of Services for Unmarried Parents and their Children, 1984

Davis, E.E., Grube, J.W. and Morgan, M., *Attitudes towards poverty and related social issues in Ireland.* Dublin: Economic and Social Research Institute (ESRI), Paper No. 117, 1984

Dean, G. *et al*, 'The opiate epidemic in Dublin, 1979-83'. *Irish Medical Journal*, Vol. 78, No. 4, 1985, pp 107-10

Dean, G. *et al*, 'The opiate epidemic in Dublin: are we over the worst?' *Irish Medical Journal*, Vol. 80, No. 5, 1987, pp 139-42

Dean, G., Bradshaw, J.S. and Lavelle, P., *Drug Misuse in Ireland, 1982-3: Investigation in a North-Central Dublin area, and in Galway, Sligo and Cork.* Dublin: Medico-Social Research Board, 1983

De'Ath, E., 'Support or intervention: help or hindrance?' *The Family in a Political Context – Proceedings of a one-day conference in London*, 11 June, 1982, E. De'Ath and D. Haldane (Eds). Aberdeen: The Association of Family Therapy, The University Press, 1983, pp 25-35

Department of Education, *Guidelines on Remedial Education.* Dublin: Stationery Office, 1987

Department of Education, *Guidelines on the Development of Sex/Relationships Education.* Circular M12/87 to the Authorities of Post-primary schools. Dublin: 1987

Department of Education, *Discipline in National Schools.* Primary Branch Circular 7/88 to the Boards of Management and Principal Teachers of National Schools. Dublin: March 1988

Department of Education, *Statistical Report* 1985-86, p. 3. Dublin: Stationery Office, 1988;

Statistical Report, 1988-89. Dublin: Stationery Office

Department of Health, *Survey of Workload of Public Health Nurses, Report of Working Group appointed by Minister for Health*. Dublin: Stationery Office, 1975

Department of Health, *Health Care for Mothers and Infants — A Review of the Maternity and Infant Care Scheme*. Dublin: Dept. of Health, 1982

Department of Health, *Adoption – Report of the Review Committee on Adoption Services*. Dublin: Stationery Office, 1984

Department of Health, *Towards a Full Life, Green Paper on services for the disabled*. Dublin: Stationery Office, 1984

Department of Health, *Report of the Working Party on the General Medical Service*, Dublin: Stationery Office, 1984

Department of Health, *The Psychiatric Services – Planning for the Future: Report of a Study Group on the Development of the Psychiatric Services*. Dublin: Stationery Office, 1985

Department of Health, *Report of the Committee on Social Work*, Dublin: Dept. of Health, 1985

Department of Health, *Minimum Legal Requirements and Standards for Day Care Services for Children – Report of a Working Party Appointed by the Minister for Health*. Dublin: Dept. of Health, 1985

Department of Health, *Comprehensive Public Expenditure Programme*, 1986. Dublin: Stationery Office, 1986

Department of Health, *Children in Care 1983*. Dublin: Dept. of Health, 1986

Department of Health, *Child Abuse Guidelines – Guidelines on Procedures for the Identification, Investigation and Management of Child Abuse* (Revised edition). Dublin: Dept. of Health, 1987

Department of Health, *Health – The Wider Dimensions (A Consultative Statement on Health Policy)*. Dublin: Dept. of Health, 1987

Department of Health, *Statistics on the Health Services, 1986*. Dublin: Stationery Office, 1987

Department of Health, *Health Statistics 1987*. Dublin: Stationery Office, 1988

Department of Health, *Children in Care in 1984*. Dublin: Dept. of Health, 1988

Department of Health, *Health Statistics 1988*. Dublin: Stationery Office, 1989

Department of Health, *Survey of Children in the Care of Health Boards, 1985*. Dublin: Child Care Division, Department of Health, 1989

Department of Health, *Survey of Children in the Care of Health Boards in 1988*, Vol 1. Dublin: Child Care Division, Department of Health, 1990

Department of Health, *Community Medicine and Public Health: The Future – Report of a Working Party appointed by the Minister for Health*. Dublin: Dept. of Health, 1990

Department of Health, *Perinatal Statistics, 1985 and 1986*. Dublin: Stationery Office, 1990

Department of Health, personal communication 11 January, 1991

Department of Health, *Guidelines for the Development of Social Work Services in Community Care Programmes*. Dublin: Dept. of Health

Department of Health, *Statistics on Child Abuse for relevant years*. Dublin: Dept. of Health

Department of Justice, *Report of the Probation and Welfare Service, with statistics for the year 1988*. Dublin: Stationery Office, 1990

Department of Justice, *Annual Report on Prisons and Places of Detention, 1990*. Dublin: Stationery Office, 1990

Department of Social Welfare, *Statistical Information on Social Welfare Services, 1988*. Dublin: Stationery Office, 1989

De Rís, N. (Chair), *Report of the Committee on Discipline in Schools*. Dublin: Stationery Office, 1985

DHSS, *The Family in Society: Dimensions of Parenthood*. London: HMSO, 1974

DHSS, *Child Abuse – A Study of Inquiry Reports, 1973-81*. London: HMSO, 1982

DHSS, *Social Work Decisions in Child Care – recent research findings and their implications*. London: HMSO, 1985

Dowling, S., *Health for a Change – The Provision of Preventive Health Care in Pregnancy and Early Childhood*. London: Child Poverty Action Group, 1983

Dowling, V.M., 'Distribution of birth weight in seven Dublin maternity units'. *British Medical Journal*, Vol. 284, p. 1901, 1983

Dublin County Council, *County Dublin areas of need – CODANS*, Volume II, Neighbourhood Profiles. Dublin: Community Department, Dublin County Council, 1987

Earls, F., 'Annotation: on the familial transmission of child psychiatric disorder'. *Journal of Child Psychology and Psychiatry*, Vol. 28, No. 6, 1987, pp 791-802

Eastern Health Board, *Community Mothers Programme*. Eastern Health Board, *Annual Report*. Dublin, 1989

Eastern Health Board, Children's section. Personal communication, 8 January, 1991

Engels, F., *Conditions of the Working Class in England (1844)*. Oxford, Beckwells, 1958

Ennis, M., 'The plight of travelling people in Dublin in 1984'. *Future Directions in Health Policy*, P. Berwick and M. Burns (Eds). Dublin: Council for Social Welfare, 1984

Eurostat, *Basic Statistics of the Community*, Luxembourg: Office for Official Publications of the European Communities, 1988

Eurostat, 'Unemployment in the Community, 1990'. *Unemployment II, 1990*, 27 Nov. 1990. Luxembourg: Office for Official Publications of the European Commission.

Fanshel, D., 'Parental failure and consequences for children – the drug-abusing mother whose children are in foster care'. *American Journal of Public Health*, Vol. 65, No. 6, 1975, pp 604-12

Fanshel, D. and Shinn, E., *Children in Foster Care – a longitudinal investigation*. New York: Columbia University Press, 1978

Farrelly, J., *Crime, Custody and Community*. Dublin: Voluntary and Statutory Bodies, 1989

Federation of Services for Unmarried Mothers and their Children (and five other organisations), *Submission to the Government in relation to Reforms in the Adoption System*. Dublin, 1981

Ferrari, M., 'Chronic illness: psychosocial effects on siblings – 1. Chronically ill boys'. *Journal of Child Psychology and Psychiatry*, Vol. 25, No. 4, 1984, pp 459-76

Festinger, T., *No one ever asked us . . . A postscript to foster care*. New York: Columbia University Press, 1983

Finch, J., 'Can skills be shared? Pre-school playgroups in disadvantaged areas'. *Community Development Journal*, Vol. 18, No. 3, 1983, pp 251-6

Findlay, C., *Child Abuse: The Dutch Response Practice (1987-88)*, 4, pp 374-381

Fine, S., 'Children in divorce, access and custody situation: An update'. *Journal of Child Psychology and Psychiatry*, Vol. 28, No. 6, 1987, pp 361-4

Finnegan, L.P., 'Outcome of children born to women dependent upon narcotics'. *The Effects of Maternal Alcohol and Drug Abuse on the Newborn*, B. Stimmel (Ed). New York: Haworth Press, 1982, pp 57-8

Fitzpatrick, D., 'Irish Emigration 1801-1921'. *Studies in Irish Economic and Social History*. Dublin: The Economic and Social History Society of Ireland, 1984

Flamm, F., *The Social System and Welfare Work in the Federal Republic of Germany*. Second English Edition. Stuttgart: W. Kohlhammer, 1983

Focus Point and The Eastern Health Board Social Work Team, *Forgotten Children – Research on Young People who are Homeless in Dublin*. Dublin: Focus Point/Eastern Health Board, 1989

Fogarty, M., Ryan, L. and Lee, J., *Irish Values and Attitudes – The Irish Report of the European Value Systems Study.* Dublin: Dominican Publications, 1984

Fontes, P. and Kellaghan, T., 'Incidence and Correlates of Illiteracy in Irish Primary Schools.' *Irish Journal of Education*, Vol. 11, No. 1 & 2, 1977, pp 5-20

Freire, P., *Cultural Action for Freedom.* Harmondsworth: Penguin, 1972a

Freire, P., *Pedagogy of the Oppressed.* Harmondsworth: Penguin, 1972b

Garda Commissioner, *Report on Crime*, 1989. Dublin: Garda Síochána 1990

Garda Síochána Complaints Board, *Annual Report, 1987-88.* Dublin: Stationery Office, 1988

Garland, O., *The Future of the Personal Social Services in the Health Boards.* Dublin: Social Workers' Group, Eastern Health Board, 1983

Gath, A., 'Mentally handicapped people as parents'. *Journal of Child Psychology and Psychiatry*, Vol. 29, No. 6, 1988, pp 739-44

Gath, A. and Gumley, D. 'Retarded children and their siblings'. *Journal of Child Psychology and Psychiatry*, Vol. 28, No. 5, 1987, pp 715-30

Gilligan, R., *Children in Care in their own Community.* Dublin: Society of St. Vincent de Paul, 1982

Gilligan, R., 'New possibilities in health and social care?' *Future Directions in Health Policy*, P. Berwick and M. Burns (Eds). Dublin: Council for Social Welfare, 1984

Gilligan, R., 'On minimising the risks of professional intervention in child welfare' in Kelly, J. (Ed) *Ireland's Troubled Children: their needs, our practice*, Proceedings of the first North-South Child Welfare Conference. Belfast: North-South Child Welfare Conference, 1986

Gilligan, R., *Foster Care for Children in Ireland: Issues and Challenges for the 1990s.* Dublin: Department of Social Studies, University of Dublin, Trinity College, Occasional Paper No. 2, 1990

Gorman, N., 'In Care'. *The Spectator*, 16 February 1985

Gould, A., *Welfare Policy – The Swedish Experience.* London: Longman, 1988, pp 77-98.

Government Information Service, *Press Release Issued on behalf of Department of Health*, 26 July 1982

Grube, J.W. and Morgan, M., *Smoking, drinking and other drug use among Dublin post-primary school pupils.* Dublin: Economic and Social Research Institute (ESRI), Paper No. 132, 1986

Grube, J.W., McGree, S. and Morgan, M., 'Smoking behaviour, intentions and beliefs among Dublin post-primary schoolchildren'. *The Economic and Social Review*, Vol. 15, 1984, pp 265-88

Gurdin, P. and Anderson, G.R., 'Quality care for ill children: AIDS-specialised foster family homes'. *Child Welfare – Journal of the Child Welfare League of America*, Vol. LXVI, No. 4, 1987, pp 291-302

Hannan, D., *Schooling and Sex Roles – Sex differences in subject provision and student choice in Irish post-primary schools.* Dublin: Economic and Social Research Institute (ESRI), Paper No. 113, 1983

Hannan, D., *Schooling and the Labour Market – Young people in transition from school to work.* Shannon: Shannon Curriculum Development Centre, 1986

Harrison, P., 'AIDS – The implications for reception of children into care'. *Irish Social Worker*, Vol. 5, No. 2, 1986, pp 9-10

Hayes, N., *State-aided Day Nurseries: An Exploratory Study.* M. Ed. Thesis, University of Dublin, Trinity College, 1983

Hegar, R., 'Sibling relationships and separations and implications for child placement.' *Social Service Review*, 1988, pp 446-467

Herbert, M., *Conduct Disorders of Childhood and Adolescence – A Social Learning Perspective*, 2nd ed. Chichester: John Wiley, 1987

Herbert, M., *Working with Children and their Families*. Leicester: British Psychological Society/London: Routledge, 1988

Heus, M. and Pincus, A., *The Creative Generalist: A Guide to Social Work Practice*. Barneveld, Wisconsin: Micamar Publishing, 1986

Higher Education Authority, *First Destination of Award Recipients in Higher Education 1988*. Dublin HEA, 1989

Hiskins, G., 'How mothers help themselves'. *Health Visitor*, Vol. 54, No. 3, 1981, pp 108-11

HM Inspectorate, 'Effective Youth Work'. *Education Observed* No. 6. London: Department of Education and Science, 1987, pp 20-21

Holland, S., *Rutland Street – The Story of an Educational Experiment for Disadvantaged Children in Dublin*. Oxford: Pergamon Press and Bernard Van Leer Foundation, 1979

Holman, B., 'Family Centres'. *Children and Society*, Vol. 1, No. 2, 1987, pp 157-73

Holman, R., 'The place of fostering in social work', *British Journal of Social Work*, Vol. 5, No. 1, 1975

Holy See, *Charter of the Rights of the Family*, 1983

Humphries, B., *Only Connect – The Report of a Three-year Project which brought together One-parent families and Volunteers*. Edinburgh: Guild of Service, 1976

Hyland, A., 'The multi-denominational experience in the national school system in Ireland', *Irish Education Studies*. Vol. 8, No. 1, 1989, pp 89-114

INBUCON, *Summary of Community Care Review Report*. Dublin, 1982

Independent Poverty Action Movement, *Poor Aid? The Supplementary Allowance Scheme, Ten Years On*. Dublin: author 1986

Ireland *Comprehensive Public Expenditure Programme 1986*. Dublin: Stationery Office, 1986

Ireland *Programme for Economic and Social Progress. Dublin:* Stationery Office, 1991, p. 77

Irish National Teachers' Organisation (INTO), *The Educational Needs of Disadvantaged Children – Report of a Special Committee*. Dublin: INTO, 1979

Irish National Teachers' Organisation (INTO), *Educational Disadvantage – Time for Action: Submission to Government*. Dublin: INTO, 1989

Irish Pre-school Playgroup Association, *IPPA Statistics for year ending 31 December 1989*. Dublin: IPPA, 1990

ISPCC, *A Chance to grow – National Children's Campaign*. Dublin: ISPCC, 1987

Jackson, P. *Migrant Women: Republic of Ireland*. Mimeograph, 19 pp. 1986

Jehu, D., *Beyond Sexual Abuse: Therapy with women who were childhood victims*. Chichester: John Wiley & Co, 1988

Jewett, *Helping Children Cope with Separation and Loss*. London: Batsford Academic and Educational, 1984

Jones, E., 'A study of those who cease to foster', *British Journal of Social Work*, Vol. 5, No. 1, 1975

Jordan, B., 'Prevention – achieving permanence', Papers from Swanick 1981. *Adoption and Fostering* 105, 1981, pp 20-22

Kadushin, A., *Child Welfare Services*. Third Edition. New York: Macmillan, 1980

Kahan, B., *Growing up in Care*. Oxford: Blackwell, 1979

Kalvesten, A.L. and Ödman, M., *Barn: 5 Länder Tecknar och Tänker*. Stockholm: Liber/Utbildning Förlaget, 1979

Kandel, D., 'Epidemiological and psychosocial perspectives on adolescent drug use'. *Journal of the American Academy of Child Psychiatry*, Vol. 21, No. 4, 1982, pp 328-47

Kaplan, L., *Working with Multi-problem Families*. Massachusetts: Lexington Books, 1986

Kavanagh, Rev. J. (Chairman of Working Party), *A Statement on Social Policy*. Dublin: Council for Social Welfare – A Committee of the Catholic Bishops' Conference, 1972

Keane, C. and Crowley, G., *Out on My Own – Report on Youth Homelessness in Limerick City*. Limerick: Mid-Western Health Board and Limerick Social Service Centre, 1990

Kellmer Pringle, M., *The Needs of Children*. London: Hutchinson, 1974

Kelly, G., 'The lost cord', *Social Work Today*, Vol. 13, No. 12, 1981, pp 7-9

Kempe, H. *et al*, 'The battered child syndrome'. *Journal of the American Medical Association*, Vol. 181, 7 July 1962, pp 17-24

Kempe, R.S. and Kempe, C.H., *Child Abuse*. London: Fontana/Open Books, 1978

Kennedy, S., *Who should care? The Development of Kilkenny Social Services*. Dublin: Turoe Press, 1981

Kennedy, S., *But where can I go? – Homeless women in Dublin*. Dublin: Arlen House, 1985

Kennedy, S. and Kelleher P., *Guidelines for Community Development Workers* (Based on the Experience of the Integrated Rural Action Projects of the Second European Programme to Combat Poverty 1985-89). Dublin: Focus Point 1989

Kenny, P., 'Letterkenny Family Resource Centre: how it developed'. *Irish Social Worker*, Vol. 5, No. 3, 1986, pp 11-13

Kent, M. and Sexton, J., 'The influence of certain social factors in the physical growth and development of a group of Dublin city children'. *Journal of the Statistical and Social Inquiry Society of Ireland*, Vol. 22, No. 5, 1973, pp 188-206

Killen, J.D., 'Annotation – prevention of adolescent tobacco smoking: the social pressure resistance training approach'. *Journal of Child Psychology and Psychiatry*, Vol. 26, No. 1, 1985, pp 7-15

Kilpatrick, R. and Mooney, P., 'Tea and sympathy: a campaign to improve mothers' involvement in a local baby clinic'. *Community Development Journal*, Vol. 22, No. 2, 1987, pp 141-46

Kirke, P., 'Sources of child health reappraised'. *Irish Medical Times*, 20 November 1981, p. 33

Kirke, P., 'Time trends in childhood accident mortality and hospitalisation rates in Ireland'. *Irish Medical Journal*, Vol. 77, No. 11, 1984, pp 347-52

Klaczynski, P.A. and Cummings, E.M., 'Responding to anger in aggressive and non-aggressive boys: A research note'. *Journal of Child Psychology and Psychiatry*, Vol. 30, No. 2, 1989, pp 309-14

Knight, B. *et al, Family Groups in the Community*. London: Voluntary Service Council, 1979

Kolvin, I. *et al, Help starts here: The Maladjusted Child in the Ordinary School*. London: Tavistock Social Science Paperback, 1987 (first published 1981)

Lavan, A., 'Tallaght Welfare Society Information Office, 1977 and 1979'. *Social Need and Community Social Services*. Dublin: Tallaght Welfare Society, 1981, pp 58-85

Law Reform Commission, *Report on Child Sexual Abuse*, Report No. 32, Dublin: Law Reform Commission, 1990

Lee, P. and Gibney, M., *Patterns of food and nutrient intake in a suburb of Dublin with chronically high unemployment*. Dublin: Combat Poverty Agency, Research Report Series No. 2, June, 1989

Levine, S., 'Primary Health Care'. *Future Directions in Health Policy*, P. Berwick and M. Burns (Eds). Dublin: Council for Social Welfare, 1984

Liegois, J.P., *Gypsies and Travellers*. Strasbourg: Council of Europe, 1987

Liffman, M., *Power for the Poor: The Family Centre Project – An experiment in self-help*. Sydney: The Brotherhood of St Laurence/George Allen & Unwin, 1978

Linehan, D., *Community Involvement – Mayfield*. Dublin: Turoe Press, 1984

Little Sisters of the Assumption, 'Non-institutional approach to caring'. *Future Directions in Health Policy*, P. Berwick and M. Burns (Eds). Dublin: Council for Social Welfare, 1984

Loppnow, D., 'Adolescents on their own' in Laird, J. and Hartman, A., *A Handbook of Child Welfare*. Free Press, 1985

Madge, N., 'Annotation – Unemployment and its effects on Children'. *Journal of Child Psychology and Psychiatry*, Vol. 24, No. 2, 1983, pp 311-19

Maguire, R., Thornton, L. and Clune, M., 'Narcotic addiction in pregnancy – problems for mother and baby'. *Irish Social Worker*, Vol. 6, No. 2, Summer 1987, pp 11-12

McAuley, R. and McAuley, P., 'The effectiveness of behaviour modification with families'. *British Journal of Social Work*, Vol. 10, No. 1, 1980, pp 43-54

McBogg, P., McQuiston, M. and Alexander, H., 'Circle house residential treatment program'. *Child Abuse and Neglect*, Vol. 3, 1979, pp 863-7

McCabe, 'What inter-country adoption really involves', *Irish Social Worker*, Autumn, Vol. 9, No. 3, 1990, pp 4-6

McCarthy, J. and Ronayne, T., *The Psychological Well-being of the Unemployed – A report prepared for the Youth Employment Agency*. Mimeograph. 1984

McCarthy, M., *Child traffic accident problem in Ireland*. Dublin: An Foras Forbartha, Research Series RS 319, 1985

McCarthy, P. and O'Boyle, C., 'Prevalence of behavioural maladjustment in a social cross-section of Irish urban schoolchildren'. *Irish Medical Journal*, Vol. 79, No. 5, 1986, pp 125-9

McCarthy, P., Fitzgerald, M. and Smith, M., 'Prevalence of childhood autism in Ireland'. *Irish Medical Journal*, Vol. 77, No. 5, 1984, pp 129-30

McCarthy, H.A., 'The supervision of delinquents in society.' *Some Problems of Child Welfare*, B.G. McCarthy (Ed). Cork: Cork University Press, 1945, pp 43-51

McConkey, R. and O'Connell, A., 'A national survey of child referrals to psychologists'. *Irish Journal of Psychology*, Vol. V, No. 2, 1982, pp 85-95

McConkey, M., 'Education for parents with mentally handicapped children'. *World Health Forum*, Vol. 8, 1987, pp 446-50

McGennis, B., Drury, C. and Murray, J., *Evaluation of Community Training Workshops – Summary Report*. Dublin: AnCO, 1986

McGreil, M., *Prejudice and Tolerance in Ireland – Based on a survey of intergroup attitudes of Dublin adults and other sources*. Dublin: Research Section, College of Industrial Relations, 1977

McInerney, T.J., *Summary of Community Care Review Report*. Dublin: INBUCON, 1982

McKenna, A., *Childcare and Equal Opportunities – Policies and Services for Childcare in Ireland*. Dublin: Employment Equality Agency, 1988

McKenna, J., 'The psychologist as expert: forensic psychology'. *Irish Journal of Psychology*, Vol. VII, No. 2, 1986, pp 75-87

McKeown, K. & Gilligan, R., 'Child sexual abuse in the Eastern Health Board area of Ireland: an analysis of all confirmed cases in 1988'. Paper presented to Sociological Association of Ireland Conference, 3 March 1990

McLaughlin, B., Gormley, T.R. and Wickham, C., *Nutritional quality of children's school pack-lunches*. Dublin: An Foras Talúntais, Technical Bulletin No. 6, 1982

McSweeney, M., *National survey of infant feeding practices, 1986*. Dublin: Health Education Bureau, 1986

McSweeney, M. and Kevany, J., *Nutrition beliefs and practices in Ireland*. Dublin: Health Education Bureau, 1981

McVeigh, F., *Women learning: An account of the women's programmes funded by the Combat Poverty Agency in 1987*. Dublin: Combat Poverty Agency, 1988

Mental Health Association of Ireland, *Good Practices in Mental Health in Tallaght*. Dublin: Mental Health Association of Ireland/Eastern Health Board, 1987

Midland Health Board, *Community Care Services Report 1986*. Tullamore: Midland Health Board, Community Care Programme, 1987

Millham, S., *et al, Lost in Care: the problem of maintaining links between children in care and their families*. Aldershot: Gower, 1986

Morrissey, T., 'Women and community development – a feminist perspective'. *Community Workers' Cooperative Newsletter*, No. 2, 1982, pp 20-23

Mulcahy, M. and Reynolds, A., *Census of Mental Handicap in the Republic of Ireland*. Dublin: Medico-Social Research Board, 1984

Murphy-Lawless, J., Redmond, D. and Ungruh, K., *Playing for Keeps: The Provision of Pre-school Facilities in the Eastern Health Board Region – A Report for OMEP*. Dublin: SUS Research Ltd., 1989

Murphy, P. *et al, A Part in Dublin – Accommodation for people out of home, 1986 and 1988*. Dublin: Focus Point, 1988

National Committee on Pilot Schemes to Combat Poverty, *Pilot Schemes to Combat Poverty in Ireland, 1974-80: Final Report*. Dublin: n.d. but very probably 1981

National Economic and Social Council (NESC), 'The Council's comments on a review of housing policy' in J. Blackwell's *A Review of Housing Policy*. Dublin: Report No. 87, NESC, 1988

National Parents' Council (Primary), Policy Document, Dublin, 1987

National Planning Board, *Proposals for Plan 1984-87*. Dublin: National Planning Board, 1984

National Social Services Board, *The Development of Voluntary Social Services in Ireland: A Discussion Document*. Dublin: National Social Services Board, 1982

National Youth Council of Ireland, personal communication to author, 30 November 1988a

National Youth Council of Ireland, *On the Margin – A study of the youth service response to young people affected by socio-economic disadvantage*. Dublin: Stationery Office, 1988b

National Youth Council of Ireland, *Youth Information – The Irish Response*. Dublin, 1989

National Youth Policy Committee, *Final Report* (Costello Report). Dublin: Stationery Office, 1984

NESC, *Community Care Services: An Overview*. Dublin: National Economic and Social Council, 1987

Nevin, M. *et al*, 'Drugs – a report on a study in Dublin post-primary schoolchildren, 1970-71'. *Journal of the Irish Medical Association*, Vol. 66, 1971, pp 231-7

Newson, E., 'Who am I – Where do I come from? *Concern* – Journal of the National Children's Bureau. Vol. 8, 1971, pp 26-7

Nic Giolla Choille, T., *Wexford Family Centre*. Dublin: ISPCC, 1983

Nic Giolla Choille, T., 'Women's Groups'. *Cork Family Centre*. Dublin: ISPCC, 1984

Nic Giolla Choille, T., *Maternity Project: Darndale Family Centre*. Dublin: ISPCC, 1985

Nic Giollaphádraig, C., *I am Important – Women's Health and Development Course*. Dublin: Combat Poverty Agency, 1988

Nylander, I., 'Children of alcoholic fathers'. *Acta Paediatrica Scandinavica*, Vol. 49, Suppl. 121, 1960

Ó Cinnéide, S., 'Including community work'. *Irish Social Worker*, Vol. 4, No. 4, 1985, pp 6-8

Ó Cinnéide, S. and O'Daly, N., 'Adoption' in Supplementary Report to *Task Force on Child Care Services: Final Report to the Minister for Health*. Dublin: Stationery Office, 1981

O'Connell, A. and McConkey, R., 'Psychological services for children in Ireland'. *Irish Medical Journal*, Vol. 75, No. 2, 1982, pp 449-51

O'Connor, A. and Walsh, D., *Activities of Irish Psychiatric Hospitals and Units, 1986*. Dublin: Health Research Board, 1989

O'Connor, J. and Daly, M., *The Smoking Habit*. Dublin: Gill and Macmillan/Health Education Bureau, 1985

O'Connor, J., Ruddle, H. and O'Gallagher, M., *Cherished Equally? Educational and behavioural adjustment of children: A study of primary schools in the mid-west region*. Limerick: Mid-Western Health Board, 1989

O'Connor, S., 'Community Care Services: An Overview (Part 2)'. In NESC (same title). Dublin: National Economic and Social Council, 1987

O'Flaherty, B., *Adult Literacy, A Survey of its Status in Dublin's Inner City*, Dublin CDVEC Curriculum Development Unit, 1984

O'Hagan, K., *Crisis Intervention in Social Services*. Basingstoke: MacMillan, 1986

O'Hare, A. *et al, Mothers Alone? A Study of Women who gave birth outside marriage – Ireland 1983*. Dublin: Federation of Services for Unmarried Parents and their Children, 1987

O'Higgins, K. and Boyle, M., *State Care – Some Children's Alternatives: An analysis of the data from the returns to the Department of Health, Child Care Division, 1982*. Dublin: Economic and Social Research Institute, 1988

O'Higgins, K., *Marital Desertion in Dublin – An Exploratory Study*. Dublin: Economic and Social Research Institute (ESRI), Broadsheet No. 9, 1974

O'Kelly, F.D. *et al*, 'The rise and fall of heroin use in an inner city area of Dublin'. *Irish Journal of Medical Science*, Vol. 157, No. 2, 1988, pp 35-8

O'Mahony, A., *Social need and the provision of social service in rural areas: A case study for the community care services*. Dublin: An Foras Talúntais, Socio-Economic Research Series No. 5, 1985

O'Mahony, A., *The Elderly in the Community: Transport and access to services in rural areas*. Dublin: National Council for the Aged, 1986

O'Mahony, P., Cullen, R. and O'Hora, M., 'Some family characteristics of Irish juvenile offenders', *The Economic and Social Review*, Vol. 17, No. 1, 1985, pp 29-37

O'Mullane, D., *et al, Children's dental health in Ireland, 1984 – A survey conducted on behalf of the Minister for Health by University College, Cork*. Dublin: Stationery Office, 1986

O'Rourke, A.H., O'Sullivan, N. and Wilson-Davis, K., 'Smoking – A study of post-primary schools, 1980-81'. *Irish Medical Journal*, Vol. 76, 1983, pp 285-9

O'Sullivan, D., 'Pre-schooling as a community resource'. *Social Studies*, Vol. 7, No. 4, 1983, pp 282-92

O'Sullivan Committee, *Development of Youth Work Services in Ireland – A report of the Committee appointed by the Minister of State at the Department of Education*. Dublin: Stationery Office, 1980

Orlin, M., 'Resolving Conflicts in Foster Care'. *Adoption and Fostering*, 90, 1977, pp 21-23

Packman, J., Randall and Jacques, N. 'Who needs care?' *Social Work Decisions about Children*. Oxford: Blackwell, 1986

Parker, R., *Caring for Separated Children*. London: Macmillan, 1980

Pelton, L., 'Child abuse and neglect: the myth of carelessness'. In L. Pelton (ed), *The Social Context of Child Abuse and Neglect*. New York: Human Sciences Press, 1985

Phillips, M., 'A case of bad treatment for social work'. *The Guardian*, 10 December 1987

Philp, M. and Duckworth, D., *Children with Disabilities and Their Families – A Review of Research*. Windsor: NFER/Nelson, 1982

Pincus, A. and Minahan, A., *Social Work Practice: Model and Method*. Itasca, IL: F.E. Peacock Publishers, 1973

Porteus, M., 'Developmental aspects of adolescent problem disclosure in England and Ireland', *Journal of Child Psychology and Psychiatry*, Vol. 26, No. 3, 1985, pp 465-478

Poulton, L., 'Support: who gives it and when?' *Parenthood, Education and Support: A Continuous Process*, G. Pugh (Ed). London: National Children's Bureau, 1982, pp 19-23

Pound, A. and Mills, M., 'A pilon evaluation of Newpin – home-visiting and befriending scheme in South London'. *Association for Child Psychology and Psychiatry Newsletter*, Vol. 7, No. 4, 1985, pp 13-15

Powell, F., 'Social policy in early modern Ireland'. *Social Studies: Irish Journal of Sociology*, Vol. 7, No. 1, 1982, pp 56-66

Power, B., *Report on heroin users in the Borough of Dun Laoghaire*. Mimeograph, 1983

Primary Education Review Body, *Report*. Dublin: Stationery Office, 1990

Psychological Society of Ireland, *A Psychological Service to Schools*. Dublin: Psychological Society of Ireland, 1974

Puckering, C., 'Annotation: Maternal Depression', *Journal of Child Psychology and Psychiatry*, Vol. 30, No. 6, pp 807-817, 1989

Pugh, G. and De'Ath, E., *The Needs of Parents – Practice and Policy in Parent Education*. London: Macmillan/National Children's Bureau, 1984

Quinton, D. and Rutter, M., 'Parents with children in care, Intergenerational Continuities', *Journal of Child Psychology and Psychiatry*, Vol. 25, No. 2, 1984, pp 231-250

Richardson, V., *Unmarried mothers delivered in the National Maternity Hospital, 1986*. Dublin: National Maternity Hospital/Department of Social Administration and Social Work, UCD, 1987

Richardson, V. and Winston, N., *Unmarried mothers delivered in the National Maternity Hospital, 1987*. Dublin: Social Work Research Unit, National Maternity Hospital/Department of Social Administration and Social Work, UCD, 1988

Richman, N., 'The effects of housing on pre-school children and their mothers'. *Developmental Medicine and Child Neurology*, 1974, pp 53-8

Richman, N., 'Behaviour problems in pre-school children: family and social factors'. *British Journal of Psychiatry*, Vol. 13, 1977, pp 523-7

Robins, J., *The Lost Children*. Dublin: Institute of Public Administration, 1980

Ronayne, T., et al, *The Living Conditions of the Long-term Unemployed: Case studies of innovations – Ireland*. Dublin: Irish Foundation for Human Development, Psychosomatic Unit, 1986

Rood de Boer, M., 'State intervention in the family in the Netherlands' in Freeman, M. (Ed), *The State, the Law and the Family*. London: Tavistock, 1986

Rosenbloom, L., 'Cerebral palsy'. *From Asthma to Thalassaemia: Medical Conditions in Childhood*, S. Curtis (Ed). London: British Agencies for Adoption and Fostering, 1986

Rosenheim, E. and Reicher, R., 'Informing children about a parent's terminal illness'. *Journal of Child Psychology and Psychiatry*, Vol. 26, No. 6, 1985, pp 995-8

Rosenstein, P., 'Family outreach: a program for the prevention of child neglect and abuse'. *Child Welfare – Journal of the Child Welfare League of America*, Vol. LVII, No. 8, 1978, pp 519-25

Rottman, D., 'The Criminal Justice System: policy and performance, Part 2', in NESC (same title) Report No. 77. Dublin: NESC, 1984

Rottman, D.B., Tussing, A.D. and Wiley, M.M., *The Population Structure and Living Circumstances of Irish Travellers: Results from the 1981 Census of Traveller Families*. Dublin: Economic and Social Research Institute, Paper No. 131, 1986

Rowe, J., et al, *Long-term Foster Care*. London: Batsford/BAAF, 1984

Russell, P., *AIDS and Children*. London: National Children's Bureau, Highlight No. 75, 1987

Rutter, M., 'Child psychiatry: looking thirty years ahead'. *Journal of Child Psychology and*

Psychiatry, Vol. 27, No. 6, 1986

Rutter, M., Quinton, D., Liddle, C., 'Parenting in two generations: Looking backwards and looking forwards'. *Families at Risk,* London: Heinemann, 1983

Rutter, M. and Giller, H., *Juvenile Delinquency: Trends and Perspectives.* Hammondsworth: Penguin Education, 1983, pp 190-91.

Rutter, M. *et al,* 'Attainment and adjustment in two geographical areas – I. The prevalence of psychiatric disorder'. *British Journal of Psychiatry,* Vol. 126, 1975, pp 493-50

Rutter, M. and Cox, A., 'Other family influences'. *Child and Adolescent Psychiatry: Modern Approaches* (Second edition), M. Rutter and L. Hersov (Eds). London: Blackwell, 1985

Rutter, M. and Gould, L., 'Classification'. *Child and Adolescent Psychiatry: Modern Approaches* (Second edition), M. Rutter and L. Hersov (Eds). London: Blackwell, 1985

Ryan, A. *et al,* 'The emergence of maternal drug addiction as a problem in Ireland, 1981'. *Irish Medical Journal,* Vol. 76, No. 2, 1983, pp 86-9

Rydelius, P.A., 'Children of alcoholic fathers'. *Acta Paediatrica Scandinavica,* Suppl. 286, 1981

Sarnacki Porter F., Canfield Blick, L. and Sgroi, S., 'Treatment of the abused child'. *Handbook of Clinical Intervention in Child Sexual Abuse,* S. Sgroi (Ed). Massachusetts: Lexington Books, 1982

Scanlan, S., 'Preventive work – what possibilities?' *Irish Social Worker,* Vol. 4, No. 4, 1985, pp 11-12

Scully, P., 'Young people out of home and the law'. *Streetwise – Homelessness among the young in Ireland and abroad,* S. Kennedy (Ed). Dublin: Glendale Press, 1987

Seanad Éireann Parliamentary Debates, G. Hussey, Vol. 96, No. 16, 17 December, 1981

Seanad Éireann Parliamentary Debates, Vol. 108, No. 4, 9 May, 1985

Secretary of State, *Report of Inquiry into Child Abuse in Cleveland.* London: HMSO, 1988

Sexton, J.J., Whelan, B.J. and Williams, J.A., *Transition from School to Work and Early Labour Market Experience.* Dublin: ESRI Paper No 141, 1988, p. 3

Sgroi, S., Canfield Blick, L. and Sarnacki Porter, F., 'A conceptual framework for child sexual abuse'. *Handbook of Clinical Intervention in Child Sexual Abuse,* S. Sgroi (Ed). Massachusetts: Lexington Books, 1982

Shamroy, J., 'Interviewing the sexually abused child with anatomically correct dolls'. *Social Work,* Vol. 32, No. 2, 1987, pp 165-6

Shatter, A., *Family Law in the Republic of Ireland* (Third Edition). Dublin: Wolfhound Press, 1986

Shaw, M. and Lebens, K., 'Foster parents talking'. *Adoption and Fostering,* No. 88, 1977, pp 11-16

Society of St Vincent de Paul, *For God's sake give . . . 1989 Annual Report.* Dublin: Society of V de P, 1989

St Michael's House, Personal communication with author, January 1988

Streetwise National Coalition, *A national survey on young people out of home in Ireland.* Dublin: Streetwise National Coalition, 1988

SUSS Centre, *A Block of Facts – Ballymun twenty-one Years on.* Dublin: SUSS Centre, 1987

Swan, T.D., *Reading Standards in Irish Schools.* Dublin: The Educational Company, 1978

Swedish Institute, 'Correctional care in Sweden'. *Fact Sheets on Sweden.* Stockholm: The Swedish Institute, 1981

Swedish Institute, 'Equality between men and women in Sweden', *Fact sheet no. 82.* Stockholm: The Swedish Institute, 1984

Taoiseach, An, Charles Haughey, *Presidential Address to the Fianna Fáil 58th Árd Fheis,* Dublin, 9 March 1991

Task Force on Child Care Services, *Interim Report.* Dublin: Stationery Office, 1975

Task Force on Child Care Services, *Final Report*. Dublin: Stationery Office, 1981

Thayer, P. *et al, Forms of Child Care*. Strasbourg: Council of Europe, 1988

Tizard, J., 'Maladjusted children in the child guidance service'. London: *Educational Review*, Summer 1973. Reprinted in *Child Development and Social Policy: The Life and Work of Jack Tizard*, A.D.B. Clarke and B. Tizard. Leicester: British Psychological Society, 1983

Trant, S. (Chairman of Working Party), *Services for the Mentally Handicapped*. Dublin: Department of Health, 1980

Trant, S. (Chairman of Study Group), *The Psychiatric Services: Planning for the Future*. Dublin: Stationery Office, 1985

Travelling People Review Body, *Report*. Dublin: Stationery Office, 1983

Treischman, A., *et al, The Other Twenty Three Hours*. Chicago: Aldine Publishing Co., 1969

Triseliotis, J. and Russell, J., *Hard to Place: the outcome of adoption and residential care*. London: Heinemann Educational, 1984

Tuairim, *Some of Our Children – A Report on the Residential Care of the Deprived Child in Ireland*. London, 1966

United Nations, *Universal Declaration of Human Rights*, 1948

United Nations, *International Covenant on Economic, Social and Cultural Rights*, 1966

United Nations, *Convention on the Rights of the Child*, New York, 1990

Van der Eyken, W., *Home Start – A Four Year Evaluation*. Leicester: Home Start Consultancy, 1982

Van Dongen-Melman, J. and Sanders-Woudstra, J., 'Psychosocial aspects of childhood cancer'. *Journal of Child Psychology and Psychiatry*, Vol. 27, No. 2, 1986

Van Rees, R., Oudendijk, N., Van Spanje, M., The Triangel (Socio-Therapeutical Institute), *Child Abuse and Neglect*, Vol. 2, pp 207-215, 1978

Vikan, A., 'Psychiatric epidemiology in a sample of 1,510 ten-year-old children: 1. Prevalence'. *Journal of Child Psychology and Psychiatry*, Vol. 26, No. 1, 1985, pp 55-75

Wadsworth, J., 'Teenage mothering: child development at five years'. *Journal of Child Psychology and Psychiatry*, Vol. 25, No. 2, 1984, pp 305-14

Wadsworth, J., 'The influence of family type on children's behaviour and development at five years'. *Journal of Child Psychology and Psychiatry*, Vol. 26, No. 2, 1985, pp 235-54

Walsh, J., 'A model scheme for children'. *Let's make friends*. London: Souvenir Press, 1986

Walsh, H., *Break Away – A Study of Short-term Family Care for Children with Mental Handicap*. Dublin: The Break Away Agencies, 1983

Whelan, C.T., *Employment Conditions and Job Satisfaction: The distribution, perception and evaluation of job rewards*. Dublin: Economic and Social Research Institute (ESRI), Paper No. 101, 1980

Whelan, B. and Whelan, C., *Social Mobility in the Republic of Ireland*. Dublin: ESRI, 1984

Whitaker Committee, *Report of Inquiry into the Penal System*. Dublin: Stationery Office, 1985

Whittaker, J., *Caring for Troubled Children – Residential Treatment in a Community Context*. San Francisco: Jossey Bass, 1979

Whittaker, J., 'Group and institutional care', in Hand, J. and Hartman, A., *A Handbook of Child Welfare*. New York: New York Free Press, 1985

Whyte, J.H., *Church and State in Modern Ireland 1923-74*, 2nd ed. Dublin: Gill and MacMillan, 1980

Wilmott, P. and Mayne, S., 'The "Downtown" Family Centre'. *Families at the Centre – A Study of seven action projects*. School of Economics Occasional Papers on Social

Administration, No. 72. London: Bedford Square Press/National Council for Voluntary Organisations, 1983

Withey, V., Anderson, R. and Lauderdale, M., 'Volunteers as mentors for abusing parents: a natural helping relationship'. *Child Welfare* – Journal of the Child Welfare League of America, Vol. LIX, No. 10, 1980, pp 637-44

Working Party on Child Care Facilities for Working Parents, *Report to the Minister for Labour*, Dublin: Stationery Office, 1983

Women's Aid, *Findings of a Common Research Project between Women's Aid, Dublin, Boys and Girls Welfare Society, Cheshire, and Northern Ireland Women's Aid, Belfast*, Dublin: 1986

Yamaguchi, K. and Kandel, D., 'Patterns of drug use from adolescence to young adulthood: II Sequences of progression'. *American Journal of Public Health*, Vol. 74, No. 7, 1984, pp 668-72

Youth Employment Agency, *Annual Report 1986*. Dublin: Youth Employment Agency, 1987

INDEX

Warrenstown House, Blanchardstown, 115
Waterford, 76, 84
  RTC, 119
Western Health Board, 46, 101, 115
  child guidance, 131
  psychologists, 125
Wexford, 166
Whelan, B. and Whelan, C., 196
Whittaker, J., 121, 194, 220
Whitaker Committee, 80, 83
Whyte, J. H., 132, 143
Wicklow, Co., 68
widowed parents, 34-5
wife battering, 27-30
Wilmott, P. and Mayne, S., 162
Wine, Hubert, District Justice, 7
Withey, V. *et al.* 158
women
  mental health of, 163-5
  unemployed, 85, 87
Women's Aid, 27-8, 144, 148
workhouses, 195
Working Party on Child Care Facilities for
  Working Parents, 137, 139
World Health Organisation (WHO), 52, 68, 114,
  124
World Summit for Children, 18

Y
Yamaguchi, K. and Kandel, D., 39
Yorkshire, 225
youth clubs, 89-90
youth counselling and support services, 90-2
Youth Employment Agency, 92
Youth Encounter Projects, 77-8, 83, 92
Youth Information Centres, 90
youth policies, lack of, 226-7
youth services, 85-93
  activity centred services, 89-90
  employment and training services, 91-2
  information, advice and counselling services,
  90-1
  youth projects and programmes for
  disadvantaged, 92-3
  youth work and services, 88-9
Youthreach, 92